CONTENTS

Involvement. Achievement needs. The self-motivated
achiever. Motivation theory and the school manager.
Opinion questionnaire. Assessing the motivation of
others.

Developing your own competence. Managing your
learning: Managing our attitudes and behaviour. Positive
and negative management. Criteria for effectiveness –
establishing priorities. Use of time analysis. Time log.
Learning styles questionnaire.

PART II MANAGING THE ORGANIZATION

The organizational dimension. Organizational goals.
Stakeholders. Environment. Models of organizations: The
classical model; The humanistic model; The systems
model; The decision model; The contingency model.
Elements of organizations. Interlocking systems.

The nature of teams. Team roles. Team-building. Self-
perception inventory for use in team-building.
Formulating objectives.

The National Curriculum. Meeting the needs of
tomorrow's citizens: Creating positive attitudes. Involving
the stakeholders. Corporate planning. Aims and value
systems. Curriculum development in practice.

Keeping pace with change. Equipment appraisal. Trends
in computing. Computer applications in the office.
Advantages of personal computing: Educational administration packages. Educational 'author' packages. New
technology and the education manager.

Resource-driven or need-driven? Investing money. Local
management in schools. Cost/benefit analysis. Budgeting
and financial control. Resource control. Adapting existing
resources to fit the need.

PREFACE

The main purpose of this book is to help teachers with senior management responsibilities, and the schools and colleges that they work in, to become more effective. It is not a book by academics for other academics, but by practitioners for practitioners. Practitioners of what? The authors have both been senior managers in industry, and we have spent much of our careers helping others, both in industry and education, to learn to become more effective managers, as well as improving the effectiveness of organizations – commercial, industrial, educational and church. So it is not only in the practice of management and the workings of organizations that we claim some expertise, but also in the methods by which both can be improved.

One of us (Morris), having taught and managed in schools and in Unilever, is managing director of a European management consultancy which has played a strong role in developing school management training since 1971; the other (Everard) has been education and training manager (= 'headteacher?') of another international company, ICI, but since 1982 has trained some hundreds of school heads in management, mostly as a visiting fellow at the University of London Institute of Education. We think this makes our book unique, because there are so few people, let alone authors, who have had enough management responsibility and training experience both in school and in industry to bridge the cultural and terminological gap fully. We both became involved, through the CNAA Education Organization and Management Board (see Glossary for unfamiliar abbreviations, etc.), in validating award-bearing courses in education management, and have both taught on such courses. So we have a foot in the academic world and are broadly familiar with what is taught in polytechnics and colleges about management, and with the value system which pervades such educational institutions. Those, then, are our credentials.

Naturally these experiences have shaped our outlook on school and college management. They have convinced us of the value of building 'learning bridges' between educational and non-educational (but particularly commercial) organizations, so that successful management practice and organizational design can be transferred to and fro. However, because industry has a longer tradition of management development, and spends more on it than does education, most (but not all) of the traffic across the bridge is towards education. We believe that only some of the available know-how should cross the bridge, and even that may need translating or adapting before it can be put to beneficial use. Everard (1984) has summarized what can be learned, in a report commissioned by the Centre for the Study of Comprehensive Schools, and it was this that led our publishers to invite him to write a longer book. Believing that, except in schools, two heads are better than one, he enlisted as a collaborator someone who also believes in learning bridges and who directed much traffic over one at Brighton Polytechnic and another at Brunel University.

It is our contention that those who do not believe that schools can learn from industry base their case on false premises and lack of first-hand knowledge of industrial management. They have a concept of industrial organizations and managers which we scarcely recognize as real – or, if real, as effective. We know of the charges of exploitation and the supposed taint of the profit motive, but we do not accept that the ethics of most businesses are malign; and we have written elsewhere to this effect (Everard, 1980). Our proposition is this:

Some firms are effective, ethical and successful,

partly because they are well managed and organized,

which is partly because their managers have learned management systematically.

Equally, some schools and colleges are effective and successful,

partly because they are well managed and organized,

which is partly because their heads and senior staff have learned management systematically.

Therefore heads and senior staff in schools and colleges can learn to manage better by studying what their counterparts do in successful firms; and across national boundaries such as the Atlantic Ocean and the North Sea.

Such learning takes time. We think nothing of investing 4–6 years in the training of a doctor, lawyer, chemist or vet, but how many managers get even as many *weeks'* training? Yet management can be just as complex and demanding as these other professions.

Just as doctors' and vets' mistakes die, managers can kill their organizations. We can learn from others' mistakes, and industry has made many (as has education). So we need to be discriminating about what we allow to cross the learning bridges. Industry has had to be discriminating in the same way, for many of the new ideas about organization and management stem from institutions of higher education; some work and some don't. This book is about those which work, and it warns the reader of some of the traps for the unwary.

Why have these learning bridges become so important recently? The notion that teachers can and should be taught to manage is still quite young – about 35 years old in the United Kingdom. Some still doubt whether it is possible: Harry Gray, a well-known editor, author and lecturer on educational management, who has taught in the United Kingdom, Canada, Nigeria and elsewhere, wrote:

> It is the experience of many professional management trainers (educators) that teachers are perceiving the same management issues that commercial and industrial managers see... in over 13 years' work in this area I have come to the conclusion that, in broad terms at least, nothing is actually achieved by teaching management skills; schools just go on as they always have.
>
> (Gray, 1984)

We do not feel as pessimistic as this, but we are aware of the size of the problem that Gray exposes, and we welcome the successive initiatives from government (circulars DES 3/83 and 4/84 and targeted grants) to encourage local education authorities to take management training more seriously. These initiatives make this book timely.

For too long books and courses on education management have been considered by students as too 'theoretical', 'academic', 'impractical' or even 'irrelevant'; they do not deal with the real condition of the manager, but with some kind of idealized role. People on courses say they learn more from each other than from the books and lectures (Hughes *et al.*, 1981). Yet the CNAA (1984), for example, is quite clear what it expects from a course (and its associated books) in practical terms. Principle 3.3

governing its awards states (author's italics):

> The direction of the students' studies must be towards greater understanding and *competence*. Thus, while it may be appropriate for a programme to include the acquisition of techniques or skills, or the learning of data, these must lead to a higher level of intellectual and creative *performance* than that intrinsic in the learning of skills, techniques or facts themselves.

We subscribe wholeheartedly to this principle, and the whole thrust of the book is aimed at improving competence and performance. We do not disparage theory; Lewin's aphorism that there is nothing so practical as a good theory rings true for us, but we believe that too many books on education management are written from a theoretician's point of view. Our aim is to redress this balance and to complement with something more practical the texts written by those academics who simply study management without practising it (excellent though many are).

Perhaps a clue to the different approaches lies in the words used to describe 'management'. It is different from 'administration' (though in North America this word comes nearer to what we mean by 'management'). We see a manager as someone who:

(1) Knows what he or she wants to happen and causes it to happen;
(2) Is responsible for controlling resources and ensuring that they are put to good use;
(3) Promotes effectiveness in work done, and a search for continual improvement;
(4) Is accountable for the performance of the unit he or she is managing, of which he or she is a part;
(5) Sets a climate or tone conducive to enabling people to give of their best.

(Everard, 1984)

Most of our readers will recognize this as the role of heads, principals, rectors and leaders in schools and colleges. Some will aspire to such posts or to the next rung down: deputies, second masters or mistresses, heads of lower school, heads of faculties, principal teachers.

We also know that education officers, advisers and inspectors who are professionally involved with education management have benefited from reading the book, because it is important that, despite LMS, institutions should be seen in the context of their LEA environment and managed as a total system.

What we have to say is directed at primary, secondary and special schools (though the parts that deal with the interdepartmental problems of large institutions will scarcely apply to a small village primary school); and it is as relevant to the independent as to the state sector.

We believe that what we say also applies to the management of colleges and polytechnics and we hope that this will be borne in mind by readers in such institutions. However, in this stratum of education, it is more to the teachers of education management on long or short courses that we offer guidance – on what, in our experience, teachers as managers really want to learn. Although the book is based on studies of effective management and successful organizations, and is pitched at a practical level, it is underpinned with theory. If it fails to do justice to important schools of thought, this is because we have quite deliberately selected approaches that we ourselves have used, and found relevant.

We have tried to help the reader interact with the book, by including short tasks which he or she can relate to his or her own school situation. Some of these exercises could be used for group discussion – group learning is a useful method which can be set up in any school or for a peer group from different schools in a locality. Wherever we can, we have included examples from schools that we have visited, including three illustrative case studies in Chapter 19.

Such conscious linking of the book to the reader's own situation helps the process of learning. We espouse the experiential learning model described by Kolb (1984, p. 33), which is based on earlier work by Lewin and Dewey. It postulates a cycle of improving competence by observing and reflecting on concrete experiences, then forming abstract concepts or generalizations, then testing the implications of these concepts in new situations. Thus learning combines the processes of experience, perception, cognition and behaviour; it is not simply the imparting and assimilation of knowledge. This book cannot supply the concrete experience, so it will not be as helpful to readers whose roles are not managerial; but we hope it will help perception, reflection and conceptualization, and we suggest ways of putting the results of these mental processes into practice.

We see the book being used: for personal study at home or work; as part of the reading for a short or a long course; for informal group discussion; and as a reference handbook for the practising manager. We don't think that this multiplicity of aims is ambitious because that is how we have used similar books on management. Our main concern is that so many of those who could benefit from it simply can't find the time for reading; their priorities leave no space for self-improvement. It is worth reflecting whether such an ordering is in the best interests of the school, for it is impossible to change a school for the better without changing oneself.

The report of the School Management Task Force (1990), *Developing*

School Management – The Way Forward, calls for a 'new approach to school management development which focuses attention on the support which should be available in and near to the school and places less emphasis on off-site training'. It sees management development as a crucial process in helping organizations achieve their purposes, and quotes Everard's definition of it as 'an approach that supports, promotes and is harmoniously related to the development of the organization'. This philosophy pervades our book, which emphasizes almost every characteristic of effective schools which the report lists, and shows how each can be developed by schools themselves. We share the Task Force's view that schools should be moving towards an integrated corporate approach to the development of the workforce, led by the head, so that achievement of corporate goals and meeting the individual's needs become matters of mutual benefit rather than of competing demands. The report advises schools to draw on industrial expertise; our book packages this in an interactive form which schools can use by themselves, selecting whichever topics, techniques and exercises meet their needs. As such, the book provides valuable support to the Task Force's new initiative, which the Secretary of State has endorsed.

We admit to being, in the writing of this book, creative plagiarists, a condition rife among management trainers. In the distant past we have picked up from lectures, handouts, articles, internal reports, books and discussions with professional colleagues, a whole host of interlocking ideas which we have built into our personal repertoires, as birds build a nest. Often the source of the original idea gets lost as it is embellished and refashioned to new use. We are conscious of our debt to many 'gurus'. As well as a general acknowledgement to all those whose ideas we have used, we have tried to give credit where we know the source. But there are some to whom we owe a special debt.

Bertie Everard had the privilege of working over several years with Professor Dick Beckhard of MIT, when he consulted with ICI, and with other ICI colleagues such as Arthur Johnston and Derek Sheane. Part 3 owes much to the insights developed during this experience. Professor Bill Reddin, the late Ralph Coverdale and his disciples, and Meredith Belbin have also helped to shape his ideas. More recently there have been colleagues at the Institute of Education and not least the superb heads he has met on courses and during his research into the problem of secondary-school management. He is much indebted to the Leverhulme Trust for funding the expenses of this research, which greatly helped him to assimilate the culture and language of schools. Then there were those who encouraged him from the sidelines and helped him make contacts –

Bob Finch late of ICI, Alan Paisey late of Bulmershe College, Harry Gray formerly at Lancaster, Andrew Pettigrew at Warwick, Frank Stoner and his colleagues at the Centre for the Study of Comprehensive Schools.

Geoffrey Morris would like to express his thanks to his colleagues in EMAS (European Management Advisory Services) who have contributed to the development of ideas used in this book, and to Tom Lea late of Brighton Polytechnic, with whom he worked on frequent courses during the last 20 years, and to Malcolm Mander of Brunel University. He would also like to acknowledge the, usually positive, criticism of his wife (a former teacher), his daughter (a teacher) and his son (a manager), and to thank them for giving him temporary leave of mental absence from the family.

Both of us have been rightly chivvied by our editor, Marianne Lagrange, and by Berteke Ibbett, Morris's secretary, who word-processed his share of the script (Everard doing his own, and recommending the technology to teachers who have text to originate and edit). To these and others unnamed, we express our thanks.

Finally, aware of the strong feelings in the teaching profession about the use of male pronouns to refer to teachers of either sex, we crave the indulgence of female readers where we have stuck to such pronouns in the interests of brevity: we know that you make very successful heads, and appreciation of your success is one of the items that should cross the learning bridge from school to industry.

Bertie Everard
Geoffrey Morris

ACKNOWLEDGEMENTS

Figure 8.2 is adapted from R.E. Boyatzis, *The Competent Manager* (1982) by permission of the publishers, John Wiley and Sons Inc.

Figure 9.4 is adapted from *The Learning Organization* (1987) by permission of the author, Bob Garratt and Collins Publishers. The learning styles description and questionnaire (Exercise 11) is reprinted from Honey and Mumford's *Manual of Learning Styles* (1986: 2nd edn) by permission of the authors.

Figure 10.2, the definitions of team roles in Chapter 10, and Exercise 12 are reprinted by permission of William Heinemann Limited, and thanks are due to Dr R Meredith Belbin, the copyright owner, for agreeing to the use of this material from his book, *Management Teams: Why They Succeed or Fail* (1981).

The quotation from *Ten Good Schools* in Chapter 16 is reproduced with the permission of the Controller of Her Majesty's Stationery Office.

The authors gratefully acknowledge their indebtedness to Professor Fullan and to Professor Beckhard and his colleagues in Part 3, which freely quotes from their work; also to their publishers, Teachers College Press and Addison-Wesley respectively, for permission to use this material.

Acknowledgement is made to the McGraw-Hill Book Company (UK) Ltd for permission to use material from V. Stewart's book, *Change: The Challenge for Management* (1983) in Chapter 16. The authors also thank Harper and Row Publishers, Inc. for permission to use material from Peters and Waterman's *In Search of Excellence* (1982); and 'Hierarchy of Needs' from *Motivation and Personality* by Abraham H. Maslow. Copyright © 1970 by Abraham H. Maslow.

The headteachers of the schools from which the case studies in Chapter 19 were written have kindly given their approval for publication, and this is gratefully acknowledged, as is the financial assistance from the Leverhulme Trust which enabled this material to be collected.

Exercises 1–4 and 7–10 and some other material in this book are the joint copyright of EMAS Business Consultants Ltd and EMAS Consultants Ltd.

The authors would like to thank Frederick Herzberg for permission to use material from *Work and the Nature of Man*, 1966.

1
INTRODUCTION

Do schoolteachers need to learn management?

Are good managers born not trained? Does management come naturally to us? Before answering these questions, you may find it useful to complete the following brief questionnaire. Answer each question in turn, without hesitating too long, and without reading ahead.

Management principles questionnaire
Award a grade of 0 (totally disagree) to 4 (totally agree) to indicate to what extent you agree or disagree with each of the statements that follow. Please do not look at Questions 6-10 until you have answered Questions 1-5.

1. One should ignore certain faults in the work of subordinates in order not to discourage them.

0	1	2	3	4

2. I spend too much time sorting out problems that my subordinates ought to be able to deal with.

0	1	2	3	4

3. I try to tell my subordinates exactly what they have to do and how I want it done.

0	1	2	3	4

4. I know enough about my area of responsibility to be able to take most decisions quickly and without having to seek the views of my subordinates.

    0   1   2   3   4

5. I always tell my staff why we are making changes.

    0   1   2   3   4

6. If anyone finds any fault at all with my work I would rather he or she told me to my face.

    0   1   2   3   4

7. If I have a problem I like my boss to take over and sort it out.

    0   1   2   3   4

8. I like to be told exactly how I am to do my job.

    0   1   2   3   4

9. If my boss is going to take a decision affecting me or my department I like him or her to consult me first.

    0   1   2   3   4

10. It is difficult to appreciate the logic behind many education office decisions.

    0   1   2   3   4

Interpreting the questionnaire
As you neared the end of the questionnaire you probably realized that there was a relationship between Questions 1 and 6, 2 and 7, etc. In fact, the first five questions all relate to the way in which we manage others or believe that we ought to manage others. Questions 6–10, on the other hand, are concerned with the way in which we believe we are or ought to *be* managed.

It seems logical that we should manage others in the way that we like to be managed. However, you will be among the vast majority of those who have answered this questionnaire if you have, by a '4' grading, firmly asserted that 'If anyone finds any fault at all with my work I would rather he or she told me to my face' (question 6), yet have at the same time suggested by a '3' or a '4' that 'One should ignore certain faults in the work of subordinates in order not to discourage them' (question 1).

Answers by a typical group of fifty headteachers of all types to the questionnaire gave the average results shown in Figure 1.1.

In looking at your own scores or at the above scores, two objections may emerge:

(1) 'The questions are not exact matches.' This is true – but necessary in the interests of not making the correspondence too obvious during the answering of the questionnaire. The match is close enough to make the point.

(2) 'The way in which you manage or wish to be managed differs from level to level. Headteachers do wish to be told of their faults (and can safely be told of their faults as they will be too mature to be discouraged!), but this is not the case with less senior staff.' However, this questionnaire has been given to groups of school staff at all levels and the mean response has been almost identical.

In the case of question 10, the wording was changed to 'Many of my headteachers' decisions... .' The responses still clearly made the point that at any level we believe that we are keeping others informed of the reasons for change. However, in the vast majority of cases we are living in a fool's paradise.

	0	1	2	3	4		0	1	2	3	4
1				X		6					X
2				X		7	X				
3				X		8		X			
4				X		9					X
5				X		10				X	

Figure 1.1 Scoring sheet for management principles questionnaire

Instinct, common sense, skills and techniques

From what we have seen above, it would appear that our 'instinct' for managing others may be less reliable than we think. We may in fact be rationalizing ourselves out of facing up to issues with our colleagues or subordinates when, in fact, this sort of evasiveness of real issues is ιιυstrating, destructive and time-wasting for all concerned.

Most of what we shall say in this book may well appear to be common sense, as it indeed is once the issues have been thought through. Unfortunately, as we often see in others, people sometimes do not behave in accordance with principles which *should* be obvious to them. The remedy is to be clearly aware of:

(1) the pitfalls;
(2) the guiding principles which will help us to avoid the pits – or to get out of those we do happen to fall into;
(3) the early warning signs of trouble.

Practice at reacting in the light of these principles will develop our management 'skills'.

Finally, the book will suggest certain techniques and 'tools' that we can use to improve the effectiveness of the 'team' for which we are responsible or of which we are members.

What is management? Who is a manager?

As all teachers will know from their college days, a great deal of ink can be expended in defining one's terms. Definitions of management are so many and varied that we could spend the next twenty pages on this subject alone. Our aim, however, is not philosophy but practical guidance. Let us therefore be brief.

What management is *not* is carrying out a prescribed task in a prescribed way. As we discussed in the Preface, management in its broadest sense is about:

(1) setting direction, aims and objectives;
(2) planning *how* progress will be made or a goal achieved;
(3) organizing available resources (people, time, materials) so that the goal can be economically achieved in the planned way;
(4) controlling the process (i.e. measuring achievement against plan and taking corrective action where appropriate);
(5) setting and improving organizational standards.

As all teaching jobs contain at least some element of 'management' in this sense, one can argue that every teacher is a manager.

More restrictive definitions of management argue that a manager must additionally 'direct' the work of others. Again, in their classroom role, this definition could apply to all teachers, and, indeed, almost all principles of management do have very direct application to 'managing' the classroom.

However, our prime concern will be with school 'managers' in the more conventional sense, i.e. those teachers who have some responsibility for planning, organizing, directing and controlling the work of other teachers.

The manager and the organization

The 'organization' – be it department, school, college, university, education authority or, indeed, the educational system *in toto* – expects of its 'managers' three things:

(1) that they will integrate its resources in the effective pursuit of its goals;
(2) that they will be the agents of effective change;
(3) that they will maintain and develop its resources.

Integration of resources
The managerial role – as opposed to the teaching role – is to be the 'glue' in the organization, not, hopefully, in the sense of 'gumming up' the works – though those whom you manage will inevitably see it that way at times – but in the sense of holding the organization together.

The first post in which a teacher has to plan, organize, direct and control the work of other teachers involves a fundamental change in the criteria for job success. Many learn the lessons the hard way.

Throughout the *educational* process, success tends to depend on demonstrating and exploiting one's own ideas and talents. This will be the focus in one's first teaching appointments. As a manager, on the other hand, success depends on using the ideas and talents of a team, on arriving at decisions and actions to which the team members feel committed and on ensuring that they are put into effect. Though you do not feel that someone else's idea is quite as good as your own, you may be wise to back that idea, particularly if the person who puts it forward has a key role in implementation.

The manager is less concerned with *being* a resource than with *using* resources. At most levels of school management, teachers are fulfilling both classroom and management roles, and the danger is that one forgets that behaviour which succeeds in the classroom is different from that required to motivate the team.

Geoffrey Morris has not forgotton the occasion when, in his first year as head of department, he made changes in textbook and curriculum without fully involving the members of his department!

Effective change

Change is an essential function of the managerial role. It may be initiated from within the school or imposed from without. It may take the form of making improvements in the way in which we achieve ongoing goals, or we may have to cope with new goals and challenges.

In the last twenty-five years, schools have had to carry through a number of radical reorganizations caused by changes in politics, philosophies and birth-rates. In the years that lie ahead, the one thing that seems certain is that the rate of technological and social change will, if anything, accelerate, and the ability of our pupils to succeed – or, indeed, survive – in a changing environment will depend on our ability to adapt the content, methods and ethos of education to the new needs.

Change features strongly in the pages which follow. By definition, strategic decisions involve change. As managers, we are involving others in that change, and we need to bear in mind that the following phenomena tend to come into play, affecting both ourselves and those whom we manage:

'Not invented here'. Next time you are in a meeting and hear someone propose a course of action, note carefully how many of the ensuing comments are positive and how many are negative. (NB 'Yes, but's' count as negative.) The natural tendency in people is to resist and even resent ideas which are not their own. The tendency is even stronger if a change is parachuted upon them. Listen to the comments when a memo from the headteacher or the local authority is posted on the staff-room notice-board announcing almost any change.

'I haven't time'. Implementing changes always takes time, and teachers' time is always in short supply. It is easier to apply a standard solution which has worked in the past, to go over the same ground, to repeat the same syllabus using the same methods, than it is to prepare and implement a new approach. However good intentions may be, crises and routine will usually take priority over preparation for change. The only way to overcome the time barrier may be to set clearly defined action deadlines. However much time may be given for these, we will often find that the action is not taken – by ourselves or others – until the last minute, when it is promoted to the 'crisis' category because someone is 'breathing down one's neck'.

'A bird in the hand'. Change means risks and unforeseen problems. Will there be timetable clashes? Will the pupils respond in the way that is hoped? Will we have the resources to cope? Can we handle the new situation?

Restricted vision. Research has shown that the most important indication of high management potential and effective managerial performance is the helicopter quality – the ability to take the broader view of one's activities and to see them in context.

However, we all have a tendency, particularly in times of stress, to move our sights down a level instead of taking this broad view. Thus we may:

(1) jealously conserve the interests of ourselves or our departments instead of relating to the interests of the total organization;
(2) take decisions to deal with instant crises and forget that the decision may create a dangerous precedent which will itself provoke more crises (the history of management/union relations is littered with catastrophic short-term expedients).

Problems of reorganization, status, demarcation, authority. As well as consuming time, such changes are seen by most people as containing 'threats'. Usually our first reaction is to concentrate on these threats instead of looking for the opportunities. A sign of individual confidence and organizational health is said to lie in the ability to reverse this trend!

Shortage of money. Change almost always costs money!

Maintaining and developing resources
The *tangible* resources of an organization can be classified as:

(1) human (the people employed by the organization);
(2) material (buildings and equipment);
(3) financial (the funds available to the organization).

If these resources are not maintained we simply do not have an organization to integrate or to change.

Alongside these are a number of *intangible* resources, of which 'image' or 'reputation' is the most generally recognized. Without the right image, the survival of any commercial enterprise, including an independent school, is certainly in doubt, and, even within the state system, image matters wherever choice comes into play, e.g. recruitment of staff, placement of pupils in jobs and parental/student choice of school or college. Reflect on what other 'intangible resources' are possessed by a school and their relative importance: ethical standards? disciplinary standards? external relationships and support? It is not enough to *maintain* resources. The process of change demands that managers focus a great deal of attention on *developing* resources to meet new challenges and needs. If the educational system is to progress and be relevant to society, it must be 'need-driven' and not 'resource-driven' – that is to say, resources must be adapted to meet needs and not vice versa. These needs will be derived from the interplay of the school's values, the trends within the environment and educational legislation.

Managerial activities particularly concerned with the maintenance and development of resources are:

(1)   human – selection, appraisal, counselling, career planning, job design, training, project work, coaching;
(2)   material – purchasing, stock control, asset management;
(3)   financial – budgeting, cost control, fund-raising, cost/benefit analysis.

While barriers to curriculum development are most often said to be financial, the real problems are often human. Do staff have the skills and knowledge needed to introduce new subjects and methods? Do they want to make the changes? The relationship between skill and knowledge on the one hand and desire to innovate on the other is a 'chicken and egg' situation. To support a new subject we need to understand it, to wish to learn about a subject, we may need to be convinced of its relevance.

A school manager needs to be able to plan, organize and control all his or her resources, but the most crucial skill is undoubtedly the development of human resources.

Ethics and the manager

As teachers we already play an important and influential role in the lives of our pupils. As managers we become, additionally, one of the most important influences on the working lives of the staff who report directly or indirectly to us. As heads we fashion the value system of the school.

On our actions and attitudes will depend to a large extent:

(1)   whether the staff are happy or unhappy in their work;
(2)   their work priorities;
(3)   the standard which they observe and reflect.

As 'leader' of a group of staff, we have a potential 'power-base' which can be used to influence decisions. The unscrupulous manager can make life hell for those of his department who do not support him in staff meetings, whether or not the issue under discussion has previously been discussed within his departmental group. Words like 'loyalty' can be corrupted to mean slavish adherence to the party line.

As we shall see, good 'meeting management' can become 'manipulation'; objectivity, honesty and justice can be lost in the emotion of conflict; all sorts of 'games' can be played.

Every manager should constantly reflect on the ethics of his or her conduct. Other people, especially more senior managers, are more perceptive of unethical manoeuvrings than ever the perpetrator imagines. Someone who fondly imagines himself to be seen as a 'brilliant young manager', or as a shrewd and sympathetic handler of people, may, in fact, be regarded as an unprincipled rogue by his colleagues.

The school's role and mission: are education and management incompatible?

Most authors on this subject readily reconcile education and management (e.g. Paisey, 1981). However, there are those who passionately believe that the manager's role and mission, as we have described them, are incompatible with those of a school. It is argued that schools, with their deep-rooted educational values and academic professionalism, are not the kind of organizations that ought to be managed by a 'linchpin head' or even a senior management group – they ought to be self-managing communities with access to power dispersed equally among the staff. This case has been argued in a London Institute of Education Paper, *Education plc?* (Maw *et al.*, 1984) which reflects the views of a number of educational sociologists and other theorists in institutions of higher education and of teachers who have been trained to embrace their thinking. The main arguments adduced in support of this stance are given below. We set them out early in this book because, unless they are confronted, much of what follows may be rejected by readers who espouse similar views:

(1) 'Managerialism' is in conflict with the values and purposes of schools.
(2) Stress on means as against ends devalues professional competence.
(3) Hierarchically organized schools deprive teachers of involvement in fundamental educational thinking.

(4) Vertical accountability is debilitating; it leads to suspicion, resentment, divisiveness, problems of legitimacy and (in the case of appraisal) attendant psychological detriment to isolated individuals.

(5) The conception of authority relationships within an educational system is contrary to democratic principles and has a miseducative effect on pupils.

(6) Pupils should not be politically educated through belonging to an institution that is run by a 'linchpin head'.

(7) The contexts of educational and commercial organizations differ fundamentally; the latter ignore important moral considerations, whereas to an educational undertaking, morality is central.

(8) Recommended management practice ('contingency theory') is tantamount to expediency and manipulation; the abrogation of such words as 'participation' is especially insidious.

(9) Management theory is a pseudo-theory, tricked out as a form of 'behavioural science', but without scientific basis; it lends a spurious legitimacy to the manipulative practices of managers.

(10) A commercially inspired management imperative may betray rather than enhance the specifically educational nature of schools, because its values, focus and style of operation are destructive and alien to progressive educational thinking.

(11) Managers surreptitiously enjoy the exercise of power, kick away much conventional morality and subjugate employees to the demands of the organization.

Therefore heads should be regarded not as 'managers' but as professionally first among equals.

We believe that these arguments rest on false premises and on a lack of understanding of what well-managed commercial organizations are really like. Some postulate a classical model of an industrial organization which has long been superseded; some do not correspond with life in such organizations as we have experienced it – as managers and managed; and others cannot be reconciled with our understanding of and belief in Christianity (taking this as a touchstone of morality). The fact is that there is great diversity in industry and commerce, and within this are to be found exemplary organizations and departments with whose managers most teachers would find some rapport. Only part of industry is concerned with the routine tasks of mass production: research, accounts and training departments resemble schools in being staffed mainly by skilled and articulate professionals, and are managed accordingly.

If we thought that the approaches we advocate in the rest of this book would have the effects that critics of 'managerialism' fear, then we should not have written it. We are more than ready to defend on moral and ethical grounds everything we have written. No less than the critics do we respect professional competence, individuality and the centrality of values in the (often hidden) curriculum of schools. For us management does not and should not imply the naked exercise of power, nor the subservience of the managed, nor insensitivity to individuals' needs, nor the renunciation of human values. It does, however, call for the knitting together of social and economic values, as warp and weft.

We readily acknowledge the cultural differences between schools and other organizations, with their different *raisons d'être*, and we are deeply aware, through bitter experience, of the pitfalls of using concepts and terminology that mean different things to people on different sides of the cultural divide. It may be that such pitfalls partly explain why we are able to accept the five conclusions about school management training with which Fielding ends his critique in *Education plc?* (Maw *et al.*, 1984), while rejecting most of the arguments on which he bases them; and why we wholeheartedly subscribe to Mitchell's view of the headteacher's role, in the same booklet, quarrelling only with his stereotype of industrial managers.

However, this is not a book about educational and managerial philosophy and ethics: it is about effective practice. Hence all we need do at this point is to outline how we perceive the school as an organization, and what its mission is:

(1) The *raison d'être* of a school is to promote its pupils' learning, within a curriculum acceptable to its stakeholders.
(2) A school organization should meet these ends efficiently and cost-effectively.
(3) In such an organization tensions will arise between social and economic values, professional autonomy and managerial control, individuality and hierarchy, structural authority and participative decision-making, the head's dual roles of 'leading professional' and 'chief executive', the educational good of the many and the self-interest of the few, high principle and pragmatic expediency – and many other dilemmas that sometimes require a decision as to the lesser of two 'evils', e.g. being cruel in order to be kind.
(4) Striking the correct balance in these dilemmas entails difficult judgements, which have to be referred to a set of values outside of and greater than those of the individuals in the organization.

(5) At the highest level of abstraction, such values apply to, and often drive, all successful organizations, be they educational or commercial, and they act as bridges between the two.

In the remainder of this book we shall often revert to these fundamental issues in exploring how the manager can best fulfil his personal role and at the same time contribute to that of the educational institution where he is set in authority.

PART I
MANAGING PEOPLE

2
THE MANAGER AS A LEADER

Interpersonal skills

Before we can set about our managerial role and mission, we need some skill in relating to other people. We need to understand the various behavioural processes which may be at work, and use our knowledge to influence or 'lead' individuals or groups. In a meeting, as we shall see, decisions can be influenced far more effectively by using the behavioural 'process' of the meeting than by simply restating one's arguments, however sound they are. How we use our awareness of behavioural processes is a key aspect of managerial ethics. Do we use it to 'manipulate' or to 'facilitate?'

In order to help us to understand managerial behaviour, a large number of 'models' have been created. Because of the commercial interest in management training, such models have proliferated to the point of confusion, and authors have at times promoted their own models by attacking those produced by others.

Our aim is to avoid adding to the list, nor do we wish to spend time carrying out a review of the differing approaches of the many theoreticians. Instead we shall focus on some generally agreed principles and on a set of well-established models which we have found to be useful to managers in general and to school managers in particular.

Those of our readers who have attended courses on management and who have read other management literature are almost certain to have some acquaintance with the contents of this and the next chapter. Having cast an eye over the subheadings, they may therefore wish to proceed directly to Chapter 4.

Management style models

The best known of the management style models are based on the premise that every manager has two main concerns:

(1) concern to achieve results (i.e. he or she is 'task' oriented);
(2) concern for relationships (i.e. he or she is 'people' oriented).

Earlier style models such as the Schmidt-Tannenbaum continuum (Tannenbaum and Schmidt, 1958) suggested that these two concerns were in conflict and that the more a person was concerned with results, the less he or she would be concerned about relationships, and vice versa. The type of style model shown in Figure 2.1 resulted.

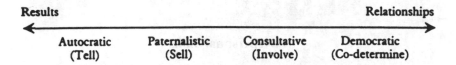

Results   Relationships

←——————————————————————————————————→

    Autocratic   Paternalistic   Consultative   Democratic
    (Tell)   (Sell)   (Involve)   (Co-determine)

Figure 2.1 Based on Tannenbaum, R. and Schmidt, W.H. (1973) 'How to choose a leadership pattern', *Harvard Business Review*, vol. 36, pp. 95–101

However, it was not long before it was realized that managers were not *either* principally concerned to get results *or* principally concerned about relationships, but that it was possible to be concerned about both at the same time (how do I best get results through people?) or, indeed, to be concerned about neither. This is the concept recognized in a number of style models which put results and relationships on two different axes of a graph and either name or number the extreme positions, e.g. the Blake Grid (Blake and Mouton, 1964).

Figure 2.2 sets out such a model which gives both the Blake numbers and verbal style descriptions. (NB The reader should note that the descriptions on the model are used in a specific context as defined. Words such as 'political' are used later in the book in a more positive context.)

Some attributes of each of the five named style positions are:

Assertive

    wants things done his or her way;
    'tells' rather than 'listens';
    doesn't worry too much about other people's feelings or opinions;

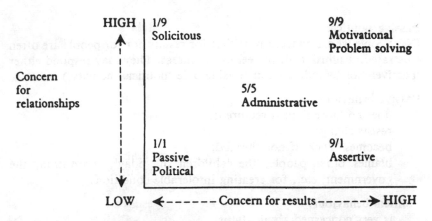

Figure 2.2 A two-dimensional model of management styles based on Blake, R.R. and Mouton, J.S. (1964).

aggressive if challenged;
'drives' things ahead;
checks up on staff.

Solicitous

cares about people;
wants to be liked;
avoids open conflict - smooths and coaxes;
'if the school is "happy", that is all that matters';
praises achievement to the point of flattering;
glosses over slackness or poor performance;
tends towards 'management by committee';
is helpful.

Motivational/problem solving

agrees goals and expects achievement;
monitors performance against goals;
helps staff members to find solutions to poor performance;
faces up to conflict calmly;
agrees and monitors action plans;
involves staff in decisions which affect them;
delegates clearly;
takes decisions as and when needed.

Passive/political

(NB People whose concern is neither for results nor for people are often frustrated, disillusioned, or feel under threat. They may respond either 'passively' or by indulging in considerable 'political' activity.)

Passive behaviour:
> does no more than is required;
> resists change;
> becomes 'slack' if not checked;
> blames other people, the 'children of today', innovation, the government, etc., for creating intolerable conditions;

Political behaviour:
> is very concerned about status;
> is quick to criticize;
> draws attention to the faults of others.

Administrative

> goes 'by the book';
> maintains the existing system;
> conscientious rather than creative or innovative;
> steady.

Orientation and behaviour

It is extremely important to realize that any such model operates at two different levels:

(1) Basic orientation (or 'dominant style'), i.e. the way in which a person most naturally behaves or wants to behave;
(2) Behaviour, i.e. the way in which a person actually does behave on any particular occasion.

Basic orientation – sometimes known as 'management approach' – will remain relatively constant. We can all think of people who tend to be 'assertive' in all they do, who are concerned to explain to their subordinates exactly what is wanted and how it is to be done and who tend to be intolerant of – or not to listen to – ideas other than their own. On the other hand, we have met basically 'solicitous' people who want above all to maintain good relationships.

Behaviour, however, will vary - and should vary - according to circumstances and people. As we shall see later, one of the characteristics of a person who truly has a high concern for both people and results is that he should be able to adapt his behaviour according to the needs of the person with whom he is dealing.

Dominant and back-up approaches

Under stress people may move automatically from their so-called 'dominant' approach into a quite different approach which is often referred to as their 'back-up' approach. For example, a head who is in the habit of doing what he wants without regard for the opinions of the staff may, if confronted, fall into profusions of apology using phrases like: 'Why didn't you tell me?', 'I had no idea you felt strongly about this', 'My door is always open.' Such a swing from assertive to solicitous is fairly common. Of course, once the crisis has passed, the head may well go on doing what he wants, but discerning members of staff will have noted the reaction for future use.

One should not count on this sort of reaction. In some cases, the dominant approach grows even harder under challenge or stress. Furthermore, just as in one individual an assertive approach may, when challenged, give way to a solicitous or even passive back-up, some helpful and caring individuals can turn into roaring lions if pushed too far.

Suiting behaviour to circumstances

If we are to manage our relationships with parents, governors, colleagues, superiors and subordinates, the important skill is to be able to suit our behaviour to circumstances and individuals. This calls for 'situational sensitivity' and 'style flexibility' (Reddin, 1971).

If there is a fire or other emergency, an assertive style by the leader is probably highly appropriate - there may not be time to consult or to let people 'do their own thing'. On the other hand, if a person is in distress, a highly solicitous approach is probably best - 'Forget your work, go home, sort things out, and come back when you can.' Such an approach may bear rich rewards in terms of future loyalty and work.

Recognizing inappropriate behaviour

While it is true that there are times when any of the range of behaviours may be equally appropriate, we must remember that there are other times when a particular behaviour is quite inappropriate. It is vitally important that we increase both:

(1)   our skill in recognizing when a particular form of behaviour is wrong; and

(2)   our ability to use alternative forms of behaviour.

Remember that as well as 'concern for results' and 'concern for relationships' everyone has a third concern – 'concern for self', or, more positively, for 'personal effectiveness'. People – and organizations – will adapt very quickly to whatever patterns of behaviour are seen to 'pay off' and will avoid patterns which do not 'pay off'. Thus there is a very interesting interaction of management styles. If it is clear in an organization that 'those who shout loudest get most', a lot of people will start to shout loudly. If esteem or salary depends on having a large number of subordinates, empires will be built.

While it is impossible to provide for every contingency, there are a number of rules of thumb which the individual manager can use in spotting an inappropriate use of behaviour on his or her part. Remember that these rules only apply to *inappropriate* uses of the different types of behaviour, and that while assertive behaviour, for example, may have a negative effect on some people, there are others who like to be dealt with in an assertive way and who will not respond to anything else.

Different individuals need to be handled in different ways. While some people may be slow to take action if not 'chased', for example, others will be sufficiently self-motivated to produce the best results when left alone.

In dealing with pupils, the technique of 'acting' an emotion is one that most of us have used. Our response to staff may need the same degree of control. The danger always is that of getting 'hooked into' behaviours which may be counterproductive.

Leadership and job experience

In dealing with subordinates the appropriate leadership style may vary according to how long they have been in the job (Hersey and Blanchard, 1977).

In the early days they may look for high task behaviour from their boss, i.e. for him or her to tell them what is expected and teach them how to do it in detail. At a second stage a more overtly 'motivational' behaviour may be called for, i.e. agreeing what is expected but leaving the subordinate more freedom to decide *how* to carry it out and giving feedback on results. At the third stage, the employee may simply need positive or negative feedback on results (a demonstration of genuine interest). Finally, a self-motivated employee may for most of the time be left to get on with his job, though this approach may *never* be right for certain subordinates.

Signs of inappropriate use of assertive behaviour

To a subordinate
(1) The subordinate may adopt a passive role: 'If my boss will not listen to my ideas, I will not contribute unless specifically asked or told to do so.' If you have a passive subordinate, you should always ask whether this is a basic orientation or whether you have caused it! A head of department recently said to us: 'I am paid to take decisions and I do so. My worst problem as head of department is that I have "turned off" teachers in my department and I can't seem to motivate them.'
(2) The subordinate may react politically, and start to bypass you by giving his ideas and suggestions to others who are more interested. He will be competing rather than contributing.
(3) There may be a direct rebellion or protest. (As we have seen, some assertive bosses when faced by this move sharply into a solicitous role. This solicitous approach is usually shortlived.)

To an equal
(1) Some equals will respond in equally assertive terms and a win–lose conflict may quickly develop (Chapter 7).
(2) Other colleagues of a 'solicitous' disposition may 'smooth' the situation by not responding strongly. However, they may then undermine your position in less obvious ways.

Signs of inappropriate use of solicitous behaviour

To a subordinate. Contrary to the expectations of many 'solicitous' managers, most people are not motivated by flattery or a style which overlooks infringements. 'If the boss does not care about my results, why should I bother?' Hence there may be slackness and low task-motivation.

To an equal. A colleague who always agrees with you on the surface (but may undermine you in your absence) loses your respect!

Personal application. You may usefully think about colleagues and try to assess their management style.

Passive/political orientation

While passive/political *behaviour* may sometimes be appropriate, an *orientation* which is directed neither towards results nor towards relationships is unlikely to be of much real value to an organization or school except in the accomplishment of purely manual tasks under strict supervision. Remember, of course, that it *may* be the school 'culture' or managerial behaviour which has produced this orientation!

Behind many a 'nine-to-four' schoolteacher is a history of being frustrated or overlooked. Some of these individuals show surprising enthusiasm and ability outside school as leading members of local societies or even councillors! What went wrong?

Style and the school manager

On any day we will see a rich variety of behaviour exhibited by our professional colleagues, our pupils, the administrative and ancillary staff and other people with whom we come into contact. In each situation the basic style orientation of the individual will be modified to a greater or lesser extent, deliberately or unthinkingly, in response to the situation with which he finds himself confronted.

Experience over the years helps us to learn to respond more effectively to many of the situations with which we are faced – to control our instinctive reactions so as better to achieve a desired result. However, there are certain behavioural patterns which we may never try unless we make a deliberate effort. Furthermore, we may become locked into assumptions about the way in which others will react.

An understanding of management style should re-open the options, cause us to challenge our assumptions and consequent behaviour and, as a result, make us more effective leaders.

Further reading

Adair, J. (1983) *Effective Leadership: A self-development manual*, Gower, Aldershot.

Adair, J. (1988) *Developing Leaders*, Talbot Adair, Guildford. (This includes a chapter on school leadership.)

Bush, T., Glatter, R., Goodey, J. and Riches, C. (1980). *Approaches to School Management*, Section IV 'Leadership in Schools', Paul Chapman Publishing, London.

John, D. (1980) *Leadership in Schools*, Heinemann, London.

Silver, P.F. (1983) *Educational Administration*, Harper and Row, New York.

3
MOTIVATING PEOPLE

Motivation

'Motivation' can be defined as 'getting results through people' or 'getting the best out of people'. The second definition is slightly preferable, since 'the best' which people can offer is not necessarily synonymous with 'the results' which we might initially want from them, though it should be in line with the overall goals and ethos of the school or college.

As Peters and Waterman (1982) quote: 'Management's principal job is to get the herd heading roughly west.'

A head of an English department may, for example, have fairly strong feelings about the choice of set books. However, if he wishes to get the best out of the teacher responsible for taking the class, he should at least allow his own choice to be modified by the teacher's preference. Both should be asking what is in the best interests of the pupils.

In motivating people we should be concerned with the needs and potential of three parties:

(1) the group which we are managing or in which we manage;
(2) the individuals who make up that group;
(3) the 'clients' (pupils, parents, etc.) of the school, college or other organization in which we all work.

A fundamental mistake is to forget that people are best motivated to work towards goals that they have been involved in setting and to which they therefore feel committed. If people do not feel committed towards a given result or activity, the only motivations at our disposal are those of the carrot and stick – reward and punishment. We therefore have to be prepared to modify our own initial perceptions of what is required. Some people have a strong 'internal' motivation – a sense of purpose or drive. Others do not.

Whom do we need to motivate?

Subordinates are obvious candidates for 'motivation'. However, it is even more important to be able to motivate equals and superiors. In the last resort, we can tell a junior member of our department what he or she is to do, but we have no such power with a schoolteacher who is our equal and even less with the headteacher, chairman of governors or local education officer. Here we are in much more of a 'selling' role, and, like all good salespeople, must be very aware of the benefits that will accrue to our 'customer'.

A cynical – but often true – maxim is: 'There is nothing I cannot achieve provided that my boss gets the credit for it!'

Satisfying needs

People work in order to satisfy some need. The need may be to achieve fame or power, to serve other people or simply to earn the money to live. It may even be the rather negative need to avoid punishment.

Most motivational theorists have therefore concentrated their attention on:

(1) examining human needs;
(2) considering how the needs are met and can be better met in work.

People work at their best when they are achieving the greatest satisfaction from their work.

Maslow's hierarchy of needs

Maslow (1943) suggested that it was useful to think of human needs as being at different levels in a hierarchy – see Figure 3.1. The principle behind the hierarchy is that, starting from the bottom, the needs at each level have to be satisfied to some extent before we think about needs at the next level up.

SELF-REALIZATION	Achievement
	Psychological growth
EGO	Status
	Respect
	Prestige
SOCIAL	Friendship, group acceptance
	Love
SECURITY	Freedom from danger
	Freedom from want
PHYSIOLOGICAL	Food, drink, shelter, sex,
	warmth, physical comfort

Figure 3.1 Based on 'Hierarchy of Needs', in Maslow, A.H. (1970) *Motivation and Personality*, 2nd edn, copyright © by Abraham H. Maslow

The physiological needs
Undoubtedly physiological needs are the most basic of all needs. For the person who is missing everything in life, it is most likely that the major motivation will be the physiological needs. A person who lacked food, security, love and esteem would probably hunger for food more strongly than for anything else.

The security needs
If the physiological needs are gratified, there then emerges a new set of needs, which are categorized roughly as the security needs. Robinson Crusoe's first thoughts on reaching his desert island were to find water, food and shelter. His second was to build a stockade and to get in reserves of food and water.

The social needs
If both the physiological and the security needs are fairly well satisfied, then there will emerge the love and affection and belongingness needs. Now the person feels keenly the need for friends, a special relationship with one person of the opposite sex, or children. There is a hunger for affectionate relationships with people in general, for a place in the group.

The ego needs
Having established a base of friendship, acceptance and affection, most

of us want to prove our worth within whatever group or groups we belong to. We seek to demonstrate to ourselves and others that we are as good, or better than, other members of the group. We pursue promotion, influence, status, power, reputation, recognition, prestige, importance, attention.

The need for self-realization
Even if all these needs are satisfied, we may still be discontented and restless if we feel that we have talent and potential within us which we are not fully exploiting.

Why do people write poetry, plays, books and music, play sports, act in plays, take up hobbies, climb mountains? We have a need to achieve, fulfil ourselves, become what we are capable of becoming, meet new challenges.

The relevance of the hierarchy

There are a number of important points to be made about the hierarchy:

(1) If an individual is really deprived at a lower level, he or she may lose interest in the higher-level needs. How often do we hear someone who suddenly finds himself in pain in hospital make a remark like: 'To think that I was worrying yesterday because I hadn't been invited to... . This puts things in perspective'? Serious financial hardship or threats of redundancy can take the mind off thoughts of achievement.

(2) On the other hand, a 'satisfying' job at the higher levels will raise the level of tolerance or deprivation at the lower levels. Teachers, doctors and nurses are prepared to tolerate conditions of employment which would not be acceptable to someone with a boring job – though even they have their limits.

(3) When a need at a given level is satisfied, the law of diminishing returns sets in. When I have eaten a meal, I do not wish to eat another immediately. While I may like friends and parties, too many become a nuisance. Even prestige can pall and those who courted publicity on their way to promotion and fame, may seek, when they have 'arrived', to avoid the limelight.

(4) 'Oversatisfying' of a need may produce a sense of guilt and/or deliberate self-deprivation. Drop-outs are often the children of well-to-do families, and young people will undertake ventures which involve frugal living and risk in order to prove themselves.

(5) Different people will feel needs with differing intensity. One person's social needs may only be satisfied when surrounded by friends, whereas another will be content simply to have the companionship and love of his or her partner. Very exceptionally, an individual will shun all company, but such 'hermits' are extremely rare.

The interesting thing is that when dealing with people with whom we work, *most of us have a tendency to behave as though the needs of others, particularly our subordinates, are at the lower levels.*

I look for satisfaction in my job but the rest of the staff are concerned only about physical conditions, being treated kindly, not being asked to work hours which are unreasonable, being given appropriate recognition of their status. This is the same sort of phenomenon as was illustrated by the questionnaire on p. 1. Furthermore, the staff themselves often reinforce our beliefs by complaining about precisely those things we have just mentioned.

The two views of work – one asserting that people seek fulfilment through work, and the other suggesting that they seek only to satisfy lower-level needs – are neatly described by Douglas McGregor (1960). McGregor called the two conflicting assumptions about the nature of work Theory X and Theory Y.

Theory X and Theory Y

Those managers who adopt 'Theory X' believe:

(1) Work is inherently distasteful to most people.
(2) Most people are not ambitious, have little desire for responsibility and prefer to be directed.
(3) Most people have little capacity for creativity in solving problems.
(4) Motivation occurs only at the physiological and security levels.
(5) Most people must be closely controlled and often coerced to achieve organization objectives.

'Theory Y' managers, on the other hand, believe:

(1) Work is as natural as play, if the conditions are favourable.
(2) Control of one's own work activities is often indispensable in achieving organizational gains.
(3) The capacity for creativity in solving organizational problems is widely distributed in the population.

(4) Motivation occurs at the social, ego and self-realization levels as well as at the physiological and security levels.
(5) People can be self-directed and creative at work if properly led.

Frederick Herzberg

Herzberg (1966) put to the practical test, through a series of experiments conducted with widely differing groups of workers, the sort of thinking developed by Maslow and McGregor.

One of his best-known experiments consisted of asking people to think of three occasions when they had felt very satisfied in their work and three occasions when they had felt dissatisfied. He then asked them to categorize the causes of satisfaction and dissatisfaction under a number of headings. Finally he recorded for all the individuals in the group the frequency with which each category had been noted as a cause of satisfaction or dissatisfaction. A typical result is shown in Figure 3.2.

From these findings, Herzberg drew some important conclusions:

(1) The things which make people happy at work are not simply the opposites of the things which make them unhappy, and vice versa. The two sets of things are different in kind. You will not make people *satisfied*, therefore, simply by removing causes of *dissatisfaction*.
(2) The things that make people dissatisfied are related to the job *environment*. The things that make people satisfied on the other hand are related to the job *content*.
(3) While those who have a satisfying job may have a higher tolerance of dissatisfiers, the dissatisfying factors can be so strong that the job becomes intolerable.
(4) Managers must therefore be concerned with ensuring both that causes of dissatisfaction are removed and that opportunities for satisfaction are increased – that, in Herzberg's terms, the job is 'enriched'. It is in this latter respect that managers usually fail. Instead of using the real 'motivation' which comes from a satisfying job, they use rewards and threats.

Herzberg calls the environmental factors which are capable of causing *un*happiness the 'hygiene' factors because he believes that these have to be reasonably well 'cleaned up' as a prerequisite for satisfaction. Among the hygiene factors are:

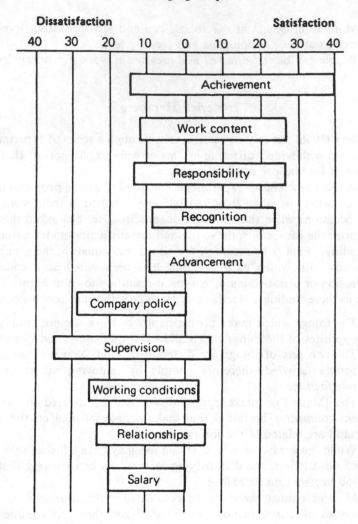

Figure 3.2 Motivators and Hygiene Factors
Source: Herzberg, F. (1966)

(1) organizational policies and administration;
(2) management.
(3) working conditions;
(4) interpersonal relationships;
(5) money, status and security.

The work content factors which lead to happiness, Herzberg calls the 'motivators' and these are:

Achievement. This is a measure of the opportunities for you to use your full capabilities and make a worthwhile contribution. It includes the possibilities for testing new and untried ideas.

Responsibility. A measure of freedom of action in decision-taking, style and job development.

Recognition. An indication of the amount and quality of all kinds of 'feedback', whether good or bad, about how you are getting on in the job.

Advancement. This shows the potential of the job in terms of promotion – inside or outside the organization in which you currently work.

Work itself. The interest of the job, usually involving variety, challenge and personal conviction of the job's significance.

Personal growth. An indication of opportunities for learning and maturing.

At this point you may like to look at how 'motivating' your own job is, in Herzberg's terms, by completing and scoring Exercise 1 at the end of this chapter.

Educators' jobs usually score fairly high in Herzberg's terms, though low scores on 'Recognition' are not uncommon. This is less a particularity of the teaching profession than a British or European cultural norm. We hesitate to tell people how they are getting on, though this knowledge is not only an element in job satisfaction but also essential for improvement and adjusting to the needs of the job. This should be the purpose of staff appraisal.

The relationship between the Herzberg 'motivators' and the top two levels of Maslow's hierarchy is self-evident.

Involvement

Where staff at any level are 'involved' in decisions taken by their superiors, peers or even subordinates, all the motivators are brought into play. This is particularly the case where the decision under discussion will affect the person 'involved'.

Involvement should produce the commitment to goals on which a sense of achievement depends. By involving people we show them recognition and increase their sense of responsibility. The interest of their job should be increased and we are providing them with the broader view which provides both a learning opportunity and experience which may be of use in seeking advancement.

Achievement needs

Motivational theorists are almost unanimous in giving a special place to the need for achievement.

In his book *Every Employee a Manager*, Myers (1970) neatly specifies that a sense of achievement arises when an individual clearly perceives a goal and is then able to:

(1) *plan* how to achieve the goal;
(2) *implement* his or her own plan;
(3) *control* (i.e. 'monitor') the results.

In this sense, whatever the other issues involved, public and internal examinations provide a motivational loop in that teachers and pupils know more or less what is expected; can plan how to achieve the required standard with freedom to choose textbooks and other means; can carry out the teaching/learning in line with the plan, and finally obtain a result. In the absence of examinations, learning goals and measures of achievement may be less clear, and we may have problems in finding motivational substitutes.

Fundamental to the concept of achievement is the perception by the individual to be motivated that the goal is relevant to him. In a world where traditional learning is no longer linked to career prospects – GCSE results do not guarantee a job – teachers and pupils have a further motivational problem.

The self-motivated achiever

As with all needs, the intensity of the need for achievement varies greatly from person to person. In some pupils, particularly at secondary level, we may feel that it has almost disappeared! McClelland's (1961) interest is in those with very strong achievement needs who offer great potential, but can also pose problems where their own perception of goals may be different from our own.

McClelland would claim that most of us have a motivation to achieve something. He would also claim, however, that only in 10 per cent of the population is this a highly developed motivation. According to McClelland, the most convincing sign of a strong achievement motivation is the tendency of a person who is not being required to think about anything in particular, that is, who is free to relax or to let his mind wander, to think about ways of accomplishing something. On a car journey the self-motivated achiever will typically set himself time-targets or fuel consumption targets. On the way to work he will try out new routes to cut mileage or time. He will work to achieve a standard in a sport, to take on new challenges in his job, to produce a play, to organize a new function.

Such tendencies emerge at a very early age. In a series of experiments McClelland provided young people with an upright pole and quoits. Some would throw the quoits aimlessly around, build towers, drop them with ease on to the pole or quickly lose interest. However, certain individuals would set themselves a challenge by attempting to hit the pole or throw the quoits over it from a distance chosen by them such that success would not come too easily nor be impossible or subject to pure luck.

Following his subjects' careers McClelland found that those who showed a strong achievement motivation in childhood tended to manifest the same drive in adult life.

Although only about 10 per cent of people are strongly motivated, the percentage in certain occupations is likely to be much higher. This is especially true of people in managerial positions, and independent entrepreneurs. A person with a strong achievement motivation is likely to surpass the accomplishments of equally able but less strongly motivated people, especially in one of the above occupations.

McClelland's studies have identified three major characteristics of the self-motivated achiever, and why supervisory tactics, which may be appropriate to other kinds of people, are often inappropriate when applied to a man or woman with a strong achievement motivation.

First, achievers like to set their own goals. They are nearly always trying to accomplish something. They are seldom content to drift aimlessly and let life happen to them. They are quite selective about which goals they commit themselves to and for this reason they are unlikely to automatically accept goals which other people, including their bosses, select for them. Neither do they seek advice or help except from experts or people who can provide needed skills or information. The achiever prefers to be as fully responsible for the attainment of his goals as it is possible to be. If he wins he wants the credit, if he loses he accepts the blame. Either way he wants the victory or defeat to be unmistakably his.

Second, the achiever tends to avoid extremes of difficulty in selecting goals. He prefers moderate goals which are neither so easy that winning them would provide no satisfaction nor so difficult that winning them would be more a matter of luck than ability. He will tend to gauge what is possible and then select a goal that is as tough as he thinks he can fulfil, i.e. the hardest practical challenge. This attitude keeps him continually straining his abilities to their realistic limits, but no further. Above all else he wants to win and, therefore, he does not knowingly commit himself to a goal that is probably too difficult to achieve.

Third, the achiever prefers tasks which provide him with more or less immediate feedback, i.e. measurements of how well he is progressing towards his goal. Because of the importance of the goal, he likes to know how well he is doing at all times.

The effect of a monetary incentive on an achiever is rather complex. Achievers usually have a fairly high opinion of the value of their services and prefer to place a fairly high price tag on them: they are unlikely to remain for long in an organization that doesn't pay them well. But it is questionable whether an incentive payment actually increases their output since they are normally working at peak efficiency anyway.

McClelland notes that monetary incentives are actually more effective with people whose achievement drives are relatively weak, because they need some kind of external reward to increase their effort. The main significance of additional income to the achiever is as a way of measuring his success. McClelland emphasizes that the achievement motive, as he defines it, is not the only source of success attainment. Other drives can also lead to high levels of attainment, but achievers have a considerable advantage.

Can the level of achievement motivation be increased in people whose achievement drives are not usually strong? McClelland believes this may be possible and indeed there are considerable reserves of latent untapped achievement motivation in most organizations. The key is to build more achievement characteristics into the job – personal responsibility, individual participation in the selection of targets, moderate goals and fast clear-cut feedback on the results each individual is achieving, etc.

For achievers themselves, McClelland believes that many standard supervisory practices are inappropriate and in some cases may even hinder their performance. Work goals should not be imposed on the achiever. He not only wants a voice in setting his own goals, but he is unlikely to set them lower than he thinks he can reach. Highly specific directions and controls are unnecessary; some general guidance and occasional follow-up will do. But if the job does not provide its own internal feedback mechanism regarding the achiever's effectiveness, as is the case, for example, in some professional or administrative jobs, then it is vitally important to the achiever that he be given frank, detailed appraisals of how well he is performing in his job.

Motivation theory and the school manager

The key to effective management is the ability to get results from other people, through other people and in conjunction with other people. If the underlying psychology is wrong, the most carefully constructed system and techniques will fail. Efficient headteachers are not necessarily effective headteachers. But if relationships and motivation are good, people will readily accept and overcome *some* administrative or environmental flaws (but see Herzberg, p. 29).

Three basic rules should underlie management relationships and the application of any technique:

(1) We should remember to use the 'motivators', i.e. people's need for achievement, recognition, responsibility, job interest, personal growth and advancement potential. We tend to underestimate the needs of other people in these areas. Involving others in decisions which affect them is one way of meeting all or most of these needs. This principle is as valid for the caretaker or the dinner lady as it is for teaching staff.

(2) The relative intensity of psychological needs will vary greatly from person to person and from time to time. There are people who simply are not interested in motivators, or who do not wish to have these needs satisfied at work. If a teacher's spouse loses his or her job, security needs may well be the most important. If there is a marriage break-up, both security and social needs may surface, though these may be followed later by a need to find renewed interest and achievement in the job.

      ·These are predictable and often recognizable behavioural phenomena. However, when symptoms and causes are less obvious, the risk is that we misjudge the needs of colleagues or friends. Some of us have a tendency to assume that the needs of others are the same as our own; others tend to assume the opposite.

As a fairly light-hearted exercise in judging your ability to assess the motivation of others, you may like to try Exercise 2 at the end of this chapter with a group of colleagues or friends.

(3) We should try to suit our management behaviour to both the personalities and the needs of the situation. Our automatic behavioural reaction may not be the right one. Think about the alternatives!

Despite every effort there will remain individuals who have no wish to be 'motivated' and who view with suspicion any attempt to increase their responsibilities, job interest or involvement. Such attitudes may typically be found in caretakers, ancillary staff or teachers who are frustrated. However, the danger is always that we give up too easily. The right approach may prompt a surprisingly warm response.

Further reading

Stewart, V. and Stewart, A. (1982) *Managing the Poor Performer*, Gower, Aldershot.
Warwick, D. (1984) *Motivating the Staff*, The Industrial Society, London.

Exercise 1: opinion questionnaire

The aim of this exercise is to discover your reaction to your job.

Instructions
Answer each question to show how you feel. Do this by circling the number of the statement which best describes your opinion. The only correct answer is your frank opinion.

Questionnaire

1. Think about the specific duties of your job. How often have you felt unable to use your full capabilities in the performance of your job?

Almost always	Very often	Fairly often	Not very often	Very seldom	Almost never
0	1	2	3	4	5

2. How many functions do you perform on your job which you consider relatively unimportant or unnecessary?

Almost all of them	Most of them	Quite a few	A few	Very few	None of them
0	1	2	3	4	5

3. As you see it, how many opportunities do you feel you have in your job for making worthwhile contributions?

Almost none	Very few	A few	Quite a few	A great many	Unlimited times
0	1	2	3	4	5

4. How often do you feel that your job is one that could be dropped?

Almost all the time	Most of the time	Quite often	Very seldom	Almost never	Never
0	1	2	3	4	5

5. How much say do you feel you have in deciding how your job is to be carried out?

None	Almost none	Very little	Fairly large amount	Very large amount	Unlimited amount
0	1	2	3	4	5

6. How frequently have you felt in your job that you could achieve more if you could have complete freedom of action to accomplish your objectives?

Almost all the time	Most of the time	Quite often	Not very often	Very seldom	Almost never
0	1	2	3	4	5

7. How frequently in your job have you received some type of recognition for your accomplishment?

Almost never	Very seldom	Not very often	Quite often	Very often	A great many times
0	1	2	3	4	5

8. How often does your job give you the opportunity for personal recognition?

Almost never	Very seldom	Not very often	Quite often	Very often	A great many times
0	1	2	3	4	5

9. How do you feel about your present post as a job where you can continually learn?

Nothing more to learn in it	Practically nothing to learn	Can learn something but not much	Can still learn a little	Can still learn a lot in it	Can still learn a vast amount
0	1	2	3	4	5

10. How do you feel about your general association with the school as an opportunity for learning?

Provides no chance for learning	Provides almost no chance	Can learn something but not much	Can learn a little	Can learn a lot	Can learn a vast amount
0	1	2	3	4	5

11. Leaving aside any regular measurements of your job (indices or performance standards), how often have you inwardly felt you have achieved something really worth while?

Very seldom	Once in a while	Fairly often	Often	Very often	All the time
0	1	2	3	4	5

12. To what extent is it possible to know whether you are doing well or poorly in your job?

No way of knowing	Almost no way of knowing	To some extent	To a large extent	To a great extent	Entirely possible
0	1	2	3	4	5

13. To what extent is it possible for you to introduce new (untried) ideas on your job?

To no extent	Almost no extent	Very little extent	Fairly large extent	Large extent	Very great extent
0	1	2	3	4	5

14. How often have you found the kind of work you are now doing to be interesting?

Never	Very seldom	Not very often	Quite often	Very often	Almost always
0	1	2	3	4	5

15. Based on your past experience in your present job, how often have you thought that you would like to resign or change jobs?

Very often	Often	Fairly often	Once in a while	Very seldom	Never
0	1	2	3	4	5

16. To what extent do you consider your present post helpful for a person who wants to get ahead?

Almost no extent	Very little extent	Not very helpful	Fairly helpful	Very helpful	Extremely helpful
0	1	2	3	4	5

17. If you wish to make any comments about your job, your chance for achievement, recognition and personal growth, use the space below.

Scoring sheet

Mark your score for each question in the appropriate space, add the total
for each group and divide as indicated.

Question	Score	Group total		
1	. . . . .			
3	. . . . .	. . . . . .	÷ 4 = ...	(ACH)
11	. . . . .			
13	. . . . .			
5	. . . . .	. . . . . .	÷ 2 = ...	(RY)
6	. . . . .			
7	. . . . .			
8	. . . . .	. . . . . .	÷ 3 = ...	(RN)
12	. . . . .			
16	. . . . .	. . . . . .	=	(AD)
2	. . . . .			
4	. . . . .			
14	. . . . .	. . . . . .	÷ 4 = ...	(WI)
15	. . . . .			
9	. . . . .	. . . . . .	÷ 2 = ...	(PG)
10	. . . . .			
Grand total				

Interpreting your score

The scoring sheet has interpreted your responses to give a rating to *your*
job under the following headings:

Achievement (ACH)   Advancement (AD)
Responsibility (RY)   Work interest (WI)
Recognition (RN)   Personal growth (PG)

Note that the rating is not of *you* but of the extent to which you feel,
according to your answers, that *your* job provides you with opportunities
for achievement, responsibility, etc.

The headings listed are the factors which, according to Herzberg, are
the 'motivators' in work.

In the grand total you have a score which reflects the relative weighting
which Herzberg gives to each motivator in determining overall job
satisfaction.

You may like to compare your own score against the European norm.

	ACH	RY	RN	AD	WI	PG	Overall
UK and European norm	3.1	3.0	2.9	3.2	3.6	3.5	51.8

As a rule of thumb, a score of 3.5 or above under any heading indicates a thoroughly satisfying job. A score of between 2.5 and 3.0 *suggests* that there may well be room for enrichment of your job. If your score is less than 2.5 under any heading, you and your manager should be asking why. There may be a simple explanation (e.g. a head of a large school may well score 0 on opportunity for further advancement!), but the likelihood is that there is an area of frustration here.

An overall score of 55+ would indicate total job satisfaction. However, between 45 and 55 should not give any cause for concern.

Note, finally, that the first three areas – 'achievement', 'responsibility' and 'recognition' – are particularly within the control of your superior and the way your work is organized.

NB   All the above remarks are equally valid if you give the test to your subordinates! It can provide the basis for a discussion which can make their jobs more interesting and your life easier and more efficient.

Exercise 2: assessing the motivation of others

The exercise that follows should be carried out with at least three (preferably five) friends or colleagues. The friends need not be connected with work – indeed, the exercise can provide a semi-serious hour's entertainment for you, your spouse and a few dinner guests. While it is essential that all the people involved in the activity should have met several times previously and spent some time together, they do not need to have a particularly close social or working relationship.

Before conducting the exercise, you are advised to familiarize yourself thoroughly with the two forms (pp. 43–44) and with the exercise instructions but you should *not* read the 'Interpretation'.

When you have completed the exercise, develop a personal strategy to remedy any problems you may have either in assessing the needs and wants of others or in ensuring that others know your own needs and wants. Put it into practice.

Instructions

Form 1, column 1. Each of the participants in the exercise should be given a copy of Form 1. On this form are listed a number of 'needs' or 'wants' which are felt to a greater or lesser extent by most people.

In the first column of the form each participant should rank the needs in order of importance to him or her by writing the figure '1' against the most important, '2' against the next most important and so on.

Usually people will find it relatively easy to rank the most important and the least important but may have some hesitation in the middle rankings. If this happens, the order probably does not matter and a choice should be made fairly quickly either way. Others may feel that two needs 'overlap' for them. If so, they should ask which is the really driving purpose for them and which is the means to the end.

The golden rule is not to spend *too* long in contemplation – first instincts are often the most accurate.

Form 1, column 2, etc. Having ranked the needs in order of importance for themselves, each participant should write at the head of column 2 the name of the first person to his right, at the head of column 3 the name of the second person to his right and so on.

The next step is for each particpant to fill in, *outside the brackets*, under the appropriate column what he thinks the person concerned will have written in column 1 of his own table, i.e. participant A tries to assess how important each need is to participants B, C, D, etc. This must obviously be done without reference to any of the other participants.

We now have the raw data to be processed.

Form 2. At this stage Form 2 should be given to each participant. Each person heads the columns with the same names as on Form 1. The purpose of Form 2 is to enable each participant to find out how each *other participant* perceived *his or her needs*.

The most efficient way of transferring the information is:

(1) Ensure that each participant has written his name clearly at the top right-hand corner of Form 1.

(2) Circulate the Form 1s and let each person enter on his Form 2, under the column bearing the name which is in the top right-hand corner of the Form 1 which has been passed to him, the ranking which on that Form 1 appears under the column bearing his own name.

Form 1, inside the brackets. When all participants have transferred the information from all Form 1s on to their Form 2, you can begin the next

Form 1 (Exercise 2) – Your own views of your own needs and those of other group members

Your name ....

Motivation

	Yourself →			Names of other group members →			
	1	2	3	4	5	6	7
(a) To be liked	.........( )	...( )	...( )	...( )	...( )	...( )	...( )
(b) To make a lot of money	.........( )	...( )	...( )	...( )	...( )	...( )	...( )
(c) To serve other people	.........( )	...( )	...( )	...( )	...( )	...( )	...( )
(d) To have a good time	.........( )	...( )	...( )	...( )	...( )	...( )	...( )
(e) To be secure	.........( )	...( )	...( )	...( )	...( )	...( )	...( )
(f) To be an expert	.........( )	...( )	...( )	...( )	...( )	...( )	...( )
(g) To become well known	.........( )	...( )	...( )	...( )	...( )	...( )	...( )
(h) To be independent	.........( )	...( )	...( )	...( )	...( )	...( )	...( )
(i) To make the most of your talents	.........( )	...( )	...( )	...( )	...( )	...( )	...( )
(j) To maximize status	.........( )	...( )	...( )	...( )	...( )	...( )	...( )
(k) To be a leader	.........( )	...( )	...( )	...( )	...( )	...( )	...( )
(l) To achieve something worthwhile	.........( )	...( )	...( )	...( )	...( )	...( )	...( )

Form 2 (Exercise 2) – Your motivation as seen by others

Motivation	1	2	3	4	5	6	7	Row Total (excl. row '1')	Ranking or Totals
	Yourself ←——— Ratings of your needs by other group members ——→								
(a) To be liked	....	....	....	....	....	....	....	....	....
(b) To make a lot of money	....	....	....	....	....	....	....	....	....
(c) To serve other people	....	....	....	....	....	....	....	....	....
(d) To have a good time	....	....	....	....	....	....	....	....	....
(e) To be secure	....	....	....	....	....	....	....	....	....
(f) To be an expert	....	....	....	....	....	....	....	....	....
(g) To become well known	....	....	....	....	....	....	....	....	....
(h) To be independent	....	....	....	....	....	....	....	....	....
(i) To make the most of your talents	....	....	....	....	....	....	....	....	....
(j) To maximize status	....	....	....	....	....	....	....	....	....
(k) To be a leader	....	....	....	....	....	....	....	....	....
(l) To achieve something worthwhile	....	....	....	....	....	....	....	....	....

process which is to let each person discover how accurate was his judgement of how others would rank themselves.

This is best done by having each person in turn read out the figures in *column 1* of his own form (e.g. how he ranked his own needs). Each other participant can then enter what is read out *inside the brackets* under the appropriate column on his own Form 1.

When this is done you can go on to the interpretation.

Interpretation

You now have data on at least two important subjects:

(1) your ability to assess the needs and wants of others and therefore to have a clue as to how to 'motivate' them by meeting these needs and wants;

(2) your ability to project your own needs and wants to others.

The first set of information is obtained by comparing the figures inside and outside the brackets under each column on Form 1. (NB The first three and the last three rankings are the most important.) The second set of information is obtained from Form 2.

In the discussion and comparisons which will inevitably arise from this exercise, it may be interesting to look for the occurrence of certain common phenomena:

(1) It often happens that the 'quieter' individuals are the best at perceiving the needs of others and vice versa.

(2) On the other hand, the needs of these quieter individuals are not so easily perceived *by* others.

(3) Certain people have a tendency to assume that all other people have the same needs as themselves.

(4) Other people display the opposite tendency and assume that their own needs are quite different from those of others.

The moral of this exercise is obvious. From the first moment we meet any other person we are making assumptions about his needs, his temperament, and his reactions, and we are acting on these assumptions. We modify our superficial assumptions very quickly as we receive back certain clear signals. For example, if we start to talk to someone about football we will learn quickly whether or not he is interested. If we start to try to impress someone with our knowledge we may be quickly cut down to size. However, even with people we know quite well, the deeper needs may remain hidden and we may therefore 'get it wrong' – if, for example, we offer a make-or-break opportunity to someone who is looking for security.

It is, finally, worth noting that the priority which people attach to needs will vary over time according to circumstances. In times of economic crisis and unemployment, 'security' rises sharply in the rankings of most people.

4
TAKING AND IMPLEMENTING
DECISIONS

Making things happen

Whether we are setting goals, planning how to achieve them, or coping with the issues which arise in organizing and carrying out day-to-day activities, making things happen as we wish them to (and preventing unwanted events!) depends on our ability to take and implement decisions. To accomplish both the taking and implementing of decisions consistently well is no mean task. Ingredients for success include self-discipline, perception, creativity, dynamism and considerable skill in handling both individuals and groups.

Taking decisions

Decision-taking can be a painful process since it usually involves:

(1) change;
(2) conflict;
(3) the risk of being wrong and being called to account;
(4) having to cope with a bewildering number of facts and alternatives.

The result is that many people would rather do almost anything than actually take a decision of any importance, though:

(1) the failure to take a decision is often worse than most of the alternatives;

(2) colleagues and subordinates are often frustrated and virtually
     paralysed by lack of decision.

In a survey at all levels of one organization, people were asked what
change they would most like to see in their boss. The most frequent reply
by a clear margin was, 'that he should take decisions'. Several added
remarks such as, 'more clearly', 'more rapidly', and there was the
frequent comment that: 'It often doesn't matter which decision as long
as he takes one or the other.'

A problem in any organization can be that the culture is such that
people are blamed heavily if a decision is proved to be wrong, whereas no
blame is attached for inertia. In fact, failure to take decisions, or
'management by default', often has the same effect as a decision and is
often worse than any considered alternative.

The risk of not deciding is often the greatest of all risks to the
organization. This is obvious when a commercial organization slides into
bankruptcy through failure to respond to market changes, for example.
Unfortunately, it is not quite so obvious if schools fail to make the
adjustments in curriculum and attitude necessary to prepare their
students for a changing society.

Logical steps in decision-taking

Whether a decision is taken by an isolated individual or in the context of
a meeting, common sense suggests a series of logical steps. These are
summarized in Figure 4.1.

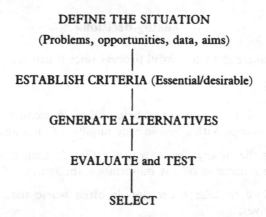

DEFINE THE SITUATION
(Problems, opportunities, data, aims)
|
ESTABLISH CRITERIA (Essential/desirable)
|
GENERATE ALTERNATIVES
|
EVALUATE and TEST
|
SELECT

Figure 4.1 Steps in decision-taking

In taking run-of-the-mill decisions we will often run through the steps subconsciously, and, indeed, time constraints dictate that we do no more. However, the risk is that in big as well as small decisions we lose creative input, and therefore quality, by short-circuiting unduly. It is all too easy to jump for the first solution that comes to mind without considering alternatives or possible side-effects.

Step 1: statement of situation
Decisions are made either to correct a situation or to improve it. Therefore the situation must be understood and its causes explored. We can often usefully compare the situation 'as is' and the 'ideal' that we should like to see. We can also ask questions such as when, where, how and why the problem occurs, or when, where, how and why there is a situation that could or should be improved. What has changed? Relevant data (facts, attitudes, events, figures) can be adduced and the total should be seen in a context of what the school is trying to achieve.

Often it can be useful to restate the problem in as many different ways as possible. The more specific we can be, the better. 'A lot of parents are complaining that their children's property has disappeared' may be able to be restated as 'Ten parents have complained that valuable items (six pens and four calculators) have gone from form rooms over the lunch-hour' or even that 'Children have no secure place to leave valuable items over the lunch-hour.' Such restatements often suggest possible solutions.

Similarly, a problem which appears as 'Parents are complaining that they have to wait around between appointments to see staff on parents' evenings' can be restated as 'Parents get bored between appointments.' This quickly suggests the solution of introducing displays of work, refreshments, opportunities to try the computers, etc., rather than playing with appointment schedules.

Step 2: establishment of criteria
When a problem has been defined and its causes identified, the needs of the situation can be determined. These should be expressed in terms of *ends* not means. To help establish priorities, it is useful to split the needs into two categories:

(1) Essential ends – those which, unless they are achieved, will mean that the situation has not been put right or improved.
(2) Desirable ends – those which are wanted but are not essential to putting right or improving the situation.

Pursuing the example of lunch-hour losses, we may feel that the criteria for a satisfactory solution are as follows:

Essential
(1) Lunch-hour thefts from form rooms will not occur.
(2) Parents will have no grounds for complaint against the school in
     this matter.

Desirable
(1) Children should not have to carry their possessions at all times, in
     particular during lunch-time.
(2) Staff should not be burdened with extra duties.
(3) Children should be able to leave their possessions anywhere on the
     premises at any time without risk of theft.
(4) Any thieves will be caught and dealt with.
(5) Would-be thieves will be deterred.

Step 3: generation of alternative courses of action
The fact that we have to take a decision implies that at least two
alternative courses of action are available, even if one alternative is to do
nothing. In the simplest cases, there are often several alternatives. The
risk is that we do not think of them. The best solution may combine two
or more alternatives.

   In more complex cases, the task of finding alternatives can call for a
high degree of original and effective thinking. Two useful approaches
are:

(1) engaging other minds (this we shall discuss shortly);
(2) using the longest possible incubation period ('sleeping on' a
     problem is a very positive technique).

Step 4: evaluation and testing of alternative courses of action
Evaluation consists of comparing the alternatives generated at Step 3
with the criteria from Step 2.

   Any alternatives which do not satisfy the 'essential' criteria can be
weeded out immediately. Thus, in our lunch-hour-losses example, we
could immediately rule out doing nothing or simply 'having a word in
Assembly'.

   Some other alternatives before us might be:

(1) Carry out an investigation to discover the thief.
(2) Set a trap.
(3) Establish a lunch-hour security duty for staff supported by prefects.
(4) Lock the form rooms at lunch-time and unlock them five minutes
     before the start of afternoon school.

(5) Tell the children that they must keep valuable and attractive items such as pens and calculators on their persons at all times during the day.
(6) Provide a secure area in which children can leave their belongings before lunch and recover them after lunch.
(7) Provide lockable personal lockers.

Each of these alternatives will to a greater or lesser extent satisfy or not satisfy our 'desirable' criteria. Solutions 3, 4 and 6 may well put an extra burden on staff. Solution 5 would partially break the criterion of children not having to carry possessions around with them. Solutions 1 and 2 applied alone might not satisfy the 'essential' criteria but could be used in combination with other actions. They would, of course, take up staff time.

Finally we need to 'test' the proposals for 'side-effects', i.e. for the fact that they might bring new problems and disadvantages. Thus solution 5 could bring the risk of loss or damage at lunch-hour play. Solution 7 could cost money. Solution 6 could bring organizational and space problems.

Step 5: selection of a course of action
Few alternatives will meet all the 'desirable' criteria and be without disadvantages. Our choice should in the end be a balanced judgement in which we are aware of the potential snags and in which we weigh the relative priority which we give to each of the desirable criteria and the extent to which each alternative satisfies each criterion.

Personal application. Before moving on to the next section, think of some problem with which you are currently faced and work through the decision-making steps systematically.

The implementation of decisions

The road to hell is paved with good intentions, and the road to managerial and organizational ruin is paved with decisions that have not been implemented – or, worse still, that have been implemented half-heartedly. There are managers who are sufficiently foolish or immodest to believe that whatever they have decided will automatically be done. The wise head knows better.

Apart from the obvious consideration of practicability, whether or not a decision is effectively implemented depends on two things:

(1)   a clearly defined and communicated structure for implementation;
(2)   the commitment of those responsible for implementation.

A structure for implementation

This is by far the simpler part of the process though it is too often forgotten in the joy of having reached an individual or group decision. Basically the structure consists of:

(1)   determining (agreeing?) *who* will do *what* by *when* (the *action plan*);
(2)   *communicating* the action plan to the parties concerned;
(3)   *ensuring* that reviews take place.

To avoid ambiguity it is usually advisable for the action plan to be communicated in writing either as a memo or as part of the minutes of a meeting. Additionally it may be necessary to speak to the people responsible for action to ensure that they have actually read the paper and that they understand exactly what is intended.

The review procedure may take the form of a special meeting, or bringing up the action plan on the agenda of a more general meeting.

Where actions involve more than one person it is important to state – and to repeat – to all those involved in implementation that anyone who at any stage feels unable to fulfil his or her part of the action plan on time should immediately inform whoever is responsible for co-ordinating the action plan. An 'update' of the plan may then prove necessary. The most vulnerable decisions are often the simplest, where, for example, one or two people agree informally that they will 'let each other have a copy of...' or that one of them will 'ring X and sort it out'. The discipline of jotting down any such action to which you have personally committed yourself is a good beginning to establishing a reputation for 'reliability'.

If you do not already have on your desk an 'action book' in which you systematically read and work through 'things to be done', you should at least try that discipline. Each morning you should review the book to ensure that actions agreed the previous day are added and that 'things left undone' are brought forward.

Styles in decision-taking

Four types of decision-taking can be identified:

(1) Autocratic: the decision is taken without consultation, then others are informed of what is to be done and what is expected of them.
(2) Persuasive: the decision is taken before consultation and then 'sold' to others.
(3) Consultative: the views of others are sought and taken into account before a decision is taken.
(4) Codeterminate: decisions are taken on either a consensus or majority basis.

The appropriate style will depend on people and circumstances.

Autocratic decision-taking
This style is acceptable for routine matters which do not deeply concern people one way or the other. It will also be accepted more easily where the decision-taker has a considerable track record of success, where he is acknowledged to be the expert or where he has 'charisma'. Though people may grumble, they may also grudgingly accept that the decisions taken at a much higher level must sometimes be handed down without opportunity for consultation.

In such situations (e.g. when the head or the LEA has issued an edict) commitment may be built by creating an opportunity for frank questions to be put and honestly answered, and by 'consulting' on *how* the edict will be implemented.

Persuasive decision-taking
This differs from the autocratic style in that the manager uses his powers of advocacy to explain and justify his decision to his staff, subsequent to the decision being taken. It is not open to negotiation. This can be perceived as dishonest, in so far as staff are manipulated by slick 'sales talk' into accepting a *fait accompli*. It would, indeed, be dishonest if such a decision masqueraded as 'consultation'; but if it is presented as what it really is, and not fudged, it is an acceptable type of decision-taking in the right circumstances, and all of us use it in our daily lives. The secret of persuading people effectively without consulting them is to try to demonstrate understanding and sincere respect for their points of view; it also helps to explain why the manager thought consultation was inappropriate (see p. 225).

Consultative decision-taking
This method combines the advantages of obtaining the ideas, suggestions and commitment of those involved, with vesting decision-taking responsibility in one person who should be able to assure consistency of

decision-taking and conformity to established guidelines. It combines motivation with effectiveness.

Codeterminate decision-taking

This approach runs the risk of inconsistency, and while having the virtue of 'collective responsibility' it may thereby avoid individual responsibility. It is the only method available when no one party has clear decision-taking authority. Negotiation and 'management by committee' are forms of co-determinate decision-taking. Many joint decisions between heads of department are of this form.

Whatever form of decision-taking is used, the important things are:

(1) The form of decision-taking should be 'open' and clear to all concerned.
(2) It should be consistent with reality.
(3) The decision-taker should understand and establish the conventions of the particular form of decision-taking.

If these conditions are not met, we may find ourselves confronted with situations like these:

(1) A group of 'votes' for a decision which is unacceptable within the school context (e.g. too expensive).
(2) A decision-taker who is trying to operate in 'consultative' mode finds himself under attack.
(3) A decision-taker says he wants people's views but ignores all that is said.
(4) Having agreed in a meeting or group to do something, the decision-taker finds that what he has agreed does not take into account the interests of another person, or some other relevant fact.

Consultative decision-taking – the 'management contract'

Consultative decision-taking imposes behavioural obligations on both the decision-taker and those who are invited to participate. There is a 'contract' to observe clear roles and conventions in going through the steps in decision-taking.

The terms of the contract are:

(1) The decision-taker will share his or her perceptions of the situation and the criteria.
(2) The other persons involved will ask questions (and give answers)

and put forward perceptions, problems and facts relevant to the situation. At the 'alternatives' step they will contribute proposals for action. (A wise decision-taker will ensure that these are recorded on a flipchart for all to see!) There can be some evaluative discussion of the various alternatives.

(3) The decision-taker will *listen* (i.e. not merely keep quiet), bearing in mind that his job is *not* primarily to *produce* the ideas but to *use* the best ideas whatever their source. (If he thinks someone else's idea is nearly as good as his own it is probably better!)

(4) *After* the meeting (or individual discussion) the decision-taker will *decide* after due consideration of the proposals and any other factors. He should then *communicate and explain* his decision, being prepared to answer any questions.

(5) Finally there is an implied contract that, having been given every opportunity to contribute to the decision, the 'doers' will each play their full part in making it work.

It should be borne in mind that this 'contract' between the decision-maker and the 'doers' can easily be broken by either side. Typical breaches of contract to be avoided are:

(1) The decision-taker suppresses key information or consults only when it suits his or her purpose.

(2) The 'doers' attack and criticize rather than make constructive proposals.

(3) The decision-taker goes on the defensive or feels that it is his duty to have all the ideas. Phrases like 'Yes I had thought of that but...' are not helpful in encouraging people to make suggestions.

(4) The decision-taker does not really listen to the ideas of others but has clearly made his mind up in advance. He is 'playing' with people.

(5) The decision-taker unreasonably refuses to explain his decision. (Note: (a) the words 'on principle' often indicate 'I have run out of logical reasons'; (b) to tell someone that you are not prepared to disclose your reasons implies a parent–child relationship.)

(6) The 'doers' do not give their full commitment to implementation.

Managing the process of consultation is not easy. It is a comparatively slow way of coming to a decision, and it brings with it a perceived risk of early confrontation. However, it has the advantages that:

(1) People who have been involved will be likely to be more committed to the decision taken. They will understand it.

(2) You have benefited from the ideas of others *before* taking the decision and are therefore less likely to have to back off and lose face because you failed to take into account some important consideration.

(3) For the above reasons, though decision-taking is slower, implementation is likely to be much more effective and faster.

Skill in managing the consultative process depends on:

(1) Being very clear on the terms of the 'contract', making them explicit ('*I* should like your views before *I* decide what to do about...' not '*We* have to decide...') and carrying them through.

(2) Dealing politely but firmly with 'breaches'. If discussion starts to become negative, you should ask very deliberately, and repeatedly if necessary: 'What do you suggest we do then?' If people are not implementing a decision, take them up on it quickly: 'Is there some problem?'

(3) Refusing to become emotionally 'hooked' on attack/defence. If people shoot at you ('If you had done what I suggested three months ago...' or 'The problem started when you...'), lie down till the bullets have passed, and then come back with a remark such as 'All that is as may be, but what do you suggest we do now?'

(4) Asking questions and collecting in ideas rather than making statements.

(5) Practice.

Commitment

While not all staff like to be involved in decision-taking, there is overwhelming evidence that *most* people would like a greater share than they have in decisions which affect them but which are the responsibility of others. A simple model putting the choices between involvement and non-involvement is shown in Figure 4.2.

If people make such remarks as: 'Don't ask me, you are paid to decide', you should ask yourself whether this reflects a real reluctance to be involved or whether, on the other hand, your own behaviour where there is such 'involvement' is seen as a charade masking an inbuilt resistance to the ideas of others. It is not enough to ask for opinions and ideas, you should also use them when reasonably possible.

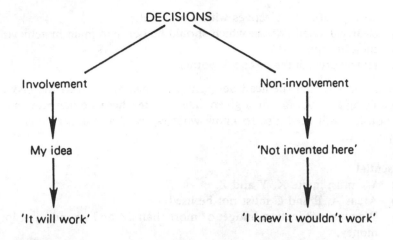

Figure 4.2

Delegation

Commitment based on the 'My idea – it will work' principle becomes even stronger if we delegate as much as possible of the decision-taking to the implementers. This is the thinking which underlies 'management by objectives'.

Ideally the head or head of department will involve his subordinates but take the decisions himself in determining:

(1) common policies;
(2) common systems;
(3) school or departmental objectives (these could derive in part from a higher level);
(4) *what* each individual is expected to achieve.

How the individual is to achieve his objectives can then be left to him, subject always to a respect for the objectives of others and to staying within the agreed policies and systems. As we saw earlier (p. 32), this puts the individual into an 'achievement loop' of planning, implementing and controlling against meaningful goals. If the goals have been agreed with his head or head of department and his colleagues, and if there is a review process, recognition of achievement is also built automatically into the process.

Effective delegation depends on:

(1) clearly defined objectives with a timetable;
(2) clearly defined criteria which should be borne in mind in achieving the objectives;
(3) review procedures or check points.

Let us suppose that the head delegates to a member of staff the task of organizing a school fair on a given date. The teacher who has been made responsible will need also to know what essential and desirable criteria apply, e.g.:

Essential
(1) We must invite X, Y and Z.
(2) Areas A, B and C must not be used.
(3) We must not incur a budget of more than £X and we must not lose money.
(4) There will no alcoholic drinks on sale.
(5) We must provide for the possibility of bad weather.

Desirable
(6) We shall raise at least £X.
(7) We shall avoid clashes with competing activities.
(8) We shall get subscriptions from local businesses.

The list is not, of course, comprehensive for even an imaginary fête. Many other items may be quite clearly implied from the school's culture or from previous experience. However, especially if there is a new head or a new organizer, a thorough briefing meeting can save a lot of wasted effort.

Job descriptions (see p. 80) are an important tool in permanently delegating authority and responsibility for decisions and actions.

Key principles

The effective taking of decisions depends in short on a logical process which ensures in particular that we:

(1) gather as many as possible of the relevant facts and opinions;
(2) consider the alternatives;
(3) take into account the criteria which we need to meet and choose accordingly.

Effective implementation depends on:

(1) a plan;
(2) reviews of progress;
(3) the involvement of the right people at the right time and through a well-controlled process.

Further reading

Poster, C. (1976) *School Decision-making*, Heinemann, London.
Sargent, A. (1980) *Decision-taking*, The Industrial Society, London.
Trethowan, D.M. (1983) *Delegation*, The Industrial Society, London.
Warwick, D. (1983) *Decision-making*, The Industrial Society, London.

5
MANAGING MEETINGS

Meetings and the manager

Though we tend to think of a meeting as a formal gathering at a pre-arranged time and place, many meetings to discuss and progress the work of the school or college are casual, informal affairs consisting of only four, three or even two people. Such meetings can have just as important or even more important outcomes for the organization. Meetings come in all shapes and sizes. They may be highly structured and highly formalized with members speaking to each other 'through the chair' and observing a rigid agenda, or there may be no formal agenda and no acknowledged chairperson. They may have many legitimate purposes, but – as we shall see – they all too often wander aimlessly and have no productive outcome. They consume a high proportion of the non-classroom time of all teachers.

Meetings are of critical importance in co-ordinating effort and effecting change, and a very important part of the manager's role is to ensure that they are vehicles for communication and action rather than for confusion and frustration. This will be achieved by 'helicoptering' above the hurly-burly of the discussion, asking what we wish to achieve, being aware of the behavioural processes at work and trying to structure the meeting in such a way as to channel positively the energies of those involved.

Tests of an effective meeting

The key criteria for judging a meeting's effectiveness are:

(1) Did the outcome of the meeting justify the time spent on it?
(2) Could there have been a better outcome for the same investment?
(3) Will the outcome be acted on?

In order to analyse whether or not these criteria have been met, further questions should be asked:

(1) Was the purpose of the meeting clear to all those who attended?
(2) Was the attendance correct for the subject under discussion? (Who else should have been there? Who was not really needed?)
(3) Were the participants adequately prepared for the meeting?
(4) Was time well used?
(5) How high was the commitment of the participants?
(6) Did the meeting achieve its purpose?
(7) What was the quality of the outcome?
(8) Was there a clear definition of:
   (a) action to be taken following the meeting?
   (b) responsibility for taking the action?
   (c) a mechanism for review of the action?

Some of the above questions need no further discussion. Below are some considerations which are relevant in answering the others.

Purpose of the meeting
The main purpose of some meetings - particularly of regularly held meetings - appears to be to fill Monday morning, the first afternoon of term, etc. In others, there is often a hidden conflict between, for example, those participants who believe that they are there to take a decision (possibly forcing it by a majority vote) and others who see the meeting as a vehicle for giving and receiving information and airing views in order to enable 'the boss' to take his or her own decisions.

Among the possible reasons for holding a meeting are:

(1) to take decisions (e.g. on the organization of parents' evenings, fêtes, curriculum changes);
(2) to collect views, information and proposals in order to enable an informed decision to be taken by an individual (e.g. on a submission to the LEA in response to a circular);
(3) to brief the meeting on, for example, policy;

(4)   to exchange information (e.g. on the progress of various aspects of a common project);
(5)   to generate ideas by use of a 'brainstorm', 'spidergram' or other creative method (these techniques are discussed later in the chapter);
(6)   to enquire into the nature and causes of a problem, such as the behaviour of a particular child or group.

Any one of these purposes is legitimate and it is quite possible that different agenda items will have different purposes. What is important is that the purpose of the discussion at any time should be clearly stated and agreed. An important function of a formal or informal chairperson is to ensure that this is done, and to 'remind' the participant whenever the discussion appears to be losing relevance. Where there is no chairperson, or where the discussion is straying wildly, any participant can often make a very telling and constructive contribution simply by asking: 'What are we trying to achieve?'

Attendance
All that needs to be said here is that attendance should be determined not by status or convention but by relevance:

'Who has the information we need?'

'Who can give a responsible undertaking?'

'Who will have to act on the outcome?'

Participants may change according to the agenda item. For some items it may be appropriate to have a fairly junior person 'sit in' or make a presentation.

It is important to ensure that the people needed at a meeting actually can and do attend. To miss a meeting can waste the valuable time of the other members, particularly if the missing member's agreement is needed to some key action. If a meeting can be missed fairly regularly the question should be asked whether the person concerned *ever* needs to attend. Should he just receive the minutes, or attend when specific items of interest to him are discussed?

Preparation
Some schools and colleges develop a vicious circle whereby people are too busy attending meetings to be able to prepare for a meeting and therefore have to attend a further meeting to present what should have been prepared for the first meeting.

Ability to prepare will depend on the circulation in good time of an agenda for the meeting. Key items for inclusion in the notice of a meeting are:

(1) date, time, place and intended duration of meeting;
(2) people attending and roles (e.g. chairperson, secretary);
(3) purposes of meeting (e.g. decision-taking, information-giving, information exchange, brainstorming);
(4) preliminary documentation, preparation, etc;
(5) agenda items with, for each item, relevant documents, etc., and a note of the persons responsible for introducing the item. (NB an early agenda item should *always* be minutes of the last meeting, if any, and *action taken*.)
(6) particulars of procedure for adding any items to the agenda.

For small informal meetings it may be enough to say 'I should like to discuss... . Could you bring X, Y and Z with you?'

The use of time – meeting structure
Efficient use of time will largely depend on having and *keeping* to a structure which is suited to the purpose and membership of the meeting.

An invaluable piece of equipment at *any* meeting is a flipchart or white board on which key ideas, information or proposals can be recorded for all to see. Advantages to be gained from this common sense but under-used item are:

(1) The discussion is focused.
(2) Ideas are not 'lost' (accidentally or otherwise).
(3) Flipcharts are a useful record on which minutes can be based (and against which minutes can be checked).
(4) Time is not wasted while individuals repeat ideas which they feel have not been heard or considered by the meeting.
(5) Recorded ideas (e.g. alternative proposals) can be dealt with in sequence, and those who have put forward an idea can take a full part in all discussions in the confidence that their own view will in due course be considered. Most people are incapable of listening to anyone else until they are sure their own view has been or will be heard. If, as often happens, there are two or more people in a meeting who feel this way, a 'dialogue of the deaf' is guaranteed.

Given the structure which is naturally created by a written record visible to all, other structural considerations will be determined by the circumstances, such as the size of the meeting.

Large meetings

The only thing which is accomplished efficiently in a large meeting is the giving of information (preferably, of course, with the help of visual aids and handouts).

If the audience is to respond with ideas or ask questions which are meaningful to more than the questioner, the meeting should be split into discussion groups (each with its own room and flipchart). Each group should be asked to formulate ideas and questions which a representative can present to the reconvened main meeting.

A typical programme for such a meeting would be:

Chairperson's introduction *(Purpose and structure of the meeting)*	5 minutes
Presentation(s) of key facts, considerations, criteria by the decision-taker with handout	10 minutes
Questions of clarification	5 minutes
Group meetings *(Groups, each containing a mix of departments, develop ideas and proposals. The decision-taker will visit groups to answer any questions.)*	40 minutes
Group presentations *(Each group will make a 3–5 minute presentation with key points on flipchart.)*	20 minutes
Questions *(After all groups have presented, questions of clarification will be put by the decision-taker and other groups.)*	15 minutes
Arrangements for follow-up	5 minutes
End of meeting	

The study-group concept can be effective with as few as eight members in a meeting (i.e. two groups of four) and should certainly be seriously considered if meaningful participation is expected from more than twelve people.

Decision-taking

As we discussed in the last chapter, 'participative' decision-taking has many advantages, and 'management by committee' does not, for the very simple reason that committees present problems of consistency and accountability. Even within the 'democratic' process of British government, the Prime Minister may overrule the Cabinet, and, on major issues, voting within the House of Commons is effectively controlled by the Government and Opposition party machines rather than by the judgement of the individual member. In the same way most company boards operate on a basis of giving the final word to one person, whether the chairman or the managing director.

Meetings at any level should therefore be clear on whether a decision is really being taken *by* the meeting or whether, on the other hand, there is, for each decision, one person who has the responsibility for taking the decision *with the help of* the meeting.

Whichever is the case, the meeting should follow a clear structure which is stated at the opening of the meeting. If the meeting is to split into groups after an initial presentation and questions, this should be made clear. If we are seeking to achieve 'involvement' in decisions, the steps described at Figure 4.1 can be followed, with key points, especially the criteria and alternatives, listed on a flipchart for all to see.

There is, however, one very important warning. In the atmosphere of the meeting, it is very easy for the decision-taker to be swept along and to forget or minimize constraints and pressures from outside the meeting. Will there be funds available? Will the governors agree? A wise manager will let it be known at the start that he does not intend to make the final choice during the meeting. He should state clearly how and when the decision will be made known and explained, and he should hold to his promise.

The aim of the decision-taker during the meeting should be to explore fully the alternatives before him by comparing them with the criteria and asking questions of the meeting to help him understand what each proposed alternative implies.

Information exchange

The important structural message under this heading is that where a series of people are to report overlapping information to a meeting (e.g. a report back from groups or progress reports on a project), questions on each report should be limited to 'clarification' until all reports have been given. Then and only then should a full discussion take place within the full meeting or in groups. If this principle is not followed, much time is wasted after early reports in discussing issues which may be covered in later reports. Also, later reporters suffer considerable frustration when their 'thunder' is 'stolen', and they are apt either to abstain from discussion or to take over the answering.

Generation of ideas

Generation of ideas can be the purpose of a total meeting or of a part of a meeting. In the decision-taking process we look to the meeting to contribute ideas during each of the first three steps, i.e.:

(1) statement of the situation;
(2) establishment of criteria;
(3) generation of alternatives.

Less familiar to many schools – though increasingly being used – are pure 'brainstorming' meetings in which the aim is to promote creative solutions to problems.

Whether in a brainstorming session or a lower-keyed session for the generation of ideas, the key to success is to gather in ideas systematically and not to allow any evaluative comments during the process. The person leading the meeting should make it clear throughout that even the merest 'Yes, but...' is unacceptable during the 'gathering' phase. All ideas must, of course, be recorded on a flipchart.

Once the ideas have been listed, then, and only then, should questions be asked to clarify what is meant or implied or involved in each suggestion. The irrelevant should be discarded; the relevant suggestions should be debated one by one in depth.

Brainstorming
In normal meetings the process of gathering ideas, prior to discussing them, will be relatively calm and rational. Sometimes, however, we may want a completely uninhibited generation of ideas and comments. Brainstorms, as we call such sessions, are particularly appropriate when we want to unleash creativity or frankness. The aim is to get as many ideas in as short a time as possible. Guidelines given to the group are:

Suspend judgement. Never evaluate the ideas being produced in a brainstorming session, whether they are yours or other people's. Never use the phrases 'That won't work' or 'That's silly' or 'We've had that before.' Laugh *with* the wild ideas, not at them. Nobody likes being laughed at, but laughing with the wild ideas encourages further ideas.

Let yourself go and freewheel. This means drifting or dreaming, and brings into play the subconscious levels of the mind. Don't be worried about putting forward wild or silly ideas. In fact, the wilder the better.

Quantity. Quality implies evaluation. Suspend judgement. Go for quantity, the more the merrier. All ideas are good.

Cross-fertilize. This is where the group comes in. Always be prepared to pick up somebody else's idea and suggest others leading from it. Don't leave it to Charlie to develop his own – after all he's going to pick up yours!

Use verbal shorthand. Don't hold things up by explaining your idea at length. Just shout out the one or two words that will convey your thinking. (You can explain later!)

Brainstorming is both fun and highly productive. Used with a group of school heads of department to answer the question 'How does the staff judge a timetable?' a list of over sixty criteria was produced within 15 minutes, reflecting interests which ranged from educational to purely personal. Some examples of the output were:

(1) good mix of subjects for children;
(2) double periods;
(3) no double periods;
(4) free periods Friday afternoon;
(5) free periods Monday morning;
(6) one free period per day;
(7) children move as little as possible;
(8) staff move as little as possible;
(9) specific criteria, such as no French after PE.

In a half-hour discussion which followed the brainstorm, the member of staff responsible for timetabling was quickly able to come to grips with her colleagues' preferences, some of which they might have hesitated to admit in a more inhibited discussion. Some guidelines on mix of subjects for the children also emerged, not to mention a review of period length and daily structure.

Spidergrams

Another approach to generating ideas is the 'spidergram' or 'mind pattern', a technique which can also be used in a group, or individually, for organizing or recalling ideas. It is an excellent basis for planning an essay or report. The technique consists of setting down the subject as a central point and adding on the other ideas around this point as they emerge. Normally the first thoughts will be immediate associations or main branches from the word but this will not always be the case, and additional main branches may emerge as we proceed.

Thus, if we start with the subject of curriculum development, the first ideas that emerge may be illustrated in Figure 5.1. We may then be 'triggered' by one of the main branches – see Figure 5.2.

Next a subject such as 'funds' may be linked with a number of other issues such as 'retraining' and 'teaching materials' – this we can illustrate by a link line between the subjects in another colour.

The value of the method is that it enables the individual or group to collect ideas in and organize them as they spring to mind, rather than hold them back until the relevant subject comes up in sequence. Furthermore, by letting our eyes wander over the chart we constantly restimulate our brains in each area. Whereas brainstorming can be used effectively in groups of up to twenty people, spidergrams are best used in smaller groups. For further reading see Buzan (1974).

As an exercise you may like to draw a spidergram linking the subjects in this or any other chapter.

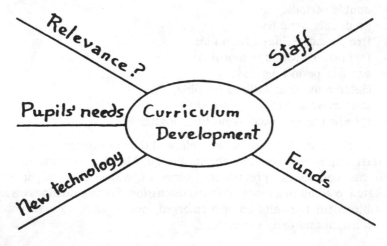

Figure 5.1

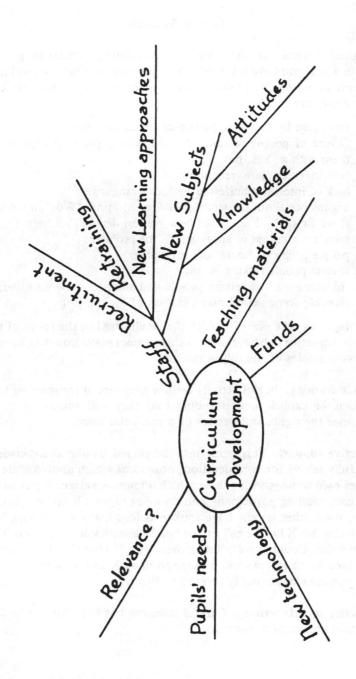

Figure 5.2

Group dynamics

A valuable exercise is to watch a video recording of a meeting, preferably one in which you have taken part. If this is not possible, you will have to rely on sitting back and observing. Among the phenomena which you may notice are:

(1) repetition by the same person of the same point;
(2) failure of people to take up each other's points except to attack them with a 'Yes, but...';
(3) 'not invented here' reactions;
(4) lack of interest manifested by 'body language';
(5) arguments about the structure of the meeting: 'Wouldn't it be best if we first...', 'I don't see how we can decide that before...', and constant changes in approach to the problem;
(6) people trying to 'score' off each other;
(7) several people talking at once;
(8) 'blocking out' of certain people and alliances between others;
(9) possibly some skilful manipulation of the meeting.

Meetings can take place in which the results are less the result of logical and constructive debate, than of skilled games play. You may have come across examples of the following:

Clique-forming. In this activity certain members of the meeting have an implicit or explicit understanding that they will support each other whatever the rights and wrongs of a particular issue.

Selective support. This game may be played by the chairperson who carefully selects for consideration those ideas which approximate to his or her own while ignoring those which do not. A variant is played by the ordinary meeting participant who does not express his own opinion but waits until other people have spoken before making a remark like: 'I think that Mr X hit the nail on the head when he said... and Mrs Y had a good point. Couldn't we build on these by...?' There is a fair chance that any idea which follows will be supported by X and Y, who are flattered that someone has actually listened to them,

Selective minute writing. Careful selection has been known to destroy the true impact of a meeting!

Failure to listen. This is the game of asking people for their views in order to ignore them.

While we don't suggest that you should use manipulative tactics, it is important that you should be able to recognize them and counteract them. Commitment to the results or decisions will depend on the apparent honesty of the decision process and conduct of meetings.

Process review

At Exercise 3 at the end of the chapter is a 'group performance check-list' which can be used to 'score' a meeting which you have attended. It highlights eight areas which are key to a meeting's success and asks you to judge to what extent various behaviours are shown.

Such check-lists can be used to powerful effect in a training context, where the various participants to a meeting first record their individual scores, and then compare scores, discuss the reasons for the scores, and in particular for any discrepancies, and finally decide how they will improve their effectiveness as a group in subsequent meetings.

Following the use of such a procedure for training purposes, some groups build a review into their normal meeting procedure, at the end or after the first 20 minutes of a lengthy meeting, or at any time when the meeting appears to be losing its effectiveness. This can become a relatively short procedure in which a practised and 'open' group will immediately bring forward perceptions such as 'We completely ignored Mrs X's point' or 'We are each defending our parochial interests again.'

There is further discussion of group dynamics in Chapter 10.

Whether or not they have a formal role, the aim of each meeting participant should be to move the meeting towards the positive behaviour outlined by the (a) items in the Group Performance Check-list. This can be done by, for example:

(1) drawing in someone who is being ignored or is remaining silent;
(2) asking quite deliberately for other views and stressing that it is 'Speak now or for ever hold your peace';
(3) asking people to talk one at a time;
(4) drawing attention to the use of time;
(5) asking exactly what decision is being minuted;
(6) summarizing the stated opinions as you now understand them.

Good questions which a consultant, an observer or an observant participant may usefully ask are:

What do you understand to be the goals of this meeting?	Whenever they have not been stated.
What order of priority should these items be in?	When the agenda looks too long.
What do you understand 'X' to have just said?	When someone has not listened.
Where is the discussion aiming now?	When you do not know.
Where are we in the systematic approach?	When the discussion rambles formlessly.
What has just been decided?	When it is not clear what has been decided.
How exactly did we reach that decision?	When it was not reached systematically.
Who is to do that?	When an action is not assigned.
When is this to be done by?	When no time has been set.
For instance?	When airy-fairy generalizations are made.
What was your purpose in saying (or asking) that?	When an unhelpful contribution has been made.
Have you followed your plan?	When they have not.
How is the time going?	When everyone has forgotten its passage.
Are we helping you?	When discussion on someone's point makes slow progress.

Preparing for a meeting

Whether you are to chair a meeting or participate, you will greatly enhance the chances of achieving the sort of outcome you want if you spend a short time in preparation. The check-lists which follow may help.

Chairman's check-list

Planning the meeting
(1)   purpose(s) of the meeting;
(2)   main agenda items (subject possibly to additions);
(3)   essential and desirable participants for the whole meeting;
(4)   participants for parts of the meeting;

(5) date and time, bearing in mind:
    (a) availability of essential and desirable participants;
    (b) degree of urgency;
    (c) need for preparation.
(6) Place.

Notification and circulation of agenda
(1) time, place, date and expected duration of meeting;
(2) purpose;
(3) proposed agenda;
(4) procedure for adding other items to the agenda;
(5) circulation list indicating who is to attend the full meeting, who will attend part only, who is being informed but will not attend.

Preparation for meeting
(1) main meeting room;
(2) group rooms if needed;
(3) visual aids (e.g. overhead projector, screen, slides);
(4) flipchart(s) and dark-coloured markers that work;
(5) seating;
(6) pads and pencils;
(7) masking tape, tacky putty or adhesive pads to stick up flipchart sheets.

Content of meeting
(1) clear objectives (inform, involve, generate ideas?);
(2) appropriate structure;
(3) clear ground rules;
(4) 'honest' procedure;
(5) use of flipcharts or whiteboard;
(6) commitment.

Follow-up
(1) Who will do what, when, where?
(2) Written minutes circulated with action responsibility;
(3) Control and review procedures.

Participants' checklist

Preliminary work

(1) What are the items on the agenda to which I shall be expected/would wish to contribute?
(2) Are there any 'hidden' agendas for which I should be prepared?
(3) Do I wish to introduce any topics? If so, how? For example:
   (a) add them to the agenda before the meeting;
   (b) add them at the beginning of the meeting;
   (c) make sure that they are considered as part of one of the agenda items;
   (d) put down a proposal.
(4) In the light of the above:
   (a) What information should I study, prepare for circulation as a handout, prepare to present?
   (b) Do I need to request any facilities such as flipcharts or overhead projector?
   (c) Do I need to talk to anyone before the meeting in order to gather information or to lobby?

Meeting content

(1) What sort of outcomes should the meeting have (e.g. a decision, an exchange of ideas, factual information, a plan of action)?
(2) Is there any outcome that I particularly want?
(3) Is there any outcome that I particularly do *not* want?
(4) Are there any conditions that I should like to see built into certain outcomes?
(5) What alternatives can I propose?
(6) What arguments should I use?
(7) What arguments can I expect to be used in opposition to my ideas?
(8) When and how should I present my ideas?
(9) Am I really thinking in the best interests of the organization?
(10) How will my views be perceived?

Follow-up

(1) To what action am I prepared to commit myself/my department?
(2) What time/cost is involved and is this reasonable in the light of other commitments?

Further reading

Marland, M. and Hill, S. (1981) *Departmental Management*, Heinemann, London.

Pemberton, M. (1982) *A Guide to Effective Meetings*, The Industrial Society, London.
Perry, P.J.C. (1983) *Hours into Minutes*, BACIE, London.
Trethowan, D. (1985) *Communication in Schools*, The Industrial Society, London.
Warwick, D. (1982) *Effective Meetings*, The Industrial Society, London.

Exercise 3: group performance check-list

According to the group's performance, distribute 100 points among the statements under the first heading below. Then do the same for the statements under the other seven headings.

1. **Objectives**
   (a) Objectives were clear, and understood and accepted by all group members.
   (b) There was no clarity or agreement on what the group's objectives were.
   (c) Though the objectives were clear, full commitment to these objectives by group members was lacking.
   (d) A significant amount of time was spent on secondary issues or unimportant detail.
   (e) Personal goals weighed more heavily than group objectives.

2. **System**
   (a) A logical procedure or method of approach was agreed and adhered to unless deliberately changed; the meeting ran smoothly.
   (b) The meeting was over-organized or rigid; following 'proper procedures' was more important than dealing effectively with the issues.
   (c) The meeting was chaotic and undisciplined.
   (d) The meeting went round in circles.
   (e) Important ideas and information took longer to emerge than they should have done.

3. **Participation**
   (a) All members participated actively; everyone contributed and all contributions received thoughtful attention; humour was a constructive element of the meeting.

(b) Several members dominated a group of relatively passive members.

(c) Members tended to interrupt one another; two or more people talked at once.

(d) Silences fell as members seemed not to know where to go next; initiatives were lacking.

(e) Frivolity, joking and irrelevant comments crept in.

4. Relationships

(a) Group members showed confidence in and trust and respect for each other.

(b) Relationships were formal and guarded.

(c) Members were not open to each other's ideas; listening was poor.

(d) Cliques or subgroups developed.

(e) Maintaining a spirit of good fellowship and friendliness was more important than dealing effectively with the issues or problems.

5. Decisions

(a) Decisions were well considered, based on facts and reason and reached by consensus.

(b) Decisions were forced by individuals; not everyone's point of view received equal attention.

(c) Decisions were reached by majority vote.

(d) Decisions were compromised rather than fully reasoned out.

(e) Few or no decisions were made; issues were left hanging; it was frequently not clear whether a decision had been made.

6. Disputes

(a) Points of disagreement were thrashed out logically until all parties were satisfied.

(b) Disagreements were smoothed over; keeping the peace was more important than getting the best decision or solution.

(c) 'Win–lose' power struggles were fought out; personal victory seemed to matter more than getting the best solution.

(d) Compromise positions were taken; 'workable solutions were accepted rather than 'best' solutions.

(e) Differences were side-stepped or ignored.

7. Leadership

(a) There was a sense of shared responsibility for the quality of the meeting; individuals took leadership initiatives as required.

(b) A leader was agreed at the start and he provided leadership initiatives as he saw fit.

(c) Two or more members of the group seemed to be engaged in a battle for the leadership of the group.

(d) The group's needs for leadership were not met.

(e) Leadership was overdone; the meeting was too tightly controlled; spontaneity and flexibility were lacking.

8. Use of resources

(a) The group made the best possible use of the resources available to it (e.g. time, special knowledge, special skills, equipment).

(b) Time available to the group was not used to the best advantage.

(c) Ideas or relevant information emerged too late or failed to emerge at all.

(d) The group did not make full use of the skills of its members.

(e) The group did not make the best use of the equipment available (e.g. by failing to capture information on a flipchart).

6
RECRUITING, APPRAISING AND DEVELOPING STAFF

People as a resource

In Chapter 13 we shall discuss in some depth the management of resources – financial, physical and human. In the educational system, it is human resources which consume the most investment. In many ways we should treat people as any other resource, selecting the best for the purpose we wish to accomplish, and maintaining, improving and adapting the resource as we would a building or piece of equipment to ensure that it meets our needs. However, there is one important difference: people are *thinking* resources who, whether we like it or not, will decide jointly with their superiors and colleagues on how their time, energy, knowledge and skill will be used. Indeed, the true human resource is not the whole person, but his or her efforts which will be jointly managed by the individual him or herself and the 'management' of the organization in which he or she works. The final arbiter in the use of a person's efforts will always be himself, since he has merely contracted to supply some of his services over a given period of time.

Teachers are often shocked at the idea of describing staff as 'human resources', yet on a continuum of attitudes towards employment (Figure 6.1) where does the average school or college management stand? Do we accept that in selecting a new member of staff we are working *with* the candidate to find out how his or her skills and personality will blend with the needs of the school and the existing skill and personality mix? Do we believe that we can sit as equals with our staff to discuss their performance *and our own performance* in order that both of us can

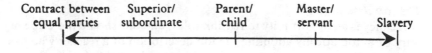

Figure 6.1 Attitudes to employment

develop as individuals and as members of a team, albeit with different roles in the team? Or do we feel that relationships are such that appraisal of our colleagues will be seen by them as 'judgement', and that it would be 'improper' for them to pass a view on the performance of their 'superior'? How do we view the caretaker and ancillary staff? Should our relationship to them be different from our relationship to our colleagues and, if so, how?

It is important to know where we stand and to behave in a coherent way which is consistent with the realities of power. In the teaching profession it is even more difficult than elsewhere to invoke sanctions against the incompetent. We are therefore almost entirely dependent on the recruitment of good staff, and the creation of open relationships in which staff at different levels will work together to make themselves, each other and the organization more effective.

Recruitment of staff

Standard elements in the recruitment process are:

(1)   the job description;
(2)   the personal profile;
(3)   attracting suitable candidates;
(4)   the application form;
(5)   references;
(6)   the interview.

The person under whose immediate direction the new recruit will work should be involved in all stages of the process. Increasingly it is also the practice to take the views of those with whom the recruit will work and also of those whom the recruit will lead. At the earlier stages this allows for creative input (e.g. a readjustment of roles within a school or department) and at the interview stage it builds staff commitment and helps the candidate to assess the environment in which he or she will have to work.

The job description

A vacancy is an opportunity to rethink roles, and one should therefore be wary of automatically adopting the job description of a teacher who has departed. Whatever job description is developed should also be open to revision after appointment as a candidate may emerge with unforeseen talents that one may wish to exploit. This is particularly true in relation to out-of-school activities, general studies or 'new' subjects such as instrumentation and control technology.

Traditionally a job description will contain:

(1)   job title;
(2)   brief description of the purpose of the job;
(3)   reporting relationships;
(4)   description of duties.

A new and very useful concept is that of:

(5)   Competences, i.e. abilities and attitudes (as opposed to qualifications) that the occupant of the post will need to possess (see Chapter 8, p. 130).

However, the most helpful element of all, both to the candidate and the person or committee charged with the appointment decision, is a sixth element, namely:

(6)   criteria for effectiveness.

Criteria for effectiveness, which can often usefully be expressed as questions, tell us how performance in the job will be assessed. For a head of French, for example, criteria might be:

(1)   Are oral standards maintained and improved?
(2)   How many pupils have visited France on exchanges, school trips or as paying guests?
(3)   Is there a thriving French club?
(4)   Are examination results satisfactory?

Additionally there will be criteria which will apply to all heads of department, for example:

(1)   Is the atmosphere in the department enthusiastic and harmonious?
(2)   Does the department work well with other departments?
(3)   Is administration accurate and timely?
(4)   Have objectives been achieved?

Personal application. As an exercise draw up a set of effectiveness criteria for: the school caretaker; the school secretary; a 'dinner lady'.

Personal profile
Starting from the job description, the next step is to define the characteristics of the sort of person able to meet the criteria. Certain of these characteristics will be 'essential' and others 'desirable'. A useful check-list is:

(1) personal characteristics and physical factors: e.g. age, speech, dress;
(2) achievements and experience; general education, degrees, etc., jobs, special projects, awards;
(3) competences: abilities, aptitudes, skills, knowledge *and* effective application;
(4) motivation: ambition (direction?), social, intellectual, level of 'drive';
(5) personality: leadership, relationships, emotional stability.

It will be immediately apparent that while the first two categories are 'factual', the last three contain judgemental elements. Some of the characteristics will – or should – depend on looking for an approach which will complement that of other members of the team. If the team is creative, mercurial but disorganized, perhaps we should look for an 'administrator' input, and vice versa. If we do not define this need the risk is always that the appointer will be attracted by someone whose approach is similar to his own, whereas the need is often for a dissimilar person who will complement him. The people we choose as friends are often similar to us; the people with whom we can most easily work (or live) are usually complementary in character (see Chapter 10).

Attracting suitable candidates
In the first edition of this book we were able at this point to talk simply in terms of 'advertising' vacant posts. With falling rolls and a plethora of applicants the problem was how to restrict applications from unsuitable candidates. It seems unbelievable that, with birth-rates giving us four years' notice of primary school staffing requirements and eleven years' notice of secondary school requirements, successive governments have failed to plan training and motivation of teachers against *future* need. However, this is the reality with which we now have to live, and, at the time of this second edition, the problem in most areas is how to find sufficient candidates to enable us to fill posts adequately.

Clearly the aim is to maintain standards in a situation where it is all too tempting to take 'anyone'. To do this requires a willingness to depart from traditional thinking in order to broaden the range of candidates from whom we can choose. A creative approach to attracting good candidates relies on four main activities:

(1) a critical re-examination of the personal profile;
(2) a scan of non-conventional target groups for recruitment;
(3) a systematic approach to these target groups;
(4) the building of an image of the school as an attractive place in which to teach.

Taking each of these in turn:

Critical examination of the personal profile. As we have already said, the personal profile should set out the characteristics which are either 'essential' or 'desirable' in the incumbent of a post. If we are not careful, we run the risk of eliminating some candidates because we define too narrowly what is 'essential'. This is particularly true in the 'factual' or 'biographical' areas ('1' and '2' above) where it is all too easy to stipulate, for example, that a candidate must have 'previous experience of teaching in a primary school', 'a degree' or 'a qualification to teach a particular subject'. In the private sector there have been examples of successful appointment to headships of those with no previous experience of teaching in schools!

Just as we may be tempted to be over-restrictive on 'factual' criteria, we may not insist sufficiently on essential competences, motivations or traits of personality – perhaps because these are harder to measure or more difficult to discuss and probe. An open mind, competence to learn and teach other subjects or to teach in new ways, positive attitudes, ability to listen may well be far more 'essential' to job success than any paper qualification or experience (though information on performance during *recent* experience will obviously be highly relevant).

The personal profile will, of course, form the basis of the job advertisement.

A scan of non-conventional target groups for recruitment. Understandably, teachers feel considerable concern lest the profession should be diluted by the introduction of staff who have not been formally trained to teach. Proposals for 'licensing' have therefore met with union resistance. This resistance has been reinforced by justified resentment at failure to provide adequate training places or incentives and the fear that recruitment of untrained staff and the use of other 'emergency' measures will provide an excuse for maintaining present inadequacies.

Whatever the politics of the situation, the school manager can only broaden his scope of choice – and therefore increase his chances of recruiting better staff – by looking outside the conventional target groups of newly qualified probationers, existing teachers and married women returners. Far from diluting quality, the experience and competence of non-conventional recruits might well enrich and broaden the profession.

Much publicity was given to the recruitment of teachers from other EEC member countries. Other groups that deserve special attention are:

(1) early retirers of all kinds;
(2) industrial managers, especially those who have worked in the training and personnel functions;
(3) local authority officers;
(4) housewives who may have no previous teaching experience, but who have relevant competences;
(5) social workers.

A systematic approach to the target groups. People in the above, and other categories may or may not have thought of teaching as a possible second career, but it is unlikely that they will have regular access to *The Times Educational Supplement* or to other lists of teaching vacancies. If they do read these lists, it is unlikely that the advertisements will encourage them to apply.

It is important therefore both to place targeted adverts in the 'job-hunting' journals read by these groups and to build up suitable contacts who will help in finding people through their own organizations. While a personnel manager will not thank you for poaching his key staff, he may be very pleased to point redundant, retiring or change-seeking executives in your direction or to encourage their wives to move into or return to the teaching profession. At least one school in the South East relies very heavily for its staff on the wives of employees of a local computer company.

The building of an image of the school as an attractive place in which to teach. One head in an area where recruitment is notoriously difficult asserts that he never has any problems because staff are 'queueing up' to come to his school. Part of this popularity can be attributed to an overall 'quality' image which attracts parents, pupils and staff alike – good academic results, good sports record, high standards of behaviour. However, specific attention has also been paid to feeding the press with articles and talking to local interest groups about the attractions of working at the school – though only the best staff will be accepted!

Image must not, of course, belie reality, and active steps have to be taken to ensure that staff conditions, facilities and, above all, motivational factors (see Herzberg, page 29) are to a high standard. We need to consider what possibilities exist, if any, to provide child-care or housing assistance where appropriate.

Application forms

Most educational institutions have a standard form and most of these forms are well designed to bring out all the factual information needed, and also to elicit data which may give us a clue to behaviour (the 'judgemental' elements in the profile). A good application form will make it clear, in asking for references, whether or not these will normally be taken up before interview.

In reading application forms, we should remember that the most relevant data is often that which is missing. An unexplained break between periods of employment, particularly in a teacher's career, may mean imprisonment, dismissal for misconduct or a clash of personalities which has led to resignation from one job before getting the next. On the other hand, it may mean illness, or having a family. Absences from work (a key question in an application form) may mean a period of illness which has been cleared up or an on-going health problem (physical or psychological) or family problems (on-going or past) or undue willingness to take advantage of minor ailments. Whether the circumstances are acceptable to us or not, the point is that we want to know. A note should be made on the form to bring the matter up at interview.

We should, of course, be comparing each form with the 'essential' and 'desirable' criteria in our profile, and assuming that 'essential' really does mean that, we will reject any applications which do not conform. We may also reject some which do not meet enough of our 'desirable' criteria.

References

As we have said, the reference procedure should have been made clear in the application form. In the teaching profession it is usual, subject to a request to the contrary, to take up references for the short list before interview.

Although a reference – unlike a testimonial – is a confidential and legally privileged document, many referees will hesitate to refer directly in writing to shortcomings in the candidate. Therefore the questions are

'What is missing?' 'Do I have a positive statement about the characteristics which I see as essential in this candidate?' If not, a telephone call to the referee can be of help. This will usually elicit a much franker view of the candidate, and, in the case of the chosen candidate for a key appointment, many would argue that a telephone call to referees is a 'must' before making a final offer.

Planning the interview

The purpose of an interview is to find which of the short-listed candidates best fits our needs. We are not looking for the most likeable person or even the one with the best track-record in his or her last job. First-class honours graduates do not necessarily make the best teachers, and first-class teachers do not necessarily make good school or college managers. Above all we want to check on those 'essential' and 'desirable' criteria about which we are not completely sure as a result of the application form and the references. Certain of these criteria will be biographical or factual; others will be behavioural or judgemental; most will be a mixture of the two, e.g. we may be able to judge a person's 'drive' by exploring in depth the results of some project he or she has undertaken, asking about the problems that occurred and whether and how these were dealt with and by whom.

Proficient interviewees will, if they can, steer us away from areas of weakness. Inexperienced candidates, on the other hand, may not know how to make the best of themselves at an interview. For both reasons it is essential that we are systematic in listing the areas we wish to explore and thinking about the questions we wish to ask. It is particularly important to think about the sort of facts and interview reactions that will help us to come to a meaningful conclusion on the behavioural/judgemental criteria.

It is essential that we make notes on each candidate as the interview progresses and that we take time at the end of each interview to consolidate these. The whole process is greatly helped if we prepare for each candidate a selection sheet (preferably on A3 paper) similar to that shown in Figure 6.2. The use and retention of such sheets can be valuable if any candidate alleges discrimination on racial, sexual or other grounds.

The interview

Educational interviews tend to be by a formal panel, possibly preceded by a 'tour' of the establishment and an informal preliminary meeting or series of meetings with the individuals with whom the successful

SELECTION SHEET

Position..............

Candidate..............

Job Description and Criteria for Effectiveness (attached)

Personal profile

E = Essential
D = Desirable

Personal and physical
.... (E)
.... (E)
.... (D)

	Application form	Reference	Interview question	Notes on candidate's response

Achievements and experience

Abilities

Motivation

Personality

Overall summary..............

Interviewer..............

Figure 6.2 Selection sheet

candidate will have to work most closely. These informal preliminaries are to be encouraged, as they help the candidate to decide whether he or she wishes to select the job as well as providing potential behavioural input to the school's side of the selection procedure. Increasingly, schools are following the example of industry in using attitude and profile questionnaires which can provide interesting insights for subsequent follow-up in interview. This input can usefully be collected up by the head or head of department before the formal panel meets.

The formal panel members should each be given a copy of the 'selection sheet' for each candidate and taken through it beforehand by the head or head of department. A decision should be taken on how the procedure will be structured. How will the candidate be welcomed, introduced and put at ease? Who will lead the panel? Who will cover what areas of questioning? How shall we allocate time?

Questioning technique is important. Some useful 'do's and 'don'ts' to bear in mind are:

Do not
(1) Start with intimate, personal, aggressive or argumentative questions. (These can come later when rapport has been established.)
(2) Use 'closed' questions which will lead to a 'yes' or 'no' answer unless there is a need to establish a clear fact which is uncertain (or about which the candidate is 'hedging') or unless you are going to follow up by an 'open-ended' supplementary.
(3) Use loaded questions, trick questions or jargon.
(4) Lead – for example 'I suppose you...', 'I think... . What do you feel?', 'No doubt you enjoy good relations with...'. (Even if the candidate would be willing to tell you about problems, you make it almost impossible for him or her to do so.)
(5) Indicate disapproval or show that you are shocked.
(6) Worry about silences.

Do
(1) Use 'open' questions which allow the candidate to express himself, to demonstrate knowledge, to add to the picture (you do not want him to repeat information that you already have).
(2) Probe tactfully, using 'Why?' 'What?' 'How?' questions or:
  'Tell me about... .'
  'What did you enjoy most about...?'
  'What was your role in...?'

'How does our job compare with...?'
'What did you enjoy least about...?'

(3) Reassure a nervous candidate by smiling, making reinforcing noises, etc.

(4) Listen for at least two-thirds of the time.

(5) Guide tactfully into the areas you wish to explore.

(6) Close down into one area and open up another with remarks such as 'OK, I think we've covered that; now, could you tell me about....'

(7) Come back to areas a candidate tries to avoid.

(8) Get his or her views on the job on offer and encourage criticism of the school.

(9) Observe behaviour (tenseness, etc).

(10) When the candidate has had time to settle down, investigate relationships by covering family, social and work life. Look for clues of difficult adjustments, loyalty, etc. (NB The inability to relate well to other people is the most frequent cause of dissatisfaction with staff members of all kinds.)

(11) Beware of your prejudices (accent, dress, men with beards, women with ear-rings, as well as colour, sex, etc).

(12) Give the candidate a chance to ask about the job, and check whether he or she is still interested and whether there are any reservations (family moves, etc).

(13) Make sure the candidate knows what the next steps are.

(14) Close when both you and the candidate have enough information.

(15) Record your overall impressions before you meet the next candidate (otherwise you will forget) and, in the case of a panel, make a brief comparison of views.

Confirming the appointment

Every employee must by law be given a written statement of terms and conditions of employment. This statement must cover a number of specific points including salary, periods of notice, holiday entitlement and grievance procedure. It is good practice to incorporate these in a written offer to the chosen candidate.

Induction

As soon as the candidate has accepted the appointment, he should be invited for an induction day and given his job description. The criteria for effectiveness should be agreed and preferably recorded in writing. An objective is seldom meaningful unless it is qualified in such a way that all parties will know whether it has been achieved. Time is the most important measure. Thus 'to put on a linguists' evening in the spring term' and 'to arrange an exchange visit to each of France and Germany next summer' are far more meaningful objectives than 'to increase out-of-school activities in modern languages'.

A pack of information, textbooks, school rules, standard forms etc., should await the new recruit, and a guided tour and meetings should be planned. Form room, locker space, pass key or other physical details should be discussed. (It is useful to establish for each school an induction check-list.) Preferably the induction day will start and finish with the recruit's immediate manager who will also become the reference point for further enquiries.

Developing staff

Fortunately the era is passing when it was assumed that a person equipped with a university degree or a teaching certificate or diploma was equipped for lifelong service as a teacher. However, it is ironic that the emphasis on in-service training, which industry and commerce have felt since the 1960s through the Industrial Training Boards, the Manpower Services Commission and latterly the Training Agency, has only in the last decade received priority in the profession which is responsible for preparing tomorrow's citizens. Even now, in some areas, teachers attending external courses may have to meet all or a part of their fees. Appraisal and development procedures, standard practice in most walks of life now, are consequently still not fully understood and are treated with suspicion in parts of the educational profession.

Types of development need

The purposes of staff development may vary and Figure 6.3 provides a useful clarification. Some needs will be specific to the individual, though two or more individuals may have a similar need; others – usually those

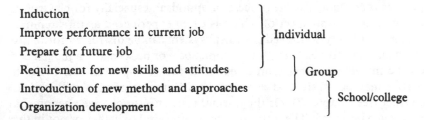

Induction
Improve performance in current job
Prepare for future job   } Individual
Requirement for new skills and attitudes } Group
Introduction of new method and approaches
Organization development   } School/college

Figure 6.3 Types of development need

related to change - will concern groups of people or even the total organization. Organizational change programmes are dealt with at some length in Part III. In the remainder of this chapter we shall be concerned with the development of individuals and groups.

Appraisal

Appraisal is, or should be, an opportunity for the individual to meet with his manager in order to take stock of their individual and joint achievements. As a result of the discussion, there should be agreement on action needed to:

(1) improve the performance of the individual;
(2) improve working relationships;
(3) develop the individual's career.

Well-developed appraisal systems are of considerable benefit to both the individual and the organization and, indeed, industrial staff will complain if their appraisal interview is overdue. At their best such systems are highly motivational to employees since they:

(1) enable them to measure their achievement;
(2) recognize their achievement;
(3) prepare them for advancement;
(4) open up opportunities for personal growth;
(5) 'clear the air' of problems and build their relationship with their manager.

The Graham Report (1985), *Those Having Torches*, and subsequent pilot work in Suffolk schools, which is leading to the introduction of a national appraisal scheme, has shown that this is true of teachers no less than of employees elsewhere. However, because of the suspicion that appraisal has aroused, it is more than ever necessary in schools to prepare thoroughly for the process of appraisal, especially for classroom observation, the prospect of which is often experienced as threatening.

A new or badly conceived appraisal system can be distrusted for many reasons. The appraisal can, for example, be - or be seen as - a judgement on the individual rather than a means to future improvement. Or both parties may be afraid that criticism or differences of view will lead to conflict (see Chapter 7). Or the normal resistance-to-change phenomena may come into play. The introduction of appraisal, whether or not in the form of a 'course', is itself a development need of organizational proportions. (See Part III.)

The appraisal of headteachers presents a special case, because there is no immediate superior to manage the process. In the Suffolk pilot scheme a triumvirate approach was used, involving another head, an LEA officer and adviser. The consultant head with whom the appraisee head was paired, was responsible for most of the data collection from governors, parents and teachers.

Essentials for effective appraisal
We can identify a number of features of constructive appraisal:

Objectivity. The basis for a constructive discussion is prior agreement on the criteria for effectiveness. A preliminary to appraisal is therefore a job description with criteria and clear objectives of the type discussed in the 'induction' section of this chapter. The focus should then be on results achieved against the criteria and objectives.

Willingness to listen. The manager's approach should not be to tell his staff member what is right or wrong but to ask for his views first. Indeed, many good systems will ask the employee to draft his answers to the appraisal form on to a separate form before the interview and to use this as a basis for the discussion.

Openness to criticism. Not just the subordinate but also a mature manager will listen very carefully to any criticism and use it as a basis for improvement. To silence criticism is to demonstrate insecurity.

Counselling not judgement. What can we do to improve the *situation* or the *results*?

Action planning. New objectives and development plans carried forward, progressed and reviewed systematically at the next appraisal.

The appraisal record
Headings for an effective appraisal record are:

(1) Development planned/carried out over the last twelve months or since the last appraisal and results.
(2) Results achieved against job criteria and objectives.
(3) Notes on 2. (NB There may be very good reasons for failure to achieve a result.)

(4) Particular strengths.
(5) Areas in which improvement could be made.
(6) Action needed by the individual, his or her manager and/or others to achieve improvement.
(7) Staff member's wishes for the future and action that will be taken to prepare him or her.
(8) Objectives or targets (quantified as far as possible).

It is of course essential that the development actions are followed through.

Meeting development needs

There are many ways of meeting development needs, and courses, if only because they are the most obvious, should be the last that we consider. Other methods are:

(1) counselling, coaching and consultancy;
(2) planned reading;
(3) self-development;
(4) projects (e.g. organizing a school event);
(5) change in responsibilities (good for all concerned);
(6) sitting in on meetings;
(7) producing a research report;
(8) visits.

The re-entry problem

Individuals emerging from any development programme in which they learn techniques, behaviours, or approaches new to themselves and/or the school are likely to feel some degree of frustration when they try to apply what they have been taught. The re-entry problem is particularly apparent after an intensive programme away from the school. Ex-autocrats who return determined to be participative managers are often surprised to find that their subordinates do not respond with 'Hallelujah' but are more disposed to say 'He's obviously been on a course; how long will this last?'. People feel uncomfortable if one of the 'norms' in their environment appears to change. They are suspicious. Unfortunately, this response may cause the returned trainee to doubt the validity of what he has learned and the development effort will have been wasted.

The re-entry problem will be eased if:

(1) The trainee is aware of it, bides his time a little (though not too much!) and makes an effort to discuss his intended change with his team and involve them in helping to implement it.

(2) The trainee's superior, who has hopefully been a key party to initiating the development, provides support and counselling on and after re-entry. This guidance should be a natural consequence of a pre-event discussion on why the trainee is undertaking the development and a post-event debriefing. Sadly, these meetings do not always take place and this is a serious dereliction of managerial duty involving waste of training investment and demotivation of staff.

Group training

Many of the re-entry problems are overcome if staff are trained in groups or as a total team, thus creating a common understanding and a 'critical mass' for implementing the learning. With the advent of LMS school managers should be viewing all their decisions in terms of investment and return; a diagrammatic comparison is at Figure 6.4.

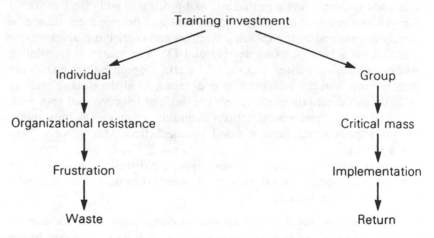

Figure 6.4

In-service training days ('Baker' days) provide a valuable opportunity to:

(1) introduce new concepts to a critical mass of staff;
(2) work through cases and exercises to ensure active learning;
(3) debate the concepts and discuss their application.
(4) make plans to implement.
(5) plan to review implementation at a specified staff meeting or at the
     next in-service day.

A valuable contribution to school effectiveness can be made by going
through such simple exercises as having individuals or departments
specify:

(1) what they expect from other individuals or departments;
(2) what they feel able to offer to other individuals or departments.

This can then be followed by reaching agreement or 'contracts' as to
how exactly individuals or departments can improve the service that they
provide to their 'internal customers'.

A coherent approach

Recruitment, appraisal and training are three activities which should not
be seen in isolation from each other but as part of a comprehensive
approach to developing a proficient, well-motivated and effective staff –
the key to a good school. Staff recruitment and development should be
largely determined by the values, objectives and curriculum development
plans of the school (see Chapters 11 and 13). The means of translating
school objectives into individual staff responsibilities are job
descriptions, and the techniques for obtaining and developing staff to
fulfil the job descriptions effectively are those of selection and appraisal,
followed up by development actions including training. The importance
of this approach has been stressed by the School Management Task
Force (1990).

The procedures advocated in this chapter, particularly appraisal, are
not easy to introduce into those schools where they do not already exist
for reasons which include:

(1) resistance to ideas which appear to come from America and/or
     industry and are *ipso facto* (in the view of some) repugnant to the
     professional world of education which is 'different';
(2) fear of being labelled incompetent;
(3) dislike of 'paperwork';

(4) discomfort at the idea that learning acquired at university may not be sufficient for a modern teacher;
(5) a feeling that teachers are by their nature people who have an instinct for choosing and developing staff;
(6) 'professional performance should be above judgement' (a misconstruction of what appraisal is about);
(7) a feeling, perhaps caught from pupils, that training and learning are unpleasant things associated with children rather than mature adults.

For all these reasons, and others which you may like to add, each step forward has to be taken carefully but purposefully and using all the strategies to which Part III is devoted.

Finally, it should not be forgotten that a 'comprehensive' approach should include administrative and ancillary staff as well as teachers. Though the recalcitrance of some school-keepers can be attributed in part to local union stances, it should never be forgotten that a show of strength is a fairly normal reaction to being underestimated or taken for granted.

Further reading

Anstey, E., Fletcher, C. and Walker, J. (1976) *Staff Appraisal and Development*, Allen and Unwin, London.

Everard, K.B. (1986) *Developing Management in Schools*, Blackwell, Oxford.

MacKay, I. (1983) *A Guide to Asking Questions*, BACIE.

Megginson, D. and Boydell, T. (1979) *A Manager's Guide to Coaching*, BACIE.

Philp, T. (1983) *Making Performance Appraisal Work*, McGraw-Hill, New York.

Randall, G., Packard, P. and Slater, J. (1984) *Staff Appraisal*, Institute of Personnel Management, London.

Singer, E.J. (1979) *Effective Management Coaching*, Institute of Personnel Management, London.

Trethowan, D.M. (1983) *Target Setting*, The Industrial Society, London.

Trethowan, D.M. and Smith, D.L. (1984) *Induction*, The Industrial Society, London.

Warwick, D. (1983) *Staff Appraisal*, The Industrial Society, London.

Warwick, D. (1984) *Interviews and Interviewing*, The Industrial Society, London.

7
MANAGING CONFLICT

A key skill

The ability to handle conflict is a key factor in managerial success. Whenever we wish to make changes, there is potential for conflict. Furthermore, we not only have to handle situations in which there is conflict between ourselves and one or more other members of staff; but may also at times have to resolve conflicts between our subordinates or, most difficult of all, to plot a course through the minefield of 'politics' when two of our peers or superiors are locked in struggle. In the last case, it often happens that one party will deliberately block anything which appears to be the initiative of, or have the backing of, the other, and progress may be difficult. On the other hand, one may have more freedom of action while the opposing parties are locked in battle: a head who is 'at war' with a local authority, his governors, a parental committee or a pressure group may be only too pleased if his staff just get on with running the school. The worst situation occurs when no one fills the vacuum caused by his preoccupation.

This chapter deals with the nature of conflict, how it builds up, its positive and negative effects and some guidelines for handling conflict situations.

The value of conflict

Conflict in the sense of an honest difference of opinion resulting from the availability of two or more alternative courses of action is not only unavoidable but also a valuable part of life. It helps to ensure that different possibilities are properly considered, and further possible courses of action may be generated from the discussion of the already recognized alternatives. Also, conflict often means that the chosen course of action is tested at an early stage, thereby reducing the risk of missing an important flaw which may emerge later.

Alfred Sloan, a former president of General Motors, would always refer for further consideration at the next meeting any proposal on which his board members were unanimous. A large proportion of such proposals were, it appears, eventually rejected! (Sloan, 1980).

The absence of conflict may indicate abdication of responsibility, lack of interest or lazy thinking.

Reason and emotion in conflict

Most conflicts have both rational and emotional components and lie somewhere along a spectrum between genuine conflict of interest on the one hand and personality clash on the other.

Examples of genuine conflict of interest occur, for example, where the vendor of a house seeks the highest price, whilst the purchaser wishes to pay as little as possible. There is also a genuine conflict of interest between employer and employee about the question of salary.

In both the above cases it is in the interest of both parties to resolve the conflict - otherwise there is no sale in the first case and a strike in the second. In order to negotiate a solution it is necessary to:

(1) Listen to and understand the point of view and needs of the other party (don't waste time reiterating your own point of view). Try to be fair.

(2) Look for trade-offs, i.e. Is there something that I can concede to the other party that means more to them than it 'costs' me?

(3) Focus on issues and facts and avoid personalising the conflict.

These are the principles of positive negotiation which should produce a 'win-win' situation.

However, it is all too easy for an emotional desire to 'beat the blighter' to creep in and, once it does, it may well spread from one party to the other.

At the other end of the spectrum many so-called 'personality clashes'

have an element of conflict of interest, and are attributable to role, system
or culture problems as much as individual cussedness.

The dangers of conflict

Conflict becomes a dangerous and disruptive force whenever personal
'glory' is staked on the outcome. The further the conflict develops, the
more 'glory' is staked, the more bitter the conflict becomes and the less
easy it is to achieve a solution. Decision-taking is paralysed because
neither party dares to make any concessions for fear (probably justified)
that these will be seized upon by the other party as a victory and a
bridgehead for further advances.

At such a point, we speak of a 'win–lose' situation since this is how the
parties approach each issue. In reality the situation is often 'lose–lose'
since the parties both do things which are against their own real
advantage (as well as wasting their own time on the conflict). Real – or
'superordinate' – goals and interests are lost sight of in the heat of battle.
Conflict may be overt, leading to a rehearsal of the same arguments at
each meeting. More dangerously it is covert, and the parties do not
actually talk to each other about the real issues but canvass support from
those whom they believe to be influential. They will each also take
actions which affect the other party, without informing him or her.

Inter-group competition

Competition, like conflict, can be of great value to an organization.
However, it can easily be destructive. The process can be seen
diagrammatically in Figure 7.1. Once inter-group competition develops
into a 'win–lose' situation it is even more difficult to handle than
between individuals. If any one member of a group departs from the
'party line' he or she may be perceived as a traitor and outcast.

Unfortunately, 'win–lose' conflict with another group is, as shown in
Figure 7.1, a very effective means of achieving allegiance within a group.
Napoleon and Galtieri both recognized this fact and used it, while the
Thatcher government, whatever may or may not have been its degree of
fault, undoubtedly benefited at the polls from the 'Falklands effect'.
Subconsciously or consciously, managers who are unsure of themselves
will use conflict to win support – often with disastrous consequences for
the organization. The head, the local authority, the examining board, or

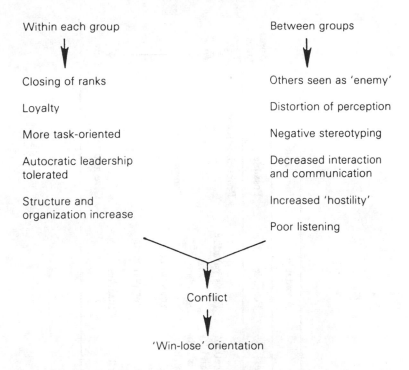

Figure 7.1 Possible consequences of inter-group competition

another department will be perceived as the 'enemy' who are always doing things wrong. 'Look what they've done now!'

Attitudes to conflict

There are basically four possible attitudes that can be adopted by the participants in any conflict and these are based on permutations of whether or not they believe that they can avoid confrontation, and whether or not they believe that they will be able to reach agreement. The combinations and their results can be represented in tabular form as in Figure 7.2.

The two central columns are self-explanatory. It is worth noting how many so-called 'communication' problems occur because there exists at the root a conflict of view which is not brought into the open. Instead, the parties each 'do their own thing' in the hope of 'getting away with it'. They may also devote a great deal of time to building up support for their

	1	2	3	4	
Confrontation	Inevitable	Avoidable	Avoidable	Inevitable	Personal Stakes
Agreement	Impossible	Impossible	Possible	Possible	
	Power battle	Frequent 'communication' problems and 'muddles' which are more or less frustrating and lead to increasing tension and stress for all concerned.	Fool's paradise	Problem-solving	High
	Arbitration		Avoiding		
			Smoothing	Compromise	↕
			Postponement		
	'Fate'		Inaction	Give and take	Low

Figure 7.2 Attitudes to conflict

point of view and talking *about* the person with whom they are in conflict rather than talking *to* him or her.

In the first and fourth columns, behaviour will depend on how high or low are the *personal* stakes. These 'stakes' are not necessarily those which have the highest monetary value or are of the greatest importance to the organization, but tend rather to be measured in terms of the ego of the parties. How strongly have they expressed their opinion on this point and to how many people? How many battles have they fought for this principle? Personal stakes may be higher on issues such as car-parking facilities, book stores and dinner duties than they are on curriculum development or provision of new teaching facilities. Indeed, any astute local government official who seeks agreement to a major project will ensure that it is preceded on the council agenda by some highly controversial, but often low-cost, subject such as the provision of an extra facility for old age pensioners or even an additional public toilet. After a heated debate on such a topic, a high-cost project may well pass 'on the nod'.

With conflicts in the first column (Confrontation Inevitable/ Agreement Impossible) the logical approach is to refer the matter to arbitration, i.e. ask the boss to decide. This may well happen if the 'personal stakes' are of medium weight. However, where personal stakes are really high, it often happens that neither party will risk 'losing'. Furthermore, a boss who steps into such a conflict and passes judgement may completely alienate the party against whom he or she decides.

If the personal stakes are low, the decision may be left to 'fate', or the conflict may easily pass into one of the other columns.

The attitude most conducive to resolving conflict is, of course, that suggested in column 4. If the stakes are low or medium, it may not be worth while for either party to spend time on in-depth problem solving, and some quick compromises or give-and-take 'horse-trading' may be the answer. Where problems are a little deeper, however, or where 'horse-trading' and give and take are leading to inconsistency and confusion, a more thorough attempt to solve problems will pay off handsomely in terms both of the effectiveness of the organization, and of reducing the stress on the protagonists.

As the contents of the columns in Figure 7.2 indicate, your attitude to conflict in general and/or any particular conflict will condition the approach that you adopt. If you would like to examine your own approach in greater depth, you may find the Conflict Orientation Questionnaire (Exercise 4) at the end of this chapter of help. You can either try to be honest in completing it about yourself or ask someone who knows you well to complete it for you.

Solving problems of conflict

The first point to make is the obvious one that no party to a conflict can solve the problem unilaterally. If the attitude of the other party is firmly locked into columns 1, 2 or 3 of Figure 7.2, the situation may prove impossible and the only resort may be to face the issues and seek arbitration. If a strong 'win–lose' orientation has been developed, resolution may be complicated by the fact that any problem-solving approach or concession may be interpreted either as a sign of weaknesses (to be exploited to maximum advantage!) or as a subtle 'ploy' to be treated with great caution and mistrust.

For these reasons conflict should be recognized and dealt with as early as possible. If you have a problem with someone, go immediately to talk to them, before acrimony builds up. If you think of the person you least want to meet and the thing that you least want to do, these are probably your first two priorities for the day!

If acrimony has built up, it may be necessary to choose your time well and to spend some time in making it clear that you really do want to solve the conflict. Some friend of both parties may be needed to act as a catalyst, to reassure both parties that intentions are sincere and to act as 'mediator' or 'process consultant'. In conflicts between other members of staff, particularly those reporting to you, your job as a manager may well be to step in as the 'process consultant', to try to understand the point of view of each protagonist individually and to bring each one into a 'problem-solving' state of mind. Having set the stage for a meeting to solve the conflict, the following principles should guide the discussions:

(1) The parties will talk to each other as openly as possible about the real issues that concern them.

(2) They will state their aims, views and feelings openly but calmly, and try to avoid reiteration.

(3) They will try to put the conflict into the context of superordinate goals and of the interest of the total organization (a 'helicopter' view). They will look for common goals.

(4) They will focus on future action rather than on the events of the past.

(5) They will listen carefully to each other's point of view and seek to

understand it. To ensure that their understanding of it is correct they may rephrase the other's point of view. However, this must be a genuine attempt at restatement and not a parody of what was said.

(6) They will try to avoid moving on to the attack or defence.
(7) They will try to build on each other's ideas.
(8) They will trust each other's good faith and try to act in good faith (see the 'OK Matrix' discussed in Chapter 8).
(9) They will plan some clear actions to follow the discussion specifying *who* will do *what* by *when*. (This is extremely important and may easily be forgotten in the euphoria of finding that the other party is not as unreasonable as had been anticipated!)
(10) They will set a date and time to review progress *and will keep this at all costs.*

If a third party is acting as a 'process consultant' in such a meeting his or her role should not be to comment on the issues (this is a dangerous trap) but simply to draw attention to any departure from these principles.

A number of useful structures can be used to help individuals or groups to overcome cultural reluctance to put conflict 'on the table'. These structures have the twin values of:

(1) Enabling strong feelings and prejudices to be expressed in a form which is less antagonistic than the spoken word. The feelings become factual (though possibly hurtful) data rather than barbed attacks.
(2) Asking for 'balance' in the data, i.e. what we like as well as what we dislike and what we do as well as what they do.

Two of these structures are set out at the end of this chapter viz:

(1) Role Revision Strategy (Exercise 5).
(2) Image Exchange (Exercise 6).

Handling 'organizational' conflicts

Conflict and frustration will often centre round the way in which a school, college or department is being run, 'the way things happen here'. Such conflicts have a tendency to build up in any organization, and they can assume more and more importance. There is often no coherent opinion about how things *should* be done - just a generally negative attitude towards the way in which things *are* being done.

For the head or head of department, the situation is very frustrating, and the feeling grows that the staff are working not for you but against you. If you bend to the suggestions of one body of opinion, another group will be even less satisfied. You feel misunderstood by everyone and alone in trying to make the organization work. You may, rightly, feel the need to bring key staff together to examine the way in which the school or department operates and hopefully to get commitment to an agreed form of amended practices. The trouble is that any such meeting can descend into chaos with all the old arguments and prejudices rehearsed.

At Exercise 7 at the end of this chapter is a structure which has been found helpful in channelling a review of school organizational practices. It may be amended to suit particular circumstances, but amendment should always be towards highlighting controversial issues, never towards avoiding them. The 'school review' uses a number of useful techniques:

(1) 'Gap' theory – asking people to state their ideal view and compare it with their actual perceptions. (The 'gap' between the two is what then has to be bridged.)

(2) Categorizing and quantifying views of what is wrong by focusing analysis round a structure of statements – always, of course, with the possibility of formulating a group statement which does not correspond exactly with any of the alternatives.

(3) Concretizing statements round 'for instances'. (These should be recorded in the 'notes' column within the exercise.)

The effect of these techniques is to take much of the heat out of the discussion and to enable deep-seated problems to be treated at a rational level. There is always a fear that individuals may be hurt by such a process, especially the head who feels responsible for the processes under review. For this reason it is important that a review meeting should be instigated from the top of the group, with a genuine desire to understand people's feelings. Provided this is done, members of the group can usually be relied on to have a high concern for feelings, and, as the 'we' spirit develops, to be able to compensate for painful home truths by supportiveness or willingness to put things right. But it is important to prepare the group by agreeing that the meeting will be based on the positive principles set out above.

Finally, it is important not to involve too many levels – or too many people – in such a review. Two levels is ideal. As soon as three or more are involved, great care has to be taken not to lay all problems unfairly at the door of the intermediate level. In a meeting involving head, deputy head and heads of department, there is real risk that the deputy head will be blamed for communication failures, for 'failing to pass on the message'.

Preventing unnecessary conflict

Certain behaviours are liable to provoke an unnecessary degree of conflict. The social policies of the European Community – and many of the member states – speak of the difference between a 'harmony model' and a 'conflict model' of relationships. In the *conflict* model:

(1) Parties are concerned only to protect their own interests. 'It is the task of management to manage in the interests of the employer and the job of the unions to look after the interests of their members', is a statement made both by some managers and by some trade unionists, and there is a risk that teachers who feel that their profession is under governmental attack (from right or left) may adopt similar attitudes.
(2) The parties involved in taking or implementing decisions will take up their positions, make their decision, possibly try to sell them to the other parties and, if necessary, fight.

In the *harmony* model, on the other hand, the aim is:

(1) Collective responsibility both for the interests of the school and for the individual interests of staff.
(2) Participative decision-taking in which the views of interested parties are sought out *before* coming to a decision (see Chapter 4). This allows differences of opinion to be handled before a position is taken up from which retreat means loss of face.

Guidelines for handling conflict

In order to minimize the destructive effects of conflict, the following principles should be observed:

(1) Maintain as much communication as possible with any party whose ideas, interests or attitudes appear to be in conflict with your own. Do not postpone discussing the problem in the hope that it will go away – it will usually get worse.

(2) Refrain from the temptation to talk *about* the other person behind their back. Do not try to build up an army of opinion on your side. Talk *with* the other person.

(3) If you see signs of inter-departmental conflict, try to establish projects, on either neutral or sensitive subjects, in which individuals from the various departments will work together. As a general principle, it is good to prevent the build-up of rigid departmental demarcation by having cross-departmental groups. Where there is competition for scarce resources – computers, overhead projectors, rehearsal space, secretarial services, or even money – it can be far more fruitful to ask a cross-departmental group of keen junior staff to meet to propose a policy to the head and heads of department than to proceed via the traditional route of inviting each department to submit its claim and thereby close ranks in battle order. Such joint projects are also an excellent personal-development activity.

(4) Try to avoid all the phenomena of the 'win–lose' orientation, and above all try to see all sides of a dispute, remembering that most staff will only behave negatively if they believe they are under threat or attack.

(5) Try to avoid setting up conflict situations through the 'reward' structure and, if they are already in the structure, change them. If two teachers see themselves as competing for your favour, a lot of their effort may be directed into 'political' activity and they may each become high consumers of your time in 'showing off' rather than getting on quietly with the job. Ensure that you recognize results and not flattery or 'show'.

Conflict-management skills

If we are to be effective managers of conflicts to which we are a party, and of conflicts between other members of staff, we need to develop certain attitudes and skills. The only way to develop these is by self-control and practice.

First, we need the ability to confront, to be able to say 'No' when a difference of opinion emerges. We should show by our attitude that we are open to reason, logical discussion and problem-solving. Second, we must be able to present our ideas and feelings clearly, concisely, calmly and honestly. Third, we need to develop listening skills, which include the ability to show someone that we understand what has been said by 'playing it back'. We also need to develop the habit of asking questions rather than making statements, remembering that successful sales people (of products or ideas) are those who ask the most questions. Fourth, we need skill in evaluating all aspects of the problem, understanding the pressure on the other party, 'helicoptering' above the limited perspective which we might normally adopt. Finally, we need to be able to articulate the common goals which should help both parties to rise above their differences about methods to look to future achievement rather than past frictions.

Personal application. A useful exercise is to think about some conflict in which you are involved and to try very deliberately to understand the position of your adversary or adversaries. Why are they behaving as they are? What are the pressures on them? What do they wish to achieve? What common goal is there? What possibilities are there for accord? Often it can be helpful to discuss your perceptions with a colleague. Much learning and many solutions have been achieved in this way.

Further reading

MacKay, I. (1984) *A Guide to Listening*, BACIE.
Sloan, A.P. (1980) *My Years with General Motors*, Sidgwick and Jackson, London.

Exercise 4: conflict orientation questionnaire

Score each of the following questions (and/or ask someone who knows you well to score them for you) on a scale of 4 (very often) to 1 (hardly ever). You may find that your answers would vary according to the person or situation: in this case you should initially try to score your conflict behaviour overall, and later you may find it useful to re-do the test for each separate conflict. When in conflict do you:

1.	Make your views and requirements very clear from the outset?	4	3	2	1
2.	Start by asking the other party what you have done wrong?	4	3	2	1
3.	Avoid meeting the other party?	4	3	2	1
4.	Tell other people about your problem?	4	3	2	1
5.	Seek the support of other people?	4	3	2	1
6.	Try to split the difference?	4	3	2	1
7.	Apologize for having to raise the issue?	4	3	2	1

8.	Listen carefully to what is said by the other party?	4	3	2	1
9.	Become aggressive?	4	3	2	1
10.	Keep calm?	4	3	2	1
11.	Explore the other party's point of view?	4	3	2	1
12.	Try to placate the other party?	4	3	2	1
13.	Go for a quick 'deal'?	4	3	2	1
14.	Speak more than the other party?	4	3	2	1
15.	Focus on a series of possible solutions?	4	3	2	1
16.	Look for a fair solution?	4	3	2	1
17.	Let the other party have his or her own way?	4	3	2	1
18.	Play down the importance of the conflict?	4	3	2	1
19.	Act as if there is no problem?	4	3	2	1
20.	Restate common interests?	4	3	2	1
21.	Try to get your own way?	4	3	2	1
22.	Apologize readily?	4	3	2	1
23.	Shift responsibility from yourself?	4	3	2	1
24.	Try to find a compromise?	4	3	2	1
25.	Give way on some issues in return for others?	4	3	2	1

Scoring the questionnaire
When you have completed the questionnaire, transfer each of your scores to the appropriate column below:

Avoiding		Smoothing		Fighting		Compromising		Problem-solving	
Question	Score	Question	Score	Question	Score	Question	Score	Question	Score
3		2		1		6		8	
4		7		5		13		10	
17		12		9		16		11	
19		18		14		24		15	
23		22		21		25		20	
TOTAL		TOTAL		TOTAL		TOTAL		TOTAL	

Interpreting your score
You now have a score for five different behaviours or orientations which are among those listed in Figure 7.2. They are set out on the next page and correspond to the management style diagram in Figure 2.2.

As with management style, and as we have indicated in this chapter, we should have an underlying high concern for both relationships and results (problem-solving). Have I really 'won' if I have sown the seeds of

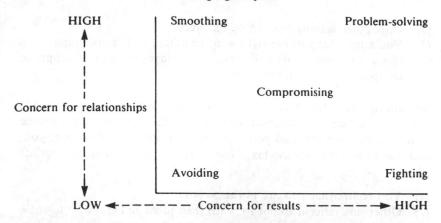

vengeance in my opponent? Has a conflict that I have smoothed over or avoided really gone away? Do I feel satisfied with the outcome?

However, there are occasions on which it may be appropriate to adopt different *behaviours* and some guidelines on these occasions are set out below:

Avoiding. This involves side-stepping conflict, postponing confrontation, hoping the problem will go away or pretending it does not exist. It usually imposes stress on all concerned, causes communication problems and means that decisions are made by default. However, it has a positive use where:

(1) The issue is a 'storm in a teacup' and will pass away of its own accord.
(2) You have no power to achieve a solution, or the potential damage of confrontation outweighs the benefits of the solution.
(3) Time is needed for cooling off or to gather information.
(4) Where others are better equipped to solve the problem than you are and you expect that they will step in.

Fighting. This may mean standing up for what you believe to be right or simply trying to score a personal victory. It involves bringing emotional, intellectual, hierarchical or any other form of power to bear in order to get your own way and implies a lack of respect for other people's interests. It often breeds resentment, 'back stabbing' and deviousness or, if your opponent is of equal status, a 'shouting match'. It can, however, be used to good effect where:

(1) There is an emergency calling for quick, decisive action.

(2) Unpopular actions have to be enforced.
(3) You know that you are right and the other party is not prepared to listen to reason or will take advantage of any attempt to compromise or problem-solve.

Smoothing. This approach is unassertive and co-operative. It puts the interests of others first. Over-use of this approach can cause other people to lose respect for you and your opinions, to ride roughshod over you, and discipline may become lax. However, the approach is appropriate where:

(1) You realize that you are in the wrong.
(2) Others are reticent to put forward their ideas and you wish to show that you respect their views and wish to hear them.
(3) The issue is very important to the other person and you wish to build up credit.

Compromising. Those who compromise seek expedient quick solutions that satisfy both parties. Focus is often less on the quality of the solution or on finding a creative solution than on finding middle ground. A compromise culture leads to wheeling and dealing that may be at the expense of principles and values. However, compromise can be used where:

(1) Two opponents of equal power are committed to mutually exclusive goals.
(2) When the issues are moderately important but there is no time to go into problem-solving mode. Often compromise can be used as a temporary expedient.

Problem-solving. This involves working with the other party or parties to try to find a solution which goes as far as is possible towards mutual satisfaction. It involves thoroughly exploring each other's interests and concerns and looking for creative alternative courses of action. The problem is that this takes time and energy and may be an excuse for postponing decisions which need to be taken.
    Problem-solving should be used when:

(1) Issues are too important to be compromised.
(2) Long-standing conflict needs to be resolved.
(3) High commitment and understanding are important.
(4) The quality of the decision is important and all possible insights,

perspectives and ideas need to be taken into account so as to produce and test creative solutions.

Exercise 5: role revision strategy

This technique is usually used with individuals and is described for such, but it can readily be adapted for inter-group application. There are seven steps which may be grouped as follows:

Steps

1	
	} problem identification
2	
3	
	} problem communication
4	
5	
6	} negotiating resolutions
7	

Step 1
The facilitator asks each participant to produce a list of:

(1) the things (s)he would like the other person(s) to do less of;
(2) the things (s)he would like the other person(s) to do more of;
(3) the things (s)he would like the other person(s) to continue doing as now.

These things should be specific actions or behaviours. The list should include everything salient to the situation; nothing important should be suppressed.

Step 2
The participants then mark their own list to indicate how strong is their desire for change in each item listed, in order to facilitate improved collaboration.

Step 3
The participants read each other's lists and through discussion seek to

clarify the changes that the other person(s) are demanding. The facilitator may well say: 'Can you give a specific example of when "X" has happened in the past, and you don't want to happen in the future?'.

Step 4
Each participant thinks for about two minutes about what the other participant(s) are demanding, and puts a ' + ' against the things (s)he thinks (s)he can do something about; also a ' – ' against things (s)he does not agree with, or will not change without a *quid pro quo*.

This completes the first round of the role revision strategy. It is based on the assumption that the *status quo* is held steady by forces (whatever people are now doing, they have reason for it) which must change if behaviour is to change. One of these forces is likely to be misapprehension of what the other people want. There are others, however. To achieve change, there must be a change in the driving or restraining forces (see force field analysis in Chapter 17), and that change must be perceived or experienced by the individual. A change strategy is needed to bring this about.

It is unrealistic to expect one participant to change his/her behaviour unless the other participants *do something different* – like giving help, or putting pressure on. One cannot assume that people of goodwill will change their behaviour merely as a result of a discussion. So we have to ask: 'What am I prepared to do to influence others to change their behaviour?' The second round of the strategy is, therefore, to obtain answers to this question.

Step 5
The facilitator may explain the foregoing, and will ask the participants to identify the areas where they think they can make progress. It is best not to tackle the tougher things first, unless there is a high degree of trust, but to go for something in the middle, success in dealing with which will lay the groundwork for dealing with the bigger issues.

Step 6
The facilitator asks the participants to talk about what could be done in the area selected, and constructs a chart under two headings:

Desires   Difficulties

The facilitator encourages the participants to offer help in overcoming the difficulties that emerge.

Step 7

When pseudo-agreement has been reached, the facilitator gets the participants to specify exactly who is going to do what by when. There is likely to be a further meeting to review progress, and this should be set up. Also there needs to be agreement on the first step to be taken to deal with those issues which have not yet been processed to *quid pro quo*.

Thus the process is iterative, and success in the first round encourages the participants to tackle the more difficult issues.

Exercise 6: image exchange

This technique is normally used with groups and is described as such, but it can also be applied to an inter-personal situation.

Step 1

The facilitator explains the phenomenon of stereotyping in such a way as to 'blame' it not on the shortcomings of the individuals or the groups, but on the organization structure; stereotyping is the natural outcome of a situation in which any two groups that have to relate are deprived (for example, through overwork) of social contact. (S)he might give examples of a humorous nature (for example, from *Yes, Prime Minister*), because by setting a mood of lightheartedness (s)he can often dispel apprehensions. Indeed, doing this exercise sometimes gives rise to much hilarity, which is an effective solvent for bitterness.

Step 2

Each group goes to a separate room, equipped with flipcharts, to produce two lists, on separate flipcharts:

(1) A list that characterizes (even caricatures) what they think and feel about the other group – their outlooks, their aims, their *modus operandi*, etc. Candour is to be encouraged.
(2) A list of what they predict the other group will be writing about them, trying to anticipate what the other group dislikes about them.

A variation on the procedure is to produce a third list, of how they would *like* to be seen by the other group.

If there is a cartoonist in the group, it is often helpful (and entertaining) to illustrate the lists.

Step 3

The two groups come together, the flipcharts are displayed, and each group in turn reads out and clarifies what it has written about the other group in the first list. No discussion is allowed but questions of clarification may be put. Then each group in turn reads out and explains their second list similarly.

Step 4

The groups return to their rooms, each with all the lists describing their own group, and they discuss which items are based on incorrect perceptions or failures to communicate.

Such items will have a rational explanation which can probably be conveyed to the other group in the expectation that they will exclaim 'Ah, so *that's* why you always keep doing so-and-so!' - or some such remark. It is probable, however, that there will be other items that cannot quite so easily be explained away, and constitute a genuine source of friction or a problem that needs to be resolved - such as a chronic shortage of resources to do what the other group needs. These items are listed, and placed in order of priority.

Step 5

The groups reconvene, share their lists, hopefully dispose of the 'easy' items, and then construct from the more difficult items a single list of problems to be resolved, in an agreed order of priority. They then draw up a plan for dealing with those problems that they agree to tackle. This plan should spell out who does what by when.

Step 6

Still meeting together, the two groups agree on a process for monitoring progress towards solving the problems, for example, regular exchange of written reports, dates for follow-up meetings to review progress, and any meeting to be held after several months have elapsed to return to the particularly difficult problems on which agreement to work on them could not be obtained.

The exercise proves more valuable if carried out in a congenial setting where it can be followed by informal social intercourse between members of the two groups - for example, in the bar of a residential centre. In such a setting, the 'ogres' become more like us, taking on a human face, and this lends credence to the facilitator's suggestion in Step 1, that the source of inter-group problems is usually structural.

A similar exercise can be carried out when three or more groups are involved, but if this gives rise to unwieldy numbers, it can be combined with a 'fish-bowl' approach, in which the key representatives (for example, managers) carry out Steps 3, 5 and 6, with an outer circle of the remaining participants looking on. Sub-groups of members drawn from each of the main groups can meet separately at the problem-solving stage, following Step 6 to work on the problem(s) allocated to them.

Exercise 7: school review

Introduction

The aims. For a school review these are:

(1) To examine frankly the way in which the school and its staff currently operate.
(2) To diagnose problems and opportunities for improvement.
(3) To set objectives for organizational improvement in the light of the diagnosis.
(4) (Starting from the second review) to examine progress towards the achievement of the organizational objectives set at the last review.

Organizing the review. In the top team (i.e. the head, the deputy head and the heads of department) responsibility for organizing review sessions lies with the head. In other groups the responsibility is that of the senior member of the group, though any other member should feel free to 'trigger' the process.

The time needed for the meeting will vary according to the size of the group, but usually six hours should be set aside for even the smallest group. It is very important that staff arrange not to be disturbed during the meeting.

The questionnaires below should be handed out by the head or senior group member before the meeting, and individuals should be asked to complete the check-list, the group development assessment and the inter-group problems questionnaire and to bring them to the meeting. There should be no consultation with other members of the group.

Check-list
Under each of the headings below are listed five alternative ways in which a work group may operate. All or most of the statements have probably been true of your own work group to some degree at some time.

Under each heading rank the statements in order (1 = 'best', 5 = 'worst') according to how well they describe:

(a) The situation in your own work group (i.e. the group to be reviewed at the meeting);

(b) The situation which should ideally obtain in your work group.

	Actual ranking	Ideal ranking	Notes

1. Decision-taking. Decisions which affect the group as a whole are:

(a) Taken by the head/department head. ....

(b) Allowed to drift. ....

(c) Thoroughly thrashed out in the group under the head/departmental head leadership. ....

(d) Left to members of the group. The head/departmental head 'falls into line'. ....

(e) Usually based on compromise or established precedent. ....

2. Communication

(a) The work of the group is hampered or effort wasted through serious lack of communication. ....

(b) Too much time is spent in exchanging irrelevant information. There is too much 'gossip' and not enough action. ....

(c) Most communication is 'vertical', e.g. between the head/departmental head and individual subordinates. ....

(d) Most communication is 'horizontal'. Subordinates exchange information and ideas but there is an absence of upward and downward interchange. ....

(e) There is a steady exchange of relevant ideas, information and problems among all members of the work group. ....

	Actual ranking	Ideal ranking	Notes

3. New ideas

(a) The group's main aim is to maintain the 'status quo'. Crises are dealt with as they arise. ....

(b) The group constantly takes up new ideas, but it fails to carry them through. ....

(c) Individuals who come up with new ideas, or show initiative are 'left to get on with it'. ....

(d) All members of the group are constantly on the look out for possible improvements and long-term solutions to problems. After careful evaluation these are systematically implemented with the active co-operation of the whole group. ....

(e) Initiative or impetus comes from above or outside the group. The group responds. ....

4. Relationships with other groups

(a) The group resents intrusions, advice or criticism from the outside. Group members staunchly defend group ideas, action and policies. ....

(b) There is a free exchange of information, ideas and help with those outside the group and with other groups. Competition with other groups is never detrimental to the effectiveness of the total organization. Responsibility for action is accepted by all. ....

(c) Some members of the group are apt to dissociate themselves from group actions when dealing with others outside the group. ....

	Actual ranking	*Ideal ranking*	*Notes*

(d) Efficiency is hampered by destructive competitiveness and lack of co-operation between this group and certain others.   ....

(e) The status of the work group is more important than the well-being of the organization.   ....

5. Review

(a) The group seldom examines the way in which it has operated. Patterns of work are either established or establish themselves.   ....

(b) Some group members discuss among themselves shortcomings in the group's operations and relationships with other groups but are afraid of hurting feelings or causing upheaval by bringing these shortcomings into the open.   ....

(c) There is a 'shake-up' from time to time, especially when there has been a clear case of inefficiency.   ....

(d) The workings of the group are examined frequently and frankly; all members seek ways of improving efficiency. The group learns from experience.   ....

(e) The group usually manages to blame some other department for any failures. It is content that it has played its own part satisfactorily.   ....

6. Objectives

(a) Group objectives and each person's role are regularly examined and realistic targets are set to which all feel committed. Objectives are updated as circumstances change.   ....

		Actual ranking	Ideal ranking	Notes

(b) While individuals are concerned for their own objectives, there is little concern for group objectives. Objectives encourage competition rather than co-operation. ....

(c) Objectives either are not set, are ignored, or are so easily attainable as to have no real value in improving performance or targeting effort. ....

(d) As reports and salary increases depend largely on achievement of fixed, annual objectives, these are pursued irrespective of changing conditions or long-term considerations. ....

(e) Effort and time are devoted to trivialities which contribute little to the fulfilment of the team's most vital functions. ....

7. Planning
(a) Many plans are made but few are executed. ....

(b) After careful consideration of circumstances, plans are made to which the group feels committed and which enable work and development to proceed in a timely and systematic fashion. ....

(c) Plans are imposed and must be strictly adhered to. ....

(d) Panics are frequent through lack of adequate planning. ....

(e) Work follows an established pattern. ....

8. Commitment
(a) All members of the group feel personally committed to achieving the highest possible standard of performance. ....

	Actual ranking	Ideal ranking	Notes

(b) There is more group loyalty than job
    commitment.   ....
(c) People do only as much as is required.   ....
(d) The head/departmental head drives the
    group hard.   ....
(e) Members of the group are anxious to
    avoid any criticisms of their operation. ....

9. Responsibility
(a) Responsibilities are clearly defined, are
    logical and are accompanied by the
    appropriate authority to take decisions. ....
(b) Many decisions which should be taken
    by an individual are referred to a group
    or to a higher level than necessary.   ....
(c) Too many decisions which should be
    taken as a group are taken by
    individuals without adequate consulta-
    tion.   ....
(d) Responsibility and authority are far
    from clear.   ....
(e) Responsibilities have become estab-
    lished in a pattern which is not the most
    effective.   ....

10. Use of resources
(a) Financial and other resources are alloc-
    ated to group members in accordance
    with a well-established pattern. They
    deploy these resources as they think fit. ....
(b) In some areas money has to be 'used
    up' while in others it is sadly lacking. ....
(c) Resource allocation is too flexible and
    money is made available to those areas
    in which the group agrees that it can be
    of most benefit to the total system.   ....
(d) Resource allocation is a matter of great
    controversy. Individuals each bid for as

	Actual ranking	*Ideal ranking*	*Notes*

much as can be got irrespective of the
needs of others.

(e) Many ventures are undertaken without
full consideration of the financial
implications.

Group Development Assessment

1. List what you believe to be at present the group's three main
   organizational problems or opportunities for improvement.
2. If the group has had a previous review, list:
   (a) The organizational objectives then set for the group.
   (b) Your own personal and organizational objectives.
3. To what extent do you consider that the above objectives have been
   attained by:
   (a) The group?
   (b) You personally?

Inter-group Problems Questionnaire

1. With what other groups does this group have to work most closely?
2. What problems prevent more effective co-operation between this
   group and any of the above groups?
3. Which three of these problems most impair effectiveness?
4. How might the above three problems be solved?

8
MANAGING YOURSELF

The manager as a resource

So far we have emphasized the fact that the manager is an organizer, a director, a controller of resources. Nevertheless, even in fulfilling these functions we are ourselves resources of the organization, and our managerial function extends to the control of our own time, skills and attitudes, to coping with stress, to the direction of our own efforts and to the development of our competence.

We have indicated already many of the ways in which we need to control our managerial behaviour in order to be effective in, for example, motivating others, taking decisions, participating in meetings and handling conflicts. This chapter is intended to focus on some key principles and to bring in some guidelines and techniques which have not been discussed elsewhere.

The use and abuse of time

It is very easy to be very busy doing the wrong thing. Those colleagues who are perpetually racing against time are seldom the most effective, and it should be recognized that just 'thinking' is one of the most positive uses of time. It is then that we are able to 'helicopter' above the hurly-burly of the school and do our managerial job of planning, organizing and controlling to make the best use of the resources available to us to achieve the desired result. Yet some teachers feel guilty if they are not seen to be bustling here and there, always doing something 'urgent'. Often the 'urgency' has arisen because they have failed to think ahead or act earlier, and they find themselves on the treadmill of crisis management. Managers will often find themselves doing things which they could - and should - have delegated if they had given the matter their attention earlier - but then they were too busy with the last crisis.

A great deal of effort can be expended to no avail. Geoffrey Morris was called in some years ago as a consultant to the head of a large comprehensive school, in which crisis management had developed to the point at which everyone was calling meetings at short notice, with the result that less than 50 per cent of the involved parties could attend because they were at other meetings. Further meetings, therefore, had to be called with many similar results, and the amount of wasted time and energy was almost unbelievable. Frustration and stress were apparent at every level. In such a situation it is very hard to get off the crisis treadmill, because no one has time to think about solving the real problems.

In this situation, despite the 'urgency' of the crisis, we had to lay down a programme of discussion, training and eventually 'school review' (Exercise 7, page 115) *well in advance* (a novelty in that school), and insist that it had absolute priority over commitments which might subsequently arise. Three months later the effect of the programme on the running and atmosphere of the school was dramatic. The time taken actually to sort things out was about 8 hours per departmental or pastoral manager, plus 12 hours each of the time of both the head and the deputy head, spread over six weeks.

Much of the success of the programme could be attributed to group work to establish new guidelines for managing the school. However, it was also essential that each manager should learn to manage his or her own time.

Establishing priorities

In determining how we use our time, we should be clear about our priorities and relate our activities to these. We should recognize that there are different kinds of priority, and the different categories have to be treated differently. The critical distinction is between what is urgent and what is important. It may well be that in time sequence we have to deal with the urgent before the important, but we must not be lured into the trap of being caught up in the urgent to the exclusion of the important. Are all the 'urgent' matters really so? Should I respond to every request to see me by allocating the next available slot of free time, or should I deliberately allocate a period of time to the important and keep that thinking, organizing or writing time as carefully as I would an appointment with Mr X? Do I myself have to deal with the things that are presented to me as urgent (or important for that matter) or can I delegate some of them, perhaps thereby motivating and developing one of my staff?

Within the 'important' category we need to think in terms of 'long-term' and 'short-term', with all the intermediate possibilities. If a priority is long-term, we need to review the shorter-term implications and lay down the intermediate steps. These then need 'do by' dates and allocation of time.

Criteria for effectiveness

A useful background to priorities is to ask yourself what your job is really about. In Chapter 6 we spoke of the importance of establishing with staff the criteria against which the performance of each one is judged. Even if there is no machinery for doing this with your own supervisor, the exercise is worth carrying out for your own guidance and it is well worth going beyond the level of the *actual* criteria by also asking:

(1) What *ought* to be the criteria against which you are judged in the interests of the organization?
(2) What personal criteria do you additionally apply in judging your performance? (For example, are you managing to achieve goals which may be related to your own interests, rather than to those of the organization?)

A format for carrying out such an analysis is in Exercise 8 at the end of this chapter.

Time-management techniques

If we have used a process such as the above to establish our priorities or if we just know them instinctively, the critical factor in management success is, of course, to control our use of time in relation to our priorities. A number of well-tried techniques are available to help us to do this. Two of these relate to an analysis of the recent past, viz:

(1) use-of-time analysis (Exercise 9 at the end of this chapter), which offers a rough and ready way of analysing your impression of how your time is being spent;

(2) time log (Exercise 10 at the end of this chapter) which enables a detailed analysis of the use of time over a relatively short period.

Both these documents are intended for occasional use and enable us to learn from what has happened and, repeated at a later date, to assess improvement. In each case the objective is, of course, to use 'gap' theory by comparing our actual use of time with the way in which we ought to use it, in line with our real priorities. Having learned from the past, the important thing is the continuous control of the present and future, and for this we need to build into our daily routine some basic administrative disciplines, i.e.:

(1) an action diary;

(2) a daily action sheet;

(3) project planning.

These disciplines are neither elaborate nor original, and most managers and headteachers come to use them sooner or later without any need for prompting from writers on management.

The action diary. This is a development of the appointments diary and the discipline consists simply in having the diary (preferably of the 'desk' variety) always in one's briefcase (possibly with a small emergency diary also in one's pocket or handbag) and writing down as they occur not only future appointments but also dates by which things have to be done Periodically, at least weekly, the diary should be reviewed and slots of time allocated for items such as 'prepare examination papers', 'plan overseas visit', 'practise with computer', or even 'administration and organization'.

The daily action sheet. This is an equally fundamental discipline. It can be a separate notebook or can be incorporated into a suitably large action diary. Here the discipline consists in starting each day by:

(1) writing a list of all the things that should be done that day;

(2) reviewing the previous day's list and carrying forward anything not done;

(3) numbering the items in order of time priority (i.e. the order in which you hope to tackle them);

(4)   starring (or whatever other system you like to use) to indicate importance.

Project planning. This is the final basic discipline which consists in thinking through, for a project involving a series of action points or check points, what has to be done by when and:

(1)   recording the total project plan on a sheet of paper or in a file;
(2)   publishing whatever parts of the plan others may need to know;
(3)   recording 'do by' dates in the action diary;
(4)   recording slots of time in the action diary for doing the actions.

Managing stress

Failure to manage our time will induce stress. As the educational environment has become more turbulent and where pupil misbehaviour has grown, so stress has become more widespread in the teaching profession. Not only does it impair the quality of life but it can also detract from performance; for both reasons, it needs managing. Stress among teachers has been studied by Kyriacou (1980) and by Dunham (1986).

There are three issues to examine: causes, symptoms and remedies. But first we need to understand that *some* stress is a valuable element in any job. It provides challenge and motivation, helps to raise performance and is an ingredient of job satisfaction. Lack of stimulation such as stress provides can lead to boredom, which paradoxically is itself stressful. Moreover, internal stress is a natural, animal response, connected with survival. In the face of external challenge, the body secretes adrenalin, which boosts the performance of the heart, muscles and brain and prepares the animal for fight or flight. But if we do nothing physical after the adrenalin flows, we remain tensed up.

It is excessive, prolonged, unmanaged stress that causes problems, especially with 'Type A' personalities (pushy, active). Some can be severe, such as ulcers, heart attacks, strokes, anxiety–depressive illnesses and even suicide. But these are largely preventable. Unfortunately our national culture is an obstacle to prevention: males particularly are conditioned not to expose their feelings or to display emotion, so stress tends to be a taboo subject for discussion. Admitting to it is felt to be tantamount to a confession of weakness or incompetence.

Causes

The causes of stress have a cumulative effect. Family crises such as divorce or bereavement pile on top of work pressures, of which the main factors in schools are:

(1) pupil misbehaviour;
(2) educational changes;
(3) poor working conditions;
(4) time pressures;
(5) role conflict, confusion or overload;
(6) a school ethos that denies information and support.

Our own attitudes can exacerbate stress: we may be perfectionists who set impossibly high standards; we may worry too much about what others think of us; we may bottle up emotion; we may not be assertive enough to say no to unreasonable demands.

Symptoms

People react in different ways to excessive stress; symptoms can be behavioural, emotional, mental or physical. Surveys among teachers identify the main symptoms as feelings of exhaustion, reduction of contacts outside school, frustration at lack of achievement, apathy, irritability, displaced aggression and a wish to leave teaching. Others are listed in Figure 8.1. Each symptom may have other causes, but if you find you have several, they could be due to stress. Experience will tell you which you usually evince and help you recognize the onset of stress. Self-diagnosis is important, so that you know when to deal with the condition. Some of the symptoms are observable and may help you to discern when a colleague needs support.

Remedies

Organizations can help to deal with stress by adopting preventative measures. Generally, industry has the edge over schools in this respect. Large firms employ occupational health specialists. They have better selection processes, which help to ensure a better fit between person and job. They practise systematic appraisal, which helps to nip incipient work-related problems in the bud. They invest more money in training so as to develop confidence in the job. There is much more team-work, which provides group support. Heads can take similar measures in their schools. They can also find out how their own management style and the school's ethos lead to unnecessary stress among the staff, and modify

Behavioural	Physical
Overeating	Headaches
Drinking too much alcohol	Upset stomach
Compulsive smoking	Dizziness
Neglect of personal appearance	Sweaty and/or trembling hands
Insomnia	Blurred vision
Restlessness – fidgeting	Skin rashes
Lethargy	Palpitations
Change in sex drive	Dry mouth
Unusual clumsiness	High blood pressure
Accident proneness	Backache
Letting things slide	Neck pains
Less communicative	Nausea

Emotional	Mental
Depression	Loss of concentration
Tenseness	Increased forgetfulness
Irritability	Increased mistakes
Remorse	Increased day-dreaming
Thoughts of suicide	Poor judgement
Defensiveness	Less rational thinking
Crying	Indecisiveness
Aggressive behaviour	
Anxiety	

Figure 8.1 Some symptoms of stress

them accordingly. They can review teachers' roles to minimize confusion, conflict and overload.

At the personal level those experiencing stress have several options open to them. Different people find help in different coping strategies, so you may have to experiment. Some things you can do by yourself are:

(1) managing your time better (see p. 124);
(2) identifying the people or tasks that steal your time and saying no more often;
(3) brain-dumping on to paper all the things that are worrying you, before you go to bed.
(4) deep breathing and other relaxation exercises (you can buy tapes for this purpose);
(5) carving out time to pursue your favourite pastime or sport after work.

Try to view yourself objectively within your environment; reason with yourself and realize that the seat of the problem may lie in the environment rather than in you, in which case self-reproach is misplaced.

Another approach is to share your concerns with a member of your family or trusted circle of friends. Let them listen and then help you to tease out the problem and come to terms with it. Agree with them the specific actions you will take, by when, to manage the stress, and arrange to meet again to review progress. Make sure that they understand the confidential nature of the discussion. The chances are that the person you choose to talk things over with will have experienced stress themselves, so you can probably count on a sympathetic understanding. However, you may do even better to meet others in the same boat; sometimes you will find a stress workshop being run locally by a trained counsellor. Such support systems can be of real help in generating the will to take effective action, especially at a time when your decision-making capacity is impaired (Baron & Thomson, 1989).

Assertiveness

We have already mentioned that one of the techniques for reducing stress is to learn to say 'no' to unreasonable demands. This is one of the principles of 'assertiveness' training which has primarily been introduced to help women to claim due recognition for their ideas and rights, but which can be of value generally in clarifying communication and preventing the build-up of commitments which cannot be met, hence stress on all parties.

'Assertiveness' in this particular sense can be summarized as 'openness, honesty and conciseness' and means:

> letting people know how you feel;
> stating your viewpoint and, if necessary, restating it until you are sure that it has been listened to;
> not hesitating to tell people what you can and cannot achieve and what will be the consequence of their pushing a demand;
> clearly stating your requirements of others;
> avoiding unnecessary padding which may soften or mask the impact of the message you wish to convey.

Being assertive must be distinguished from being aggressive. The latter usually involves some degree of emotion and a positive desire to impose one's will on the other party or to dominate. The 'assertive' person, on the other hand, should:

Keep calm and keep the emotions under control.

Make factual, objective statements. (This also applies to statements about one's feelings.)

Respect the interests and feelings of the other party and seek fair solutions in which neither party uses undue pressure to subjugate or dominate the other.

The simple techniques of 'assertiveness' are surprisingly powerful. The only danger is that those who practise them may over-compensate for their previous submissiveness and that, despite all warnings, the dominated may become dominators or even 'aggressors'.

Developing your own competence

The increased emphasis on competency-based national vocational qualifications is leading to the development of 'occupational competency frameworks'. For management occupations this is being led by the 'Management Charter Initiative'. The implications (and limitations) for education management have been discussed by one of us (Everard, 1989a). Not only are organizations being invited to subscribe to a code of practice that actively promotes competence development, but individual managers are being encouraged to take responsibility for systematic self-development, as part of their professionalism. The steps in the development process are:

(1) recognition of the various elements or units of competence;
(2) understanding their nature and how they relate to managerial effectiveness;
(3) self-assessment or other feedback (such as appraisal) on the level of competence;
(4) experimentation with displaying the competence, or demonstrating it at a higher level of effectiveness, with systematic feedback;
(5) continuing conscious practice in using the competence;
(6) applying it, along with other relevant competences as an integral whole, in a range of work situations.

While training courses are helpful in taking groups of individuals through steps 1-5, the process can also be followed on the job, especially if facilitated by a trusted colleague, adviser or consultant.

Competence is a combination of knowledge and skill plus the ability and will to apply them to particular situations. It thus includes motives, traits, attitudes and aspects of self-image and role. Competence is related to performance in regard to both the functions and demands of the particular management job and the requirements and constraints of the organizational setting (e.g. LEA policy). In developing competence, therefore, there has to be some definition of what constitutes effective performance (effectiveness criteria – see p. 124 and Chapter 6).

The functions that managers are required to perform (p. 4) call for a variety of competences which are largely generic, in that they are needed in all kinds of settings. These have been classified in various ways; one of us (Everard, 1986) used Burgoyne's taxonomy (Burgoyne, 1976) to group the qualities that senior teachers associate with managerial competence. Boyatzis (1982) identified six clusters of competences that were statistically related to superior performance (Figure 8.2).

However, it is insufficient to analyse competence, which is a holistic concept, into its elements; there is also a need for an overarching 'integrative competence', which enables a manager to assemble and orchestrate the necessary elements in dealing with particular situations.

Lists such as these can be used for rating by self and others and for identifying key areas for self-development. Each of these competences can be improved by systematic development and training; none is so innate that it cannot be influenced, although people's aptitudes for acquiring particular competences differ widely.

Managing your learning

Competence is developed by repeatedly going round an experiential learning cycle (page xiii). The most effective learning occurs when all four stages of the cycle are fully used (concrete experience, reflective observation, abstract conceptualization, active experimentation). However, people have different preferences for the four stages; they are said to have different 'learning styles' (Kolb, 1984). Honey and Mumford (1982) call these styles Activist, Reflector, Theorist and Pragmatist, and have developed a useful questionnaire for determining one's learning style profile. They have kindly allowed us to reproduce this (Exercise 11 at the end of this chapter), asking that readers use it only for themselves. If you want to use it more widely or purchase copies either of their manual or the inexpensive booklet *Using Your Learning Styles* which helps you to interpret your scores, use your learning strengths and improve your learning style, write to Dr Peter Honey, 10 Linden Avenue, Maidenhead, SL6 6HB. A summary of the features of each style is included at the end of Exercise 11.

Cluster	Competence
1. Goal and action management (needed for planning, organizing and controlling functions)	Efficiency orientation (concern to improve) Proactivity (disposition towards action) Diagnostic use of concepts (deductive thinking) Concern for impact (good at influencing)
2. Leadership (needed for planning, organizing, motivating and co-ordinating)	Self-confidence Public speaking ability Logical thought (placing events in a causal sequence)* Conceptualization (recognition of patterns in an assortment of information)
3. Human resource management (needed for organizing, controlling, motivating and co-ordinating)	Use of influence to build teams, networks and coalitions Positive regard (belief in others)* Managing group process (getting others to work together effectively) Accurate self-assessment*
4. Directing subordinates (needed for controlling and motivating)	Developing others (coaching)* Influencing to obtain compliance Spontaneity (ability to express oneself freely)*
5. Focus on others (needed for co-ordinating)	Self-control (ability to inhibit own needs in service of organization) Perceptual objectivity (low level of prejudice) Stamina and adaptability

6. Specialized knowledge*

* A threshold competence: needed to a certain level, but not causally related to superior performance beyond.

Figure 8.2 Competence clusters related to management functions, from R.E. Boyatzis, *The Competent Manager*, copyright © 1982 (reprinted by permission of John Wiley & Sons Inc.)

In interpreting your profile you need to compare your results with the norms for your occupational group. Butcher is finding that there is a distinct difference between the norms (which are subject to revision as the sample grows) for primary and secondary heads (the manual contains norms for other occupations, which may be used for careers guidance; and there are applications to teaching).

	Activist	Reflector	Theorist	Pragmatist
Primary	10.6	9.0	10.0	10.6
Secondary	8.9	13.9	12.9	12.8

This is reflected in their different responses to management training courses, so you can use your score to select courses that suit your learning style. Remember, however, that practice in a less preferred mode helps you to enlarge your repertoire and thus to take better advantage of different sorts of learning opportunity; also, that competence develops as you follow round every stage of the learning cycle.

The learning styles and team role questionnaires (Exercise 11, p. 141 and Exercise 12, p. 184) are examples of self-perception tools that we recommend for getting to know yourself better; accurate self-perception is a key management competence and vital to self-development. Other do-it-yourself tools will be found in Pedler's books (see below). We also recommend the Myers–Briggs test as particularly suitable for teachers, but this requires a psychologist to adminster, as does the 16PF, OPQ and Firo B, which are also used.

Managing our attitudes and behaviour

In the preceding chapters in this section we have seen that 'natural' reactions to situations are not always the best. We can, in fact, easily become 'hooked' into behavioural patterns which are counter-productive, such as developing inter-group conflict in order to cover up our own feelings of insecurity or threat. We may be unduly ready to perceive an attack and respond defensively when suggestions are offered.

We have already looked at models, check-lists and guidelines which may help us to check on our behaviour in one-to-one or group situations, and to adopt constructive approaches. Other helpful models exist, and we would recommend, as a perceptive (though not to be taken too seriously) insight into behaviour, the theories of transactional analysis (Berne, 1967), which starts from the premise that behavioural patterns can be classified as those of the Parent, the Adult or the Child with classic attitudes of:

(1)   Parent – telling, guiding, asserting, dominating, criticizing;
(2)   Adult – reasoning, listening, suggesting;
(3)   Child – feeling, creating/destroying, accepting/resisting, enquiring.

It is surprising how often we can catch ourselves, especially as teachers, treating our colleagues or social contacts as 'children' by adopting 'know-all' or 'patronizing' attitudes. How often are we instantly recognized as teachers?

In a book of this scope it is impossible to do justice to this or other helpful theories. However, this author has found the following adaptation of another of the transactional analysis concepts particularly helpful in helping managers to understand and control their own behaviour (Harris, 1973). It is a useful model in dealing with conflict, since it enables us to recognize the psychological realities that may underlie the reactions of ourselves and/or others.

The OK Matrix

The OK Matrix (Figure 8.3) illustrates four basic ways in which we may feel about ourselves and other people.

	You're OK	You're not OK
I'm OK	We can work together effectively	I don't trust you
I'm not OK	I must prove that I'm worth something or opt out	I may be able to prove myself at your expense

Figure 8.3   The OK matrix, from Harris, T.A. (1973), reprinted by permission of Jonathon Cape Ltd.

However self-confident we are, there are bound to be times when each of us will not feel 'OK', i.e. sure of ourselves. For example, no one feels completely 'OK' on his or her first day in a new job. The adolescent does not basically feel 'OK' in an adult world. Some people consistently feel less 'OK' than others and are then said to have an inferiority complex.

At times when we do not feel 'OK' most of us will try to prove ourselves in a variety of ways. If these ways fit into the value system of the organization to which we belong, the effect will be perceived as positive – a teenager may strive for distinction in the examination room or on the sports field; a salesman will seek to achieve his targets and possibly to be the best; a manager will seek to demonstrate his effectiveness to his superior.

However, if these methods do not succeed, the individual may, in his underconfidence, adopt less constructive approaches. The teenager may seek the approbation of his fellows by being disruptive; the salesman may blame the market, the system, the targets; the manager may feel that he must suppress the initiatives of his subordinate which he perceives as a threat. Ironically, people with inferiority complexes do not behave modestly but, on the contrary, often behave in an aggressive, patronizing, arrogant way in an attempt to prove themselves. Finally, there is the possibility of withdrawing into one's shell and opting out.

Such patterns of behaviour can be disturbing enough when directed towards someone else whom we see as 'OK'. However, they have the potential to become really vicious when someone, who does not himself feel 'OK', takes the opportunity to prove himself at the expense of someone whom he perceives to be also 'not OK'. This is the behaviour of the bully. It is also the behaviour of the manager who tries to shift blame on to, or take advantage of, a weaker colleague.

In the top right-hand corner of the matrix we have the situation where 'I' may feel 'OK' but may find someone else 'not OK'. This means that I do not trust him or have confidence in his ability. Such an attitude may be justified. However, there is the risk in a conflict situation that I am stereotyping him negatively – inclined to attribute the wrong motives to his actions. I may well be right, particularly if he and I have become locked into a vicious circle where neither trusts the other and where the actions of both will therefore be loaded.

The important thing to bear in mind is that most negative behaviour occurs because people feel unsure or threatened – perhaps not by us but by others or by circumstances.

Finally, it must be remembered that how a person perceives himself and others in terms of the OK Matrix depends to a large extent on that person. If we treat others as though they are 'not OK' in our eyes they will seldom prove the contrary.

As far as possible the aim should be to feel 'OK' in ourselves and try to accept others in a positive way. This is the basis for a sound working relationship or friendship. In attempting to resolve conflict, the parties must make a real effort to move towards the 'I'm OK/You're OK' corner, though it will never be easy! (Harris, 1973).

Positive and negative management

Finally, we suggest that the behavioural check-list in Figure 8.4 may serve to crystallize the key behavioural issues for the manager.

THE POSITIVE MANAGER	THE NEGATIVE MANAGER
Acts	Is a victim
Accepts responsibility	Blames others
Is objective	Is subjective
Listens and responds	Rejects suggestions
Proposes solutions	Criticizes
Delegates	Is incapable of delegation
Sees opportunities	Sees threats
Has breadth of vision	Is preoccupied with detail
Faces up to problems	Conceals problems
Confronts the source of problems	Talks about the source of problems
Learns	Is taught
Has foresight	Has hindsight

Figure 8.4 Positive and negative management

Further reading

Adair, J. (1987) *How to Manage Your Time*, Talbot Adair, Guildford.
Cooper, C.L. and Payne, R. (eds.) (1978) *Stress at Work*, Wiley, London.
Dunham, J. Helping with stress, in Marland, M. (ed.) (1986) *School Management Skills*, Heinemann, Oxford.
Gray, H. and Freeman, A. (1987) *Teaching Without Stress*, Paul Chapman, London.
Honey, P. and Mumford, A. (1982) *Manual of Learning Styles*, Honey, Maidenhead.
Mumford, A. (1980) *Making Experience Pay*, McGraw-Hill, London.
Pedler, M., Burgoyne, J. and Boydell, T. (1978) *A Manager's Guide to Self-Development*, McGraw-Hill, London.
Pedler, M. and Boydell, T. (1985) *Managing Yourself*, Fontana, London.
Stewart, R. (1982) *Choices for the Manager*, McGraw-Hill, London.

Exercise 8: criteria for effectiveness – establishing priorities

List criteria detailed, and then rank them in order of importance to you:

1. The main criteria against which you believe that your performance is

judged by your immediate superior and by others who can affect your career.

2. *Additional* criteria against which you feel that your performance ought to be judged in the interests of the school or college.

3. *Further* criteria against which you personally judge your success or failure.

Exercise 9: use of time analysis

This exercise is fully intended to help you think about how you spend your time currently, and how you would like to spend your working day, with a view to developing some concrete action plans directed towards improving your overall effectiveness.

1. Using the activity categories shown on the analysis sheet and *any others you feel are applicable*, estimate the amount of your time you have spent on each activity during the past three months, expressed as a percentage of your total working time. Use the first column ('Actual') for recording your estimates.

2. Use the second column ('Ideal') to fill in the time allocations as percentages which you feel you would like to be able to record for a future period.

3. Which five (approximately) activities show the greatest discrepancy between 'actual' and 'ideal' in terms of time commitment? Enter these below.

4. Which major obstacle (if any) do you see preventing you from achieving the sort of time allocation which you think would be ideal for you in your job?

5. What concrete steps can *you* take in order to come closer to your ideal in terms of spending time on the job? Be specific.

6. What can others (who?) do to help you or indeed make it possible for you to achieve this ideal? Be specific.

Analysis sheet

		Actual	Ideal
(a) Teaching	(overall)	. . . .	. . . .
– lesson preparation		. . . .	. . . .
– practical teaching		. . . .	. . . .

	Actual	*Ideal*
– marking	....	....
–	....	....
–	....	....
–	....	....

(b) Administration   (overall)

– staff management	....	....
– tidying up, sorting out, 'getting organized'	....	....
– reports	....	....
– general adminstration	....	....
–	....	....
–	....	....
–	....	....

(c) Miscellaneous   (overall)

– meetings (if not covered above)	....	....
– reading, studying, thinking	....	....
– parent/teacher co-operation	....	....
– 'out-of-school' activities (including clubs,	....	....
societies, one-day and extended visits – UK	....	....
and abroad)	....	....
–	....	....

(d) Specialized activities (please list)

–	....	....
–	....	....
–	....	....
–	....	....
–	....	....
–	....	....

Exercise 10: time log

Day ....

Date ....

Describe *what happens* in detail – the subject of meetings, telephone calls, letters, reading, conversations. Note the *duration* of each happening. Note the *name* and *position of other people involved*. Include even casual encounters.

Time	What happened?	Duration	People involved	Comments
8.00 8.30				
9.00 9.30				
9.30 10.00				
10.00 10.30				
10.30 11.00				
11.00 11.30				
11.30 12.00				

Time	What happened?	Duration	People involved	Comments
12.00				
12.30				
12.30				
1.00				
1.00				
1.30				
1.30				
2.00				
2.00				
2.30				
2.30				
3.00				
3.00				
3.30				
3.30				
4.00				
4.00				
4.30				
4.30				
5.00				
5.00				
5.30				

Exercise 11: learning styles questionnaire

This questionnaire is designed to find out your preferred learning style(s). Over the years you have probably developed learning 'habits' that help you benefit more from some experiences than from others. Since you are probably unaware of this, this questionnaire will help you pinpoint your learning preferences so that you are in a better position to select learning experiences that suit your style.

There is no time limit to this questionnaire. It will probably take you 10–15 minutes. The accuracy of the results depends on how honest you can be. There are no right or wrong answers. If you agree more than you disagree with a statement put a tick by it ($\checkmark$). If you disagree more than you agree put a cross by it ($\times$). Be sure to mark each item with either a tick or cross.

☐   1. I have strong beliefs about what is right and wrong, good and bad.

☐   2. I often act without considering the possible consequences.

☐   3. I tend to solve problems using a step-by-step approach.

☐   4. I believe that formal procedures and policies restrict people.

☐   5. I have a reputation for saying what I think, simply and directly.

☐   6. I often find that actions based on feelings are as sound as those based on careful thought and analysis.

☐   7. I like the sort of work where I have time for thorough preparation and implementation.

☐   8. I regularly question people about their basic assumptions.

☐   9. What matters most is whether something works in practice.

☐ 10. I actively seek out new experiences.

☐ 11. When I hear about a new idea or approach I immediately start working out how to apply it in practice.

☐ 12. I am keen on self discipline such as watching my diet, taking regular exercise, sticking to a fixed routine, etc.

☐ 13. I take pride in doing a thorough job.

☐ 14. I get on best with logical, analytical people and less well with spontaneous, 'irrational' people.

☐ 15. I take care over the interpretation of data available to me and avoid jumping to conclusions.

☐ 16. I like to reach a decision carefully after weighing up many alternatives.

☐ 17. I'm attracted more to novel, unusual ideas than to practical ones.

☐ 18. I don't like disorganised things and prefer to fit things into a coherent pattern.

☐ 19. I accept and stick to laid down procedures and policies so long as I regard them as an efficient way of getting the job done.

☐ 20. I like to relate my actions to a general principle.

☐ 21. In discussions I like to get straight to the point.

☐ 22. I tend to have distant, rather formal relationships with people at work.

☐ 23. I thrive on the challenge of tackling something new and different.

☐ 24. I enjoy fun-loving, spontaneous people.

☐ 25. I pay meticulous attention to detail before coming to a conclusion.

☐ 26. I find it difficult to produce ideas on impulse.

☐ 27. I believe in coming to the point immediately.

☐ 28. I am careful not to jump to conclusions too quickly.

☐ 29. I prefer to have as many sources of information as possible – the more data to think over the better.

☐ 30. Flippant people who don't take things seriously enough usually irritate me.

☐ 31. I listen to other people's points of view before putting my own forward.

☐ 32. I tend to be open about how I'm feeling.

☐ 33. In discussions I enjoy watching the manoeuvrings of the other participants.

☐ 34. I prefer to respond to events on a spontaneous, flexible basis rather than plan things out in advance.

☐ 35. I tend to be attracted to techniques such as network analysis, flow charts, branching programmes, contingency planning, etc.

☐ 36. It worries me if I have to rush out a piece of work to meet a tight deadline.

☐ 37. I tend to judge people's ideas on their practical merits.

☐ 38. Quiet, thoughtful people tend to make me feel uneasy.

☐ 39. I often get irritated by people who want to rush things.

☐ 40. It is more important to enjoy the present moment than to think about the past or future.

☐ 41. I think that decisions based on a thorough analysis of all the information are sounder than those based on intuition.

☐ 42. I tend to be a perfectionist.

☐ 43. In discussions I usually produce lots of spontaneous ideas.

☐ 44. In meetings I put forward practical realistic ideas.

☐ 45. More often than not, rules are there to be broken.

☐ 46. I prefer to stand back from a situation and consider all the perspectives.

☐ 47. I can often see inconsistencies and weaknesses in other people's arguments.

☐ 48. On balance I talk more than I listen.

☐ 49. I can often see better, more practical ways to get things done.

☐ 50. I think written reports should be short and to the point.

☐ 51. I believe that rational, logical thinking should win the day.

☐ 52. I tend to discuss specific things with people rather than engaging in social discussion.

☐ 53. I like people who approach things realistically rather than theoretically.

☐ 54. In discussions I get impatient with irrelevancies and digressions.

☐ 55. If I have a report to write I tend to produce lots of drafts before settling on the final version.

☐ 56. I am keen to try things out to see if they work in practice.

☐ 57. I am keen to reach answers via a logical approach.

☐ 58. I enjoy being the one that talks a lot.

☐ 59. In discussions I often find I am the realist, keeping people to the point and avoiding wild speculations.

☐ 60. I like to ponder many alternatives before making up my mind.

☐ 61. In discussions with people I often find I am the most dispassionate and objective.

☐ 62. In discussions I'm more likely to adopt a 'low profile' than to take the lead and do most of the talking.

☐ 63. I like to be able to relate current actions to a longer term bigger picture.

☐ 64. When things go wrong I am happy to shrug it off and 'put it down to experience'.

☐ 65. I tend to reject wild, spontaneous ideas as being impractical.

☐ 66. It's best to to think carefully before taking action.

☐ 67. On balance I do the listening rather than the talking.

☐ 68. I tend to be tough on people who find it difficult to adopt a logical approach.

☐ 69. Most times I believe the end justifies the means.

☐ 70. I don't mind hurting people's feelings so long as the job gets done.

☐ 71. I find the formality of having specific objectives and plans stifling.

☐ 72. I'm usually one of the people who puts life into a party.

☐ 73. I do whatever is expedient to get the job done.

☐ 74. I quickly get bored with methodical, detailed work.

☐ 75. I am keen on exploring the basic assumptions, principles and theories underpinning things and events.

☐ 76. I'm always interested to find out what people think.

☐ 77. I like meetings to be run on methodical lines, sticking to laid down agenda, etc.

☐ 78. I steer clear of subjective or ambiguous topics.

☐ 79. I enjoy the drama and excitement of a crisis situation.

☐ 80. People often find me insensitive to their feelings.

Scoring

You score one point for each item you ticked (√). There are no points for items you crossed (×). Simply indicate on the lists below which items were ticked.

2	7	1	5
4	13	3	9
6	15	8	11
10	16	12	19
17	25	14	21
23	28	18	27
24	29	20	35
32	31	22	37
34	33	26	44
38	36	30	49
40	39	42	50
43	41	47	53
45	46	51	54
48	52	57	56
58	55	61	59
64	60	63	65
71	62	68	69
72	66	75	70
74	67	77	73
79	76	78	80

Totals:

Activist	*Reflector*	*Theorist*	*Pragmatist*

Plot the scores on the arms of the cross below and apply the appropriate norms given in the text (see p. 133).

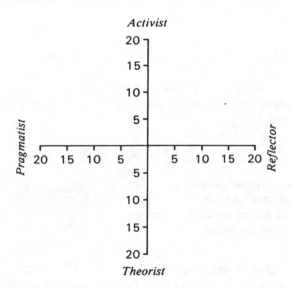

Learning styles – general descriptions

Activist
Strengths:
Flexible and open minded.
Happy to have a go.
Happy to be exposed to new situations.
Optimistic about anything new and therefore unlikely to resist change.

Weaknesses:
Tendency to take the immediately obvious action without thinking.
Often take unnecessary risks.
Tendency to do too much themselves and hog the limelight.
Rush into action without sufficient preparation.
Get bored with implementation/consolidation.

Reflector
Strengths:
Careful.

Thorough and methodical.
Thoughtful.
Good at listening to others and assimilating information.
Rarely jump to conclusions.

Weaknesses:
Tendency to hold back from direct participation.
Slow to make up their minds and reach a decision.
Tendency to be too cautious and not take enough risks.
Not assertive - they aren't particularly forthcoming and have no 'small talk'.

Theorist
Strengths:
Logical 'vertical' thinkers.
Rational and objective.
Good at asking probing questions.
Disciplined approach.

Weaknesses:
Restricted in lateral thinking.
Low tolerance for uncertainty, disorder and ambiguity.
Intolerant of anything subjective or intuitive.
Full of 'shoulds, oughts and musts'.

Pragmatist
Strengths:
Keen to test things out in practice.
Practical, down to earth, realistic.
Businesslike - gets straight to the point.
Technique oriented.

Weaknesses:
Tendency to reject anything without an obvious application.
Not very interested in theory or basic principles.
Tendency to seize on the first expedient solution to a problem.
Impatient with waffle.
On balance, task oriented not people oriented.

© Honey and Mumford (1986), pp. 141–46.

PART II
MANAGING THE ORGANIZATION

9
ORGANIZATIONS

The organizational dimension

Most of Part I was addressed to the ways in which managers deal with people as individuals. However, managers also have to operate at points further along the organizational dimension (Figure 9.1) and this is tackled in Part II. We shall first look at some of the characteristics of organizations and their implications for managers, then, in Chapter 10, at groups. Forming groups of individuals, building them into effective working units or teams, and getting these teams to work together effectively in pursuing the organization's purpose and goals, is at the heart of organization management. Teams, or whatever word is used to describe these groupings of collaborating individuals, are the building blocks of organizations, and managers (as we have seen) are the glue that holds them together. But first we look at organizations as a whole.

Organizational goals

We believe that all organizations, including educational ones, should be actively managed against goals; in other words, not only should there be a clear sense of the direction in which the organization is being steered, but also markers whereby we can assess progress. The words that we use to describe concepts of direction and progress vary from the broad to the more specific. At the specific end, we have words like 'goals', 'objectives', 'targets' and 'success criteria', which more or less define

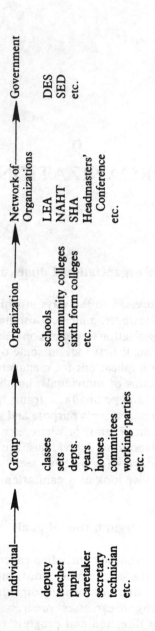

Figure 9.1 The organizational dimension

Individual ⟶	Group ⟶	Organization ⟶	Network of Organizations ⟶	Government
deputy	classes	schools	LEA	DES
teacher	sets	community colleges	NAHT	SED
pupil	depts.	sixth form colleges	SHA	etc.
caretaker	years	etc.	Headmasters'	
secretary	houses		Conference	
technician	committees		etc.	
etc.	working parties			
	etc.			

endpoints or milestones. 'Aims' are broader in concept, and subsuming the rest, we can talk of a 'central purpose', a 'reason for being' or a 'core mission' for the organization. A sense of purpose is like gravity – a continuous force that moves the organization in a particular direction. There is no agreed generic word that describes these concepts collectively, but we usually speak of 'opening' and 'closing' an objective when we want to indicate a movement towards, respectively, breadth or specificity.

Organizational aims (used here in a generic sense) nurture and steer creative tension and release and harness human energy; they keep the organization on the move, heading in a certain direction. Some heads we interviewed conceive it as one of their most important tasks to keep their schools moving. 'My recurring nightmare is stagnation and not moving forward', said one.

Interestingly, this same idea of inducing movement was picked up as a key activity of executives of successful companies by Peters and Waterman in *In Search of Excellence* (1982, p. 119). For instance, they quote a Cadbury's executive as saying 'Ready. Fire. Aim.' And (p. 107): 'organizations are to be sailed rather than driven... . the effectiveness of leadership often depends on being able to time interventions so that the force of natural organizational processes amplifies the interventions rather than damps them... . organizational design is more like building a snow fence to deflect drifting snow than like building a snowman.' Similarly, John Harvey-Jones, chairman of ICI, said in a nautical metaphor: 'I know this sounds terrible, but I'm more interested in speed than direction. Once you get moving, you can sort of veer and tack. But the important thing is, you're moving.' (Huxley, 1984.)

So the message to organization managers is: Get moving! Don't drive it; steer it. Use the force of the wind and snowstorm, not just letting them buffet you around like a cork, but to help you *aim* in roughly the right direction. Once you have got it on the right course and everyone knows in what direction you are trying to head, you can start to close down the broad objectives and set more specific markers of progress, such as targets. For example, if you want to stimulate new thinking on curriculum development, you could assemble a small informal group of, perhaps, staff, pupils and parents who are constructively dissatisfied with the present curriculum, and give them the general aim of helping you to decide what most needs change. You may not agree with all they say, but you will probably like at least one suggestion which you might give to, say, the English department to shape into a concrete proposal by the end of the Easter term. After discussion, you might agree a target date for incorporating the change in next year's curriculum.

The same approach is needed for the constituent parts of the organization – the departments, the teams, the committees. Their aims should be kept aligned with those of the school. The setting of organizational and departmental aims should normally involve the people in them, together with other stakeholders (see next section), but it is ultimately for the manager to decide what these should be. This is laid down as the first professional duty of headteachers under their conditions of employment (DES 1988): 'formulating the overall aims and objectives of the school'. Peters and Waterman (1985, p. 85) state: 'The inbuilding of purpose is a challenge to creativity because it involves transforming men and groups from neutral, technical units into participants who have a particular stamp, sensitivity and commitment.'

Organizations usually have more than one objective: it is a fallacy, for example, to suppose that business organizations only exist to make the maximum profit. Study of the published objectives of such companies as Shell, ICI and Securicor show that they pursue social as well as economic objectives, which it is the task of management to keep in balance. Similarly, those schools that make their aims explicit often find that they are having to harmonize different though compatible aims.

Stakeholders

Take, for example, the set of aims of a comprehensive school, reproduced in Figure 9.2. Not only does the school aim to serve the needs of the individual pupil, but it also seeks to respond to the legitimate demands of employers, colleges, universities, polytechnics, examining

---

Aims are ideals and they are like stars in that though we may not reach them we use them to guide us. If we do not know where we are going, it is likely that we will end up somewhere else!

To recognize the individual's talents of all kinds and degrees and to develop this intellectual, physical and creative capacity.

To ensure that the curriculum serves the individual's needs.

To develop a curriculum which is flexible enough to respond to the sensible needs of students at different ages and stages.

To recognize the legitimate demands of employers, colleges, universities, polytechnics and examining bodies.

To recognize the legitimate demands of society as a whole with respect to adequate numeracy, literacy and other fundamental skills relating to the processes of communication; oral, written and visual.

To enable students to acquire the required education relating to the necessity to earn a living and, when appropriate, to enter into skilled occupations and professions.

To seek to measure the extent to which an individual is being successful in making the maximum use of natural gifts and opportunities.

To be rigorously selective in the material presented to students, bearing in mind the above aims and having particular regard to the following aims:

> The instilling of an attitude to learning that shows it to be a life-long process.
>
> The stimulation of intellectual curiosity.
>
> The direction and exercising of the emotions.
>
> The encouragement of discrimination.
>
> The development of the art of learning.
>
> The fostering of a capacity to tackle unfamiliar problems.
>
> The emphasizing of the need to differentiate between truth and lies and between fact and feeling with the associated understanding of the nature of evidence.
>
> The growth of understanding of the nature and importance of knowledge plus the involvement with the processes and resources of learning.

To recognize and accept differences in natural endowment and environment and to hold every individual in esteem as of right.

To accept responsibility for identifying the physical, aesthetic, creative, emotional and social needs of each individual student as a necessary starting point to satisfy these needs.

To maintain the school as a caring community emphasizing the central importance of good human relationships based upon sensitivity, tolerance, good will and a sense of humour.

To promote the understanding of the fact that the individual and the community have a reciprocal responsibility and that individual needs must at times be secondary to the greater need of a large group; that collaboration and co-operation is a two-way activity.

To foster habits of responsibility, self-discipline, initiative, endeavour and individual judgement.

To obtain a positive response to the needs of a changing society whilst emphasizing established fundamental values and standards.

To promote the idea that the school is the servant of the community in both local and national terms and to accept the responsibilities which flow from this understanding.

To secure the active involvement of all people concerned with the school's welfare, staff, students, governors, parents and the Authority, in the continuous re-assessment of the aims and objectives of the school.

Figure 9.2 Aims of a comprehensive school

bodies and society as a whole. There are different 'stakeholders' in all organizations: businesses need to serve customers, offer a market to suppliers, reward shareholders, look after employees and be good corporate citizens in society; likewise schools have as stakeholders pupils, parents, LEAs, governors, teachers, feeder schools, higher education, employers and the local community.

The management's task is to look after the interests of all the stakeholders and keep some sort of balance between them. An industrial manager is no more the paid lackey of the shareholders (or expected by them to be so) than a headteacher is of the LEA. Both have a right and duty to resist demands that seriously upset the balance and health of the organization. Not all organizational aims are perfectly aligned, and the manager has to resolve conflicts of interest, some of which are more apparent than real. It is a help when the different stakeholders recognize and respect each other's legitimate aims for the organization, and can see that its best interests are served when any conflict is resolved by consensus: hence the importance of the last objective in the list in Figure 9.2.

Another objective in the list mentions the concept of 'reciprocal responsibility'. Organizations have to strike deals with their stakeholders whereby, in return for certain advantages flowing one way, other advantages will flow the other way. The head may well have to supervise unwritten contracts of this kind.

Personal application. List the stakeholders in your school. What aims does each stakeholder have for the school? Is there any conflict, actual or potential? Is there an 'umbrella' statement of purpose that subsumes all these aims? Do all the stakeholders subscribe to this? How well are these aims articulated and used in directing the affairs of the school? What more can you do to generate a sense of common purpose and commitment to agreed aims or ends?

Environment

Much criticism is levelled at schools for being out of touch with the world outside them. Some of it may be justified in the sense that few teachers have had an opportunity of working anywhere other than in an educational establishment: those who have held a responsible post in industry or in the public service outside education develop a useful frame of reference by which to judge what goes on in school.

Those who manage organizations should remember that they are part of a bigger system; they are interdependent with the rest of society, which they serve as society serves them. To ensure that they keep track of what is going on around them, successful organization managers make a point of having a wide circle of contacts and of staying interested in developments outside their immediate sphere. Blinkered managers are unlikely to pick up from the flow of events what may hit them tomorrow. They fail to anticipate what new demands may be made on them, and are caught unprepared. Managers have to take into account prevailing currents of opinion, to track the changing stance of the DES, for example, and to aim not at where the environment is now, but at where it will be when they are able to respond. It is not easy to distinguish a fundamental shift from an ephemeral straying off course; but we have to try.

One way of picturing an organization such as a school in the context of its environment is shown in Figure 9.3. Rather like a living organism, it pursues its central purpose, denoted by the big arrow, within an environment with which it makes continuous transactions. It takes in various inputs (in the case of organisms, food and energy: for schools, younger pupils, funds, learning materials, etc.) and it gives out various outputs – older, educated pupils, service to the community, a livelihood for teachers and their families, etc. The organism or organization is designed to achieve the efficient transformation of all the inputs into the desired outputs – 'efficient' signifying that the transformation takes place with the minimum expenditure of internal energy (using an electrical metaphor, the battery has low internal resistance).

Such a model does not always appeal to schools as it suggests that they are a kind of sausage machine. No model tells the whole story, yet there is a sense in which schools exist to 'school' or socialize children and to equip them as future mature members of society.

The model also depicts the other important properties of organizations: the existence of a basic aim to provide a sense of purpose and direction, and the effect of the interactions with the environment which arise from pursuing this aim. The arrows on the right show that the turbulent environment may tend to thwart the fulfilment of the school's central purpose; the double-headed arrow in the middle indicates that there is some feedback mechanism to enable the organization to know how well it is faring in pursuit of its aims, so that the helm can be set accordingly.

Many long-serving heads we have talked to have remarked how much over the past two or three decades the nature of their jobs has changed to

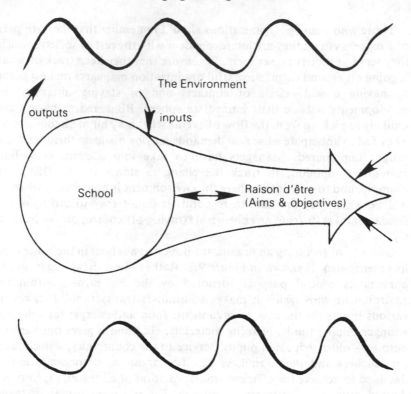

Figure 9.3　A school in its environment

one of 'boundary management' (Chapter 14): that is, they spend much more of their time managing transactions between their school and its environment. They are being forced to keep a weather eye on what is happening around them, so that they can successfully pilot their schools through the ruffled waters that lie ahead. Garratt (1987) depicts the dual role of top people in organizations in a double-loop model (Figure 9.4 - adapted) and enjoins them to spend more time 'looking upwards and outwards', delegating more of the operational management to subordinates. This is a key part of organization management. In Part III we shall explore further what this involves, and how to influence the environment's demands.

Models of organizations

The way in which managers conceptualize organizations influences the

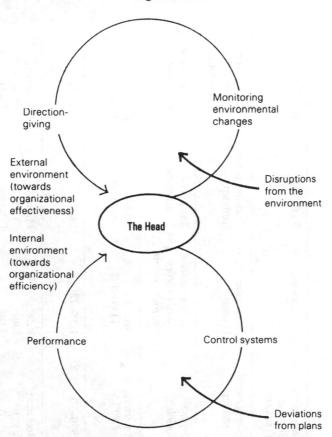

Figure 9.4 The learning organization model (after Garratt, 1987)

way they manage them, so it is worth exploring some of the main models that are used, in relation to organizations, in addition to the simple one described in the last section. Managers familiar with the various models or schools of thought about organizations are better able to select an appropriate one to deal with the particular situation they need to manage.

There is no one 'right' model of so complex an entity as an organization: different models are different approximations to the truth. On management courses we have found that people are helped by having a map of the various models or schools of thought which have had an important influence. Such a map appears in Figure 9.5.

Descriptions	Classical Mechanistic Bureaucratic	Behavioural Organic Human relations	Systems Cybernetics Socio-technical	Decisions	Technological or contingency
Dominant management style	Theory X	Theory Y	Situational	Authoritarian	Situational
Organizational structure	Formal Rigid Long-lived	Informal Flexible Transient	Interlocking	Stratified	Variable
Emphasis on	Specialization Rationality	Interpersonal relations	Information flows Groups	Decision bands Authority	Environmental Process technology
Source of ideas	Army Mass-production	Psychologists Sociologists	Instrumentation Control theory Nervous system	Business enterprises	Investigational field-work
Predominant nationality	British French American	American (NTL)	British (Tavistock)	British American	British American
Period of main development	1900–40	1950–70	1950–72	1960	1950–55
Some key names	Urwick Fayol Taylor	Beckhard Argyris Likert Blake McGregor	Rice Emery Trist Beer	March Cyert Paterson	Woodward, Burns and Stalker Lawrence and Lorsch Reddin Perrow

The classical model
This model emphasizes characteristics such as rationality, high job specialization, centralization, a command system, a tight hierarchy, strong vertical communication, tight control, rigid procedures and an autocratic approach. Though it bears some resemblance to certain bad companies and schools, it is the antithesis of the way in which the best companies are organized: 'The rational model causes us to denigrate the importance of values... . The top performer's ability to extract extraordinary contributions from very large numbers of people turns on the ability to create a sense of highly valued purpose.' (Peters and Waterman, 1982, p. 51.)

The humanistic model
The model is characterized by respect for the individual and other human values, job breadth, consultation, consensus, decentralization, loose project organization, flexible procedures, multidirectional communication, management by objectives and a participative approach. It comes closer to describing how the best companies are organized and it is a good deal more attractive to schools. However, without care, it tends to lead people to undervalue the achievement of the tasks of the organization and thereby to detract from the organization's effectiveness in achieving its aims. It can also give managers a sense of impotence and loss of control.

Nevertheless, a humanistic model has played a key part in the development of thought about organizations, counteracting the rational thinking of the classical school. Incidentally, the term 'rational' is usually misused in the literature on organizations: it actually means sensible, logical and reasonable. However, it has come to have a narrow meaning which excludes the messy, human stuff. Yet there is a great deal of rationality in the humanistic model: it takes human behaviour into full account, by postulating that human beings act rationally towards situations *as they perceive them*. The trick is to find out how they perceive them, at the level of emotions as well as intellect; then you can predict how they will respond.

The Systems Model has been popular in industry for the last decade or two and is particularly useful to organizations having to adapt rapidly to change. Although one of the conceptual roots of the model, control engineering, is alien to schools, the other root is more acceptable: it comes from a study of how living organisms work and survive, and especially of the properties of the central nervous system of the human organism. By comparing organizations to organisms that adapt and survive in a changing environment, this approach brings out a number of factors important to schools today.

Stafford Beer, in his *Brain of the Firm* (1971), has taken the metaphor of the living organism a stage further. He has used knowledge of human physiology to develop a theory that has been applied to industrial organizations, governments and a church. It states that there are five tiers of subsystems in the human central nervous system, which have their counterparts in all organizations. The successful survival and development of the human race is evidence of the effectiveness of such a system. The assumption is made that organizations can be made more effective by comparing them to the central nervous system, diagnosing in what respects they fall short and strengthening the subsystem that seems weakly developed.

Three of the tiers (systems 5, 3 and 1) are easily recognizable (Figure 9.6). They are associated with the functions of policy-making, managing the execution of policy and finally the actual 'doing' operation. In practice, the 'doing' can be complex – teachers share pupils, plant and equipment, crises arise, etc., so there is a cloud of buzzing communication across the 'doing' groups: a bit of give and take, borrowing and lending, reciprocal adjustment, ironing out problems. On the whole this tends to be fairly informal, but it is nevertheless vital to the smooth operation of the school. Its equivalent in the human body is the subconscious co-ordination of movement; when the system fails, this smooth co-ordination is lost.

This system (2 in Figure 9.6), which liaises, harmonizes, smooths and provides lateral information exchange to avoid imbalance or rocking of the boat, differs in kind from any of the three main tiers: it has no authority to *tell* anyone to do anything. It can, however, feed information upwards to suggest that plans are impractical and need to be changed.

Someone operating as just plain 'doing' often cannot see the need for liaison, or policy, both of which are apt to seem to him unnecessarily constraining because he cannot see the whole picture. We are all familiar with the apparently crass acts of management, yet from the management vantage point it all seems so obviously sensible. So it is important for organization managers to develop in staff some understanding of how organizations work.

Systems 5, 3, 2 and 1 are largely concerned with getting things done *now* within the organization. The model needs another function (system 4) which looks into the outer world and into the future: we need to know the future trends in pedagogy, educational technology, demography,

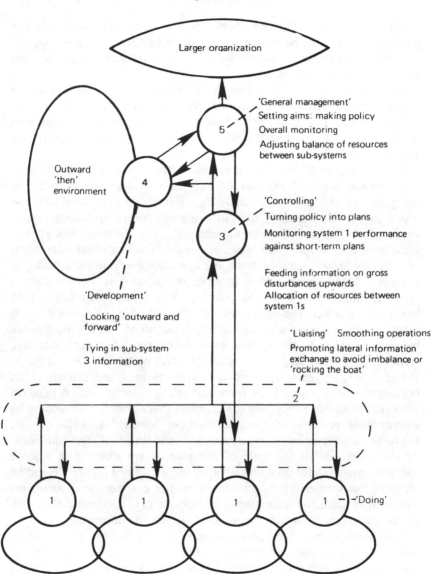

Figure 9.6 The systems model (after Beer, 1971)

legislation and so on. This is not to say that every department needs its own research institute; but somebody, somewhere, needs to spend some 'panic-free time' thinking about the future. Like the liaison function, it has no authority, except that of expert knowledge. It influences policy by making proposals for future action. It does the 'staff work' for the policy group. It must be in touch with what is happening inside as well as outside the organization; indeed its need for information is just as vital as its need for panic-free time.

The counterpart of this system in the human body is the five senses which scan the environment continuously and send messages to the other systems about future danger or opportunities, either at conscious 'policy' level or at the unconscious 'execution' level, as when we remove a finger from a hot stove.

Another aspect of the sensing system is the scanning of the internal environment. We need a system that tells us when we have an abscess in our gums, by giving us toothache. Organizations likewise need to know where they hurt. Normally such information comes up through other systems, if the communication channels are flowing freely, but sometimes it is necessary to 'poke a thermometer' or other instrument (an attitude survey, perhaps?) into the organization from the outside, to sense how it feels in relation to its environment and its 'normal state'.

In the model, system 5 – the policy-makers – are shown linked to a larger organization. The head needs to talk to the LEA, for example, on school policy. System 5 also has the key function of keeping the balance between systems 3 and 4. It cannot allow the neglect of scanning activities by overloading the same people with operational activities.

The theory suggests that all five systems must be present if an organization is to work. Their form and relative strength will depend on what the organization is trying to do, on its management style and on its environment. A one-teacher primary school does not need five people, but to be successful the one teacher must spend time in all five functions. At the other end of the scale of complexity, for example in a large comprehensive school on a divided site, the pattern of Figure 9.6 will be repeated many times. Thus each subsystem 1 (e.g. the maths department) will itself contain five subsystems, its subsystem 5 communicating with the larger organization, i.e. the school's senior management.

Individuals in such a complex organization may find themselves with a role in more than one subsystem in different parts of the organization; for example, a head with teaching duties may operate in a department's subsystem 1, and a head of year appointed to a policy-making working party will be operating in the school's subsystem 5. It is important to distinguish between these roles and to know in what capacity one is operating at any given time.

The model can be used in three main ways:

(1)   to examine the health or viability of an existing organization;
(2)   to evaluate proposals for new organization structures;
(3)   to clarify the purpose of committees or of roles.

It is not intended as a blueprint for an organization: it is more like a template to test an organization for fit.

Personal application. Apply the model to your school or department. Identify the subsystems in the organization: of what do they consist? Pay special attention to subsystem 4, because it is often found to be underdeveloped. Also assess whether vertical communication links operate as well upwards as downwards. Do you need to improve internal sensing? Are any 'organizational pathologies' apparent in your school? Which subsystems most need to be brought into a state of health?

The decision model
This model, which depicts organizations as an assembly of elements for taking decisions of varying levels of importance, has had its exponents in a number of firms, such as the Glacier Metal Company (Brown, 1971). It is not thought to offer much to schools, except that it does throw light on the different purposes of meetings and conferences. These are dealt with in Part I of this book.

The contingency model
The central idea in the contingency theory is that organizations are, and should be, different both from one another and from part to part. The appropriate structure, management style, etc., are contingent upon what the organization (or part of it) is there to do. There is no perfect organizational structure: the choice of structure depends on which set of problems you prefer to live with. For example, take the 'generalist-specialist' argument: is it better to let people specialize deeply in their subject so that they achieve mastery over it, or should one encourage the 'jack of all trades' who can turn his or her hand to anything? The compartmentalization of secondary schools by subject discipline may have contributed to academic excellence, but how effective is it in developing the whole person?

   Contingency theory accepts that, left to themselves, organizations, departments and individuals tend towards specialization, carving out a more and more distinctive niche for themselves. In other words, the units tend to get more and more *differentiated* from one another, as the expertise builds up and becomes increasingly specialized. If this process continues, each unit begins to regard its own excellence as an end in itself, divorced from the interests of the organization, forgetting that the unit was set up in the first place to help the whole organization pursue common aims. People then complain that the organization is becoming fragmented, that departments are drifting apart, that empire-building is taking place, that overall objectives are obscured, that there is too much upward delegation and that they are becoming frustrated. The head of the organization feels that he or she is dealing with a set of mediaeval barons in charge of their various departments.

Integration is probably a key issue in many secondary schools, because of the high commitment of most teachers towards their subject disciplines. It also becomes more important under conditions of resource constraint, as a means of making the whole more than the sum of the parts. Somehow departments and staff have to enhance one another's contributions to the achievement of the main purpose of the school.

Effective integration calls for careful attention to relationships, a high degree of mutual trust, candour and respect, and an insight into organizational behaviour and complexities. Conflict has to be confronted and managed constructively: i.e. intead of being avoided altogether, smoothed over or resolved by the exercise of crude power, it is treated as a matter susceptible to a systematic problem-solving approach (Chapter 7). If this fails, there are other devices that can be used to secure a constructive resolution:

(1) Each unit or individual can report to a manager (e.g. a deputy head) who is made accountable for 'synergizing' the two roles (bringing them together so that the sum is greater than the parts).
(2) A third unit or individual (e.g. a head of year), seen by the other two as understanding their roles and as standing midway between them, is interposed to act as intermediary.
(3) Some kind of training or 'image exchange' can be undertaken to help each unit understand more accurately why the other unit behaves as it does (see Exercise 6, p. 113).
(4) Interdepartmental groups or task forces, with members selected from the two departments, can be formed on a temporary or permanent basis to resolve issues between the two departments.

However, rather than rely solely on formal mechanisms for cross-linking departments, the best organizations encourage an informal approach. Peters and Waterman (1982, p. 117) comment on this as follows: 'All of them [previous commentators on excellence] fall far, far short of depicting the richness, the variety of linkages that we observed in the excellent companies.'

Personal application. What problems arise in your school which can be attributed to high differentiation and low integration? How effective are the integrating mechanisms and lateral processes? What methods are used to get departments to work synergistically? What else needs to be done?

Elements of organizations

There is a temptation to think of organizations solely in structural terms – as in an organization chart. However, organizations can be said to consist of four interdependent elements, of which structure is only one (Figure 9.7). The elements are:

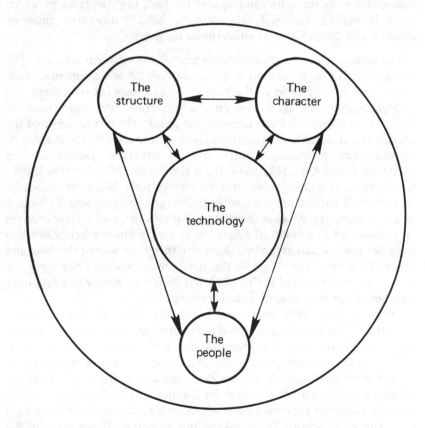

Figure 9.7 Elements of organizations

Technology. The 'technology' of an organization is its processes – in the case of a school, the process of education and the plant (classrooms, workshops, gymnasia, blackboards, etc.) that goes with it.

Structure. An organization's structure embraces the organization chart, the committees, the departments, the roles, the hierarchical levels and authority, the procedures in the staff manual, the timetable, etc.

People. The people in a school organization are the teachers, their professionalism, their knowledge, experience, skills and attitudes; also the pupils and non-teaching staff.

Culture. The character (or culture) of the organization covers such intangibles as its tone, its value system (p. 196), the standards by which merit is judged, personal relationships, habits, unwritten rules of conduct and the practice of educational judgement.

The arrows in the diagram indicate that all the elements interact. The management of organizations involves not only the management of each of the elements, but also of the balance or harmony between them.

Organization managers are apt to underrate the importance of character as a formative influence on the people, the technology and the appropriate structure, and therefore give too little attention to shaping it. Instead, they constantly tighten up the structure. Goldsmith and Clutterback (1984, p. 162) show from their study of successful British firms that organizations can and do change their character radically: attitudes and culture are constantly evolving. Managers seek to build a unity of perception of what the company stands for, and culture changes take place, not as a result of edict, but as people observe behaviour and attitudes at work and assimilate them into their own way of thinking and doing. They conclude: 'One of the strengths of many of the company leaders we have featured in this book has been their ability to adapt their own behaviour to stimulate cultural change.'

Rutter *et al.* (1980) have shown how the ethos of Inner London Education Authority schools affects the outcome of the pupil's education. Indeed, in few organizations is the influence of ethos or culture on the product greater than in a school, or its consequences for society more profound. Mant, an experienced management consultant, devotes a whole chapter ('School for Scoundrels') to this (Mant, 1983). He writes that the problem about school goes to its very heart: what's it *for*? The good school keeps asking this question. If we don't really know, the school and its functionaries are without clear authority. The good school is an *authority structure* rather than a *power system* where survival is all.

In too many schools all the children learn to survive in a naughty world. They explicitly reject the basis of the school's authority and the teachers begin to see schools as anti-educational child-minding institutions, in which the children's peer groups determine attitudes for life more effectively than do the teachers. By contrast the good schools are sculpted with a respect for the intrinsic value of ideas and materials and not simply because they will help you 'get on'. With good schools you can almost smell the calm and quiet purposefulness when you walk in the door. Their heads reflect some higher purpose than the 'getting ahead' mentality. They confront their staff as to standards, notwithstanding 'academic freedom', and are highly intolerant of the irredeemably incapable teacher.

In a well-known independent school that we visited, a master who had spent much of his career in industry was as critical of the culture of his present school as Mant is of some state schools. He was shocked by the school's organization structure and culture, because they depended so much on command and the wielding of power. The head exerted more coercive power than company chairmen, and this characteristic ran right through the organization. As a result, the boys, who were given very little responsibility, even as prefects, modelled their view of how organizations are run on an unrealistic concept. Thus the school was still preparing boys to work in or manage in organizations in which people did as they were told. What was needed, he said, was a major cultural shift in the school regime to prepare boys for entering tomorrow's real world, in which management is by consent that is earned. Needless to say, his colleagues thought him eccentric!

Evidently this school was an example of the 'power' culture identified as one of four organizational stereotypes by Harrison (1977) and discussed by Handy (1986). The others are 'role' culture, 'task' culture and 'person' culture. Power culture organizations are proud and strong; their managers are power-oriented, politically minded and risk-taking. They put a lot of faith in the individual manager, and judge by results. They may or may not be successful: so much depends on the man at the top.

In the task culture, influence is more widely dispersed; individuals identify with the objectives of the organization; and they often work in transient teams. It is the culture most in tune with current approaches to change and adaptation, individual freedom and low status differentials (Peters and Waterman 1982). But it is not always the appropriate culture for the technology of the organization. It would not be appropriate for schools that see their basic purpose as primarily custodial, for example.

Personal application. How would you characterize the culture of your school? What effect does it have on the behaviour of the people in it, including the pupils? Does it influence the educational process? Does the structure reflect it? Are the four elements in harmony, and consistent with the *raison d'être* of the school?

Interlocking systems

One aspect of systems theory deserving a brief mention is the way in which systems interlock. The pioneer work of the Tavistock Institute for Human Relations on organizations (Rice, 1963 and Trist, 1960) distinguished between two systems, the social and the technical, which together constituted the arrangements for getting tasks performed. We prefer to add a third system, the economic system, overlapping with the other two as in Figure 9.8. The idea is to show that where the groups in the social system overlap with the plant (buildings, etc.) in the technical system, there is work; where the technical system (say, a factory) overlaps with the economic system, wealth is generated; and at the remaining interface, between the economic and the social system, we find reward.

The manager has to operate in all three systems, and solutions to problems in one of them which ignore the effect on the other two are no solutions at all. The systems interlock. Failure to recognize this, e.g. trying to save money without allowing for the effect of this on people's livelihoods, or settling disputes by paying people more money without asking where it is to come from, is simply to transfer the locus of the problem without solving it.

It may be objected that schools are not factories generating wealth by making goods and therefore this is irrelevant. We do not think so. Although the bulk of a school's resources are invested in people, the 'plant' is worth a tidy sum and is costly to maintain. It is important to turn these physical assets to account as fully and efficiently as possible. A school is of economic value to the community, too, because it adds economic worth to children by educating them. Those who see schools simply as drains into which taxpayers' money is poured ignore the investment element in such expenditure. Heads, however, should be very aware of the economic contribution that schools make to society, albeit

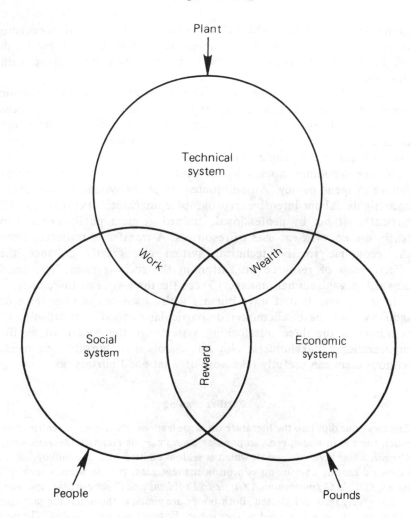

Figure 9.8 Interlocking systems

indirectly, and should be able to defend their use of resources within the economic system.

Such an argument becomes more convincing, and applications for funds become more likely to succeed, if it can be shown that money is being used cost-effectively, i.e. good value is being obtained from the resources used by the school. We do not suggest that the drive to improve the productivity of capital and labour should be as central a concern as in a factory, but good stewardship in any organization requires attention to the effectiveness with which all resources are used. Effectiveness is to be judged by useful outcomes achieved, rather than by work put in, in relation to the resources used. Local financial management will highlight this point.

Stakeholders in the school who are more familiar with the economic system than are some teachers are more likely to be impressed by pleas for additional resources if they sense that the school appreciates and cares about good economic and technical management, as well as good management of the people in the social system.

We are sometimes shocked by the waste in schools which is caused by failure to spend money. An antiquated telephone system, a dilapidated and highly labour-intensive reprographic machine, operated not by clerical staff but by professionals trained at great public expense to teach, are not efficient uses of resources. A transfer of resources from the economic to the technical system can greatly enhance the effectiveness of resource utilization in the social system. The good steward (organizational manager) keeps the three systems in balance.

In those schools that have bursars with experience in commerce or industry, we have encountered particularly good stewardship of resources in the three interlocking systems, to the benefit of all the organization's stakeholders. Not all schools need bursars, but heads without them can usefully take note of what good bursars do.

Further reading

The more one dips into the literature on organizations, the more one realizes how much there is to know; even so popular a summary as Handy's *Understanding Organizations* (1985, 3rd edn), which is seldom omitted from the bibliographies of award-bearing courses on education management, runs to no less than 450 pages. Child's *Organization: A Guide to Problems and Practice* (1984, 2nd edn) is also widely read and quoted. Both books are aimed at the practising manager rather than the academic, but neither is specific to school organization. The best book on the latter is Handy's *Taken for Granted: Looking at Schools as Organizations* (1984), followed by his *Understanding Schools as Organizations* (Handy and Aitken, 1986).

Handy adeptly captures the essence of schools as organizations and compares them with other organizations, especially those described by Peters and Waterman (1982). Among his suggestions for improving effectiveness are the following:

(1) Distinguish between 'leadership' and 'administration', relying more on bursars, secretaries and junior teaching staff for the latter.

(2) Separate policy and execution, with different mechanisms for each (this is equivalent to systems 5 and 3 in the Beer model).

(3) Turn teachers into managers, preferring the primary school model of co-workers (pupils) with a teacher managing their learning, rather than the factory model of the secondary school, with its functional division of labour.

(4) Cut down secondary schools to a manageable size and federate them.

(5) Find more faces for success, instead of relying so heavily on norm-referenced exams.

He concludes that 'schools need not be prisoners of their own, or anyone else's, past'. We agree, and devote most of Part III to suggesting how to change them.

10
TEAMS

The nature of teams

We turn now to a different aspect of organizations, the building-block which we call 'the team'. A team is a group of people that can effectively tackle any task which it has been set up to do. 'Effectively' means that the quality of the task accomplishment is the best achievable within the time available and makes full and economic use of the resources (internal and external) available to the team. The contribution drawn from each member is of the highest possible quality, and is one which could not have been called into play other than in the context of a supportive team.

There is always dynamic interaction between the individual member and the team, such that each continuously adapts to optimize the quality of the team's work. This optimization consists of matching the individual and the team to the progressively developing technical requirements of the task.

Although this is how a team should work, it is often found that a group of people brought together to form a team (such as a head and his or her deputies) do not really 'gel', and a good deal of time is wasted because tasks are not handled effectively. When many groups in the school (departments, heads of department committees, pastoral teams, etc.) fail to work at peak efficiency, then the effectiveness of the whole organization suffers. If groups cannot work effectively by themselves, they are not likely to relate effectively to other teams with which they have to do business.

The head of an organization plays a key role in making the best choices of whom to bring together to make what happens for the good of the organization. He or she then has to ensure that these groups work effectively and collaborate with one another 'synergistically' to achieve the task of the organization. ('Synergistically' means that they enhance one another's contribution, so that the whole is greater than the sum of the parts.) The head's role may be compared to that of the conductor of an orchestra, drawing from each group and player the highest possible quality of performance.

There are two complementary components in the building of an effective team: the selection of the members and the training of the team. Training begins either with some kind of instruction so that members know what makes for an effective team, or with some task that enables them to discover it for themselves. Then they practise and repeatedly review their own progress, so that they finally become proficient at any new skills required. Collaboration between teams can also be improved through practice and review, so that a process for developing effectiveness is at work throughout the organization (Figure 10.1).

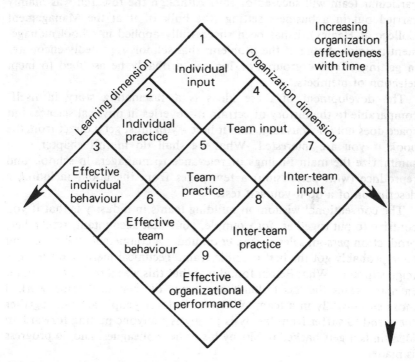

Figure 10.1 Training and organization development matrix

Although in industry a good deal of team building training has been systematically carried out along these lines over the last twenty-five years (see below), it is only in the last ten that the selection of team members has got much beyond the point of intuitive judgment. It was Meredith Belbin, a Cambridge psychologist, who made the breakthrough, in what has been described as one of the most imaginative and original pieces of research in management for two decades. His book *Management Teams: Why They Succeed or Fail* (1981) is a classic. His ideas have been used for ICI graduate recruitment and for building research-project teams; Marks and Spencer and the BBC are also among his clients.

Team roles

The essence of Belbin's research findings is that the mix of personal characteristics in members of a team is a major determinant of the team's success. It is not simply the technical expertise that the members bring, for this can be of second-order importance – it is the way they interact. Moreover, astonishingly accurate predictions can be made of whether a particular team will succeed or fail. Although the research was mainly carried out in a business setting (the bulk of it at the Management College at Henley), it has been successfully applied in school management training. Some of the problems that schools repeatedly encounter in getting effective group working can probably be ascribed to inept selection of members.

The development of these ideas is a fascinating story in itself, comparable to the history of certain discoveries in physical science, but space does not allow us to go into it here – you must get it direct from the book if you are interested. What we shall do in this chapter is to summarize the main findings of relevance to managers in schools and reproduce (with permission) a few pages from the book, including a description of a do-it-yourself test.

The conventional wisdom in building teams in industry is that if you contrive to put together, for example, your best accountant, researcher, production person, sales person *et al.* under a competent chairman, you have probably got the best possible team. Technical merit and expertise reign supreme. What Belbin found was that this was a recipe for failure. In many cases the less brilliant exponents of their profession worked more successfully in a team. When very clever people are put together they tend to suffer from 'analysis paralysis'; anyone putting forward an idea finds it gets hacked to bits by his or her colleagues, and no progress is made.

By contrast, the meticulous observation of winning teams shows that the members individually adopt one or more of certain team roles which are indispensable to the successful completion of the task. There are eight such roles (although further work since the book was first published has shown that in some instances it may be useful to add another role, that of 'specialist').

The roles are listed in Figure 10.2, together with the typical features, positive qualities and allowable weaknesses of the role incumbents. A short description of each role and associated common traits is given below (in a school setting you may prefer to substitute 'implementor' and 'co-ordinator' for the first and second labels).

Company worker. Turns concepts and plans into practical working procedures, and carries out agreed plans systematically and efficiently. Traits: stable and controlled.

Chairman. Controls the way in which a team moves towards the group objectives by making the best use of team resources; recognizes where the team's strengths and weaknesses lie; and ensures that the best use is made of each team member's potential. Traits: stable, dominant, extravert.

Shaper. Shapes the way in which the team effort is applied; directs attention generally to the setting of objectives and priorities; and seeks to impose some shape or pattern on group discussion and on the outcome of group activities. Traits: anxious, dominant, extravert.

Plant. Advances new ideas and strategies with special attention to major issues, and tries to initiate breakthroughs in the team's approach to the problems with which it is confronted. Traits: dominant, intelligent, introvert.

Resource investigator. Explores and reports on ideas, developments and resources outside the group; creates external contacts that may be useful to the team; and conducts any subsequent negotiations. Traits: stable, dominant, extravert.

Monitor–evaluator. Analyses problems and evaluates ideas and suggestions so that the team is better placed to take balanced decisions. Traits: intelligent, stable, introvert.

Team worker. Supports members in their strengths (e.g. building on suggestions); underpins members in their shortcomings; and improves

Type	Symbol	Typical features	Positive qualities	Allowable weaknesses
Company worker	CW	Conservative, dutiful, predictable	Organizing ability, practical common sense, hard-working, self-discipline	Lack of flexibility, unresponsiveness to unproven ideas
Chairman	CH	Calm, self-confident, controlled	A capacity for treating and welcoming all potential contributors on their merits and without prejudice. A strong sense of objectives	No more than ordinary in terms of intellect or creative ability
Shaper	SH	Highly strung, outgoing, dynamic	Drive and a readiness to challenge inertia, ineffectiveness, complacency or self-deception	Proneness to provocation irritation and impatience
Plant	PL	Individualistic, serious-minded, unorthodox	Genius, imagination, intellect, knowledge	Up in the clouds, inclined to disregard practical details or protocol
Resource investigator	RI	Extraverted, enthusiastic curious, communicative	A capacity for contacting people and exploring anything new. An ability to respond to challenge	Liable to lose interest once the initial fascination has passed

Monitor-evaluator	ME	Sober, unemotional, prudent	Judgment, discretion, hard-headedness	Lacks inspiration or the ability to motivate others
Team worker	TW	Socially orientated, rather mild, sensitive	An ability to respond to people and to situations, and to promote team spirit	Indecisiveness at moments of crisis
Completer-finisher	CF	Painstaking, orderly, conscientious, anxious	A capacity for follow-through. Perfectionism	A tendency to worry about small things. A reluctance to 'let go'

Figure 10.2 Useful people to have in teams

communications between members, fostering team spirit generally. Traits: stable, extravert, not dominant.

Completer-finisher. Ensures that the team is protected as far as possible from mistakes of both commission and omission; actively searches for aspects of work which need a more than usual degree of attention; and maintains a sense of urgency within the team. Anxious, introvert.

The two most crucial roles are probably those of chairman and plant, and the incumbents need to relate to one another well: if they don't the plant's ideas never bear any fruit. The essence of skilfully employing a plant (a role which some people prefer to think of as that of creative catalyst) lies in recognizing the member's potential, giving him scope and not allowing him to pursue unrewarding lines of thought. The successful chairman does not have to be brainy: his characteristics are commonplace, but they are put together in an uncommon way, which earns the respect of everyone in the team. Often he is a good shaper as well.

Different people are good at different team roles; although they may have one dominant role, they may still be reasonably competent in another one. In teams smaller than eight in number, people may have to play more than one role. By contrast, two dominant chairmen, two plants or too many monitor-evaluators are apt to cause problems.

Associated with these team roles are personality characteristics such as intelligence, dominance, introversion/extraversion and anxiety/stability. Stable extraverts, who often excel in jobs that place a high premium on liaison work and where co-operation is sought from others, are generally good team members. Anxious introverts, on the other hand, usually lack cohesion in a group, yet as individuals they are often very creative; they distinguish themselves in jobs (such as teaching?) which call for self-direction and self-sustaining persistence.

Anxious extraverts are commonly found in places where people need to work at a high pace and exert pressure on others: they form good teams in rapidly changing situations. Stable introverts plan well, are strong in organization, but are slow-moving and tend to be blind to new factors in a situation. They excel in bureaucratic occupations.

While co-operative stable extraverts form the most effective homogeneous teams (i.e. in which all team members are of the same personality type), they are excelled by heterogenous teams (composed of different personality types) because stable extraverts on their own are prone to complacency and euphoria. The best teams also have a mix of mental abilities, usually with the highest belonging to the plant, then the chairman. The advantage of having people of relatively low mental ability appears to lie in the fact that these members tend to be willing to adopt the less 'dynamic' team roles.

Another type of successful team is one dominated by a chairman who has unrivalled superiority in intellectual or creative ability over his colleagues, and his office and natural talents reinforce each other in establishing his ascendancy. It is not a recommended formula because of the gulf left when the chairman leaves the team.

Whatever the composition of the team, all its members must learn 'teamsmanship'. This goes beyond fitness for any particular team role. Good teamsmen time their interventions, vary their role, limit their contributions (often difficult for teachers), create roles for others and do some of the jobs that others deliberately avoid. Most of these behaviours can be learned through training.

One of the problems in a hierarchical organization is that it is not always easy to bring the most suitable people into teams. The wise manager avoids building teams solely on the basis of *ex-officio* membership. Meetings of heads of department, for instance, often lead to disappointing results. It is often better to set up project or study teams of a mixed composition of people at different levels in the hierarchy; what such a team may lack in structural authority, it may gain in effectiveness, if the team roles have been well chosen. To give it authority, let it report to a project steering group, e.g. heads of department, which meets occasionally to advise on guidelines and objectives; or let both report to the head independently.

Finally, you may like to rate your own preferred team role by completing the self-perception inventory given in Exercise 12 (p. 184). It was developed from a number of earlier versions which have been used at Henley by managers undergoing training there, and also in industry. A word of warning is needed about its use: it should not be assumed by managers that they have failed if they do not come out as chairmen. Managers can make their mark on an organization in a variety of ways, including being shapers and team workers. The test specifically assesses predisposition for roles in a working team.

Knowledge of one's colleagues' preferred team roles, and of the roles that have to be played in effective teams, assists the manager both in composing teams and in helping them to work more effectively once they are formed. For instance, if it is noticed that the team is missing its deadlines, it could look to its completer-finisher to inject a greater sense of urgency.

Team-building

There are several successful methods of building teams. The approach most often used in the United Kingdom is probably that of Coverdale training in 'the practice of teamwork' (Taylor, 1979). ICI and Unigate are among the satisfied clients of this organization. Recently it has been successfully used by Newham LEA staff and applied to Oxfordshire primary school pupils with impressive results. A related approach is 'development training', usually undertaken outdoors. Brathay Hall, Ambleside, for example, trained the project team that developed Austin-Rover's K-series engine and also the senior managers in Cheshire and Salford local authorities.

Because so much of the work of teachers is done alone with children in the classroom, there are fewer opportunities for practising team-work than is usual among professionals in industry. Moreover, there is less of a tradition of using consultants or short courses for developing effective team-work. Nevertheless, teams are an essential part of healthy organizations, especially those undergoing rapid change, and heads would do well to encourage the formation of more teams such as task groups and working parties to get new things done. Most large schools operate with a top management team, which is an obvious place to start trying to improve effectiveness.

Teams are trained by encouraging them to follow a systematic approach to getting things done. Individuals who have the talent and skill to solve problems intuitively may feel that they do not need to follow a systematic approach. The intuitive thinker tends to solve a problem by devising solutions and testing them until he is satisfied with the quality of his decision. Most individuals, however, are more effective when their thought processes and actions are systematic; even an intuitive thinker meets situations when he needs a systematic approach.

It is when people are working in groups that a commonly understood systematic approach becomes essential, since an intuitive approach cannot be followed and understood by other members of the group. A simple systematic approach provides a foundation for team-work, and a basis from which to develop ways of meeting the needs of the team when tackling problems.

Such an approach consists of a logical series of steps that are followed in order to achieve a given task or deal with a particular problem. We met an example of this when considering decision-taking in Chapter 4. The main steps in problem-solving and team-building are similar:

(1)   Define *what we are seeking to achieve* in the specific situation to solve the problem, including the criteria by which we shall judge success.

(2)   Identify *why* we are seeking to achieve this. Because... .

(3)   Generate *alternative means* of achieving this.

(4)   Decide *which means* to adopt.

(5)   *Act* on the decision.

(6)   *Review* successes and failures in order to improve performance.

The acronym TOSIPAR helps to fix these stages in the memory:

> tuning in to the problem;
> objective-setting;
> success criteria;
> information and ideas;
> plan;
> action;
> review.

Time spent on the TOS stages is time saved later on. Everyone needs to know exactly what the team's product is for and how it will be used.

The last stage is also very important in team-building. Teams should set some time aside before the end of each meeting so that they can review the way in which they work together to accomplish tasks. Such a 'process review' provides an opportunity for members to make observations about the behaviour of a group (e.g. uneven frequency of member's contributions), from which it can deduce reasons for successes and difficulties. When important points emerge, they should be processed into group decisions, e.g. on how to remedy the situation or to consolidate good practice. Then a plan is needed to implement each decision, i.e. a specific statement of who does what, when.

All systematic approaches lay stress on the importance of the team defining and agreeing its objectives (what has to be achieved), for no team can work effectively unless everyone in it knows where it is going. This may sound trite, but the authors have repeatedly found that teachers are not good at defining what has to be done and formulating sound objectives, either for themselves or for groups or organizations in which they work.

Soundly framed objectives are as specific, as clear, as concise, as time-bound and as observable or measurable as possible. They tend to be quantitative rather than qualitative, results-centred rather than activity-centred, and realistic rather than pessimistic. A small degree of overreach helps to motivate those who respond to challenge; a minimum objective, likely to be met anyway, provides little stimulus.

Objectives can be broadened by asking the question 'In order to achieve what?' and can be narrowed down by asking 'What has to be achieved to attain this?' Objectives that appear vague and woolly should be narrowed down.

Another device for increasing specificity is the definition of 'success criteria': these define the situation that will exist when the objective has been attained.

An example of an objective that is too broad to lead to effective action is 'To maintain sound communication in the school'. A soundly framed objective, dealing with the same problem, would be: 'To have introduced a two-page weekly staff bulletin, which all staff use and read, by half-term, edited by Miss X.' The success criterion for this objective might be: 'During the second half of the term, no more than five staff will complain to the head that something has been done without their being told.'

These techniques need to be assiduously practised before it becomes second nature for teams to use them. Exercise 13 (p. 189), for use by teams, will help to improve objective-setting skills.

Apart from unclear objectives and other manifestations of failure to define the problem, teams sometimes waste time by not listening actively to what is being said, with the result that one contribution does not build on another. One way of following the process of discussion is to use a form down the vertical axis of which are listed various categories of contribution, and along the top are listed the names of the team members (see Rackham *et al.*, 1971). Categories of contribution can include:

Seeking suggestions. This label is used when someone invites others to contribute their ideas, suggestions or proposals.

Suggesting. Can take a number of forms, e.g. 'I suggest we do so and so', 'Let's do the following', 'Shall we do X, Y and Z?', 'Can I take your idea a stage further?'

Agreeing. Covers all types of supporting or backing what has just been said; this includes nodding.

Disagreeing. Covers all ways of opposing or withholding support for what has just been said: i.e. not only an outright disagreement ('No, I can't go along with that!') but also stating a difficulty, whether valid or not: 'The snag with that is... .' or 'We are running short of time again.'

Seeking clarification. Whenever anyone asks for a recap or checks that he has understood what was intended: e.g. 'Do you mean...?', 'What happens if A and B coincide?'

Clarifying. Responses to requests for explanations; also spontaneous summaries of a discussion.

Interrupting. Whenever someone breaks in to stop a member from finishing his or her contribution; or when everyone seems to be speaking at once.

Miscellaneous. In practice, it is difficult to assess all contributions quickly enough to categorize them, so any unspecified contribution can be put in this category rather than go unrecorded.

In order to analyse the discussion in this way it is necessary to detach from the group an observer, who does not take part in the discussion, but is given the task of leading a process review later, to help the team discover how effectively it is operating. With a bit of practice, the observer not only gets quicker at recognizing categories of contribution, but can study sequences of contributions from which he can deduce what types help and hinder the team in particular situations. He can observe, for example, how ideas get lost when the next contributor after a suggestion is made completely ignores the contribution; or the effect of timing of a proposal, and the style or tone in which it is made; or the different ways in which different individuals habitually contribute, e.g. by making positive proposals, asking relevant questions, encouraging action, controlling use of time.

Other aspects of teamwork can also be brought out: the degree of openness and trust in the team; the quality of chairmanship; the use of resources; the clarity of decisions; and non-verbal communication.

Teams (including school management teams) sometimes invite an outsider to be a consultant to the group, and to coach it in improving effectiveness. A consultant, such as an industrial trainer or college lecturer, experienced in group processes, can bring a useful amount of objectivity and detachment into the proceedings, and get the team to confront issues that, left to itself, it would probably suppress.

The main object of these techniques is to heighten the team's awareness of the process by which it tackles its task, then to make use of the insights in order to improve. It certainly entails some members changing their behaviour, which can feel threatening, but the only way a team can improve is by individuals continually adapting their behaviour to meet the needs of the team.

Personal application. Next time you attend a meeting of a task group to which you belong, try to focus for some of the time on the process by which the group tackles its task. Does it start with clear, agreed objectives? Is use of time properly planned? Do some members impede the work of the group? Is a systematic approach consciously followed? Do ideas get lost? How do you rate the degree of openness and candour in the group? Do people listen to one another? Are the resources available to the group well used? Does it hold a process review? If not, try getting it to agree at the next meeting to set ten minutes aside to reflect together on how effectively it operates.

Further reading

Adair, J. (1987) *Effective Teambuilding*, Pan, London.
Belbin, M. (1981) *Management Teams: Why They Succeed or Fail*, Heinemann, London.
Hastings, C., Bixby, P. and Chaudhry-Lawton, R. (1986) *Superteams*, Fontana, London.
Trethowan, D.M. (1985) *Teamwork in Schools*, Industrial Society, London.

Exercise 12: a self-perception inventory for use in team-building

This inventory is taken from Belbin (1981) *Management Teams: Why They Succeed or Fail*, Heinemann, London. © Belbin, 1981.

Directions
For each section distribute a total of ten points among the statements that you think best describe your behaviour. These points may be distributed among as many statements as you like: in extreme cases they might be spread among all the statements, or ten points may be given to a single statement. Enter the points in the table that appears after the last section of statements.

The highest score on team role will indicate how best you can make your mark in a management or project team. The next highest scores can denote back-up team roles towards which you should shift if for some reason there is less group need for your primary team role.

The two lowest scores in team role imply possible areas of weakness. But rather than attempting to reform in this area, you may be better advised to seek a colleague with complementary strengths.

Descriptions of the team roles featuring in this analysis sheet are given in Figure 10.2.

The statements
1. What I believe I can contribute to a team:
    (a) I think I can quickly see and take advantage of new opportunities.
    (b) I can work well with a very wide range of people.
    (c) Producing ideas is one of my natural assets.
    (d) My ability rests in being able to draw people out whenever I detect they have something of value to contribute to group objectives.
    (e) My capacity to follow through has much to do with my personal effectiveness.
    (f) I am ready to face temporary unpopularity if it leads to worthwhile results in the end.
    (g) I can usually sense what is realistic and likely to work.
    (h) I can offer a reasoned case for alternative courses of action without introducing bias or prejudice.
2. If I have a possible shortcoming in teamwork, it could be that:
    (a) I am not at ease unless meetings are well structured and controlled and generally well conducted.
    (b) I am inclined to be too generous towards others who have a valid viewpoint that has not been given a proper airing.
    (c) I have a tendency to talk too much once the group gets on to new ideas.
    (d) My objective outlook makes it difficult for me to join in readily and enthusiastically with colleagues.
    (e) I am sometimes seen as forceful and authoritarian if there is a need to get something done.
    (f) I find it difficult to lead from the front, perhaps because I am over-responsive to group atmosphere.
    (g) I am apt to get too caught up in ideas that occur to me and so lose track of what is happening.
    (h) My colleagues tend to see me as worrying unnecessarily over detail and the possibility that things may go wrong.
3. When involved in a project with other people:

    (a) I have an aptitude for influencing people without pressurizing them.

    (b) My general vigilance prevents careless mistakes and omissions being made.

    (c) I am ready to press for action to make sure that the meeting does not waste time or lose sight of the main objective.

    (d) I can be counted on to contribute something original.

    (e) I am always ready to back a good suggestion in the common interest.

    (f) I am keen to look for the latest in new ideas and developments.

    (g) I believe my capacity for judgment can help to bring about the right decisions.

    (h) I can be relied upon to see that all essential work is organized.

4. My characteristic approach to group work is that:

    (a) I have a quiet interest in getting to know colleagues better.

    (b) I am not reluctant to challenge the views of others or to hold a minority view myself.

    (c) I can usually find a line of argument to refute unsound propositions.

    (d) I think I have a talent for making things work once a plan has to be put into operation.

    (e) I have a tendency to avoid the obvious and come out with the unexpected.

    (f) I bring a touch of perfectionism to any job I undertake.

    (g) I am ready to make use of contacts outside the group itself.

    (h) While I am interested in all views I have no hesitation in making up my mind once a decision has to be made.

5. I gain satisfaction in a job because:

    (a) I enjoy analysing situations and weighing up all the possible choices.

    (b) I am interested in finding practical solutions to problems.

    (c) I like to feel I am fostering good working relationships.

    (d) I can have a strong influence on decisions.

    (e) I can meet people who may have something new to offer.

    (f) I can get people to agree on a necessary course of action.

    (g) I feel in my element where I can give a task my full attention.

    (h) I like to find a field that stretches my imagination.

6. If I am suddenly given a difficult task with limited time and unfamiliar people:

    (a) I would feel like retiring to a corner to devise a way out of the impasse before developing a line.

(b) I would be ready to work with the person who showed the most positive approach.

(c) I would find some way of reducing the size of the task by establishing what different individuals might best contribute.

(d) My natural sense of urgency would help to ensure that we did not fall behind schedule.

(e) I believe I would keep cool and maintain my capacity to think straight.

(f) I would retain a steadiness of purpose in spite of the pressures.

(g) I would be prepared to take a positive lead if I felt the group was making no progress.

(h) I would open up discussions with a view to stimulating new thoughts and getting something moving.

7. With reference to the problems to which I am subject in working in groups:

(a) I am apt to show my impatience with those who are obstructing progress.

(b) Others may criticize me for being too analytical and insufficiently intuitive.

(c) My desire to ensure that work is properly done can hold up proceedings.

(d) I tend to get bored rather easily and rely on one or two stimulating members to spark me off.

(e) I find it difficult to get started unless the goals are clear.

(f) I am sometimes poor at explaining and clarifying complex points that occur to me.

(g) I am conscious of demanding from others the things I cannot do myself.

(h) I hesitate to get my points across when I run up against real opposition.

Points table

Section	Item (a)	(b)	(c)	(d)	(e)	(f)	(g)	(h)
1								
2								
3								
4								
5								
6								
7								

Analysis sheet

Transpose the scores taken from the points table above, entering them section by section in the table below. Then add up the points in each column to give a total team-role distribution score.

Section	CW	CH	SH	PL	RI	ME	TW	CF
1	g......	d......	f......	c......	a......	h......	b......	e......
2	a......	b......	e......	g......	c......	d......	f......	h......
3	h......	a......	c......	d......	f......	g......	e......	b......
4	d......	h......	b......	e......	g......	c......	a......	f......
5	b......	f......	d......	h......	e......	a......	c......	g......
6	f......	c......	g......	a......	h......	e......	b......	d......
7	e......	g......	a......	f......	d......	b......	h......	c......

Exercise 13: Formulating objectives

In 15 minutes, as individuals, write legibly on flipchart sheets:

1. A personal objective in your job, for improving your competence or effectiveness:
2. An organizational objective for your school, for improving its effectiveness.

For each objective, establish success criteria and write them immediately beneath the objective to which they apply.

In one hour, working as a group:

1. Display the flipcharts and read them;
2. By marking the sheets in silence, each individual should distribute five points only, among up to five objectives and related success criteria (other than your own), so as to identify those that come nearest to being soundly formulated. You are *not* judging whether the objectives are intrinsically worthwhile: only how well they are formulated.
3. In discussion, agree in your team and list succinctly on a flipchart the criteria you used in judging how to distribute your five points each.
4. Still as a team, take the objective and related success criteria that scored the most points and use the listed criteria to improve them (in case of a tie, take either or both).
5. If time permits, form pairs to improve one another's objectives and success criteria, again applying the agreed group criteria.

11
MANAGING THE CURRICULUM

The National Curriculum

The National Curriculum represents a major change in our approach to education. While the 'core' and 'foundation' subjects prescribed by the 1988 Education Reform Act are not substantially different from those set out in the 1904 regulations (the biggest change is that 'manual work/housewifery' is replaced by 'technology'), the introduction of 'key stages', 'attainment targets', 'programmes of study' and 'standard assessment tasks' ensures a common structure that schools in the United Kingdom have never previously known. To many teachers and heads, the National Curriculum appears as yet another unwarranted restriction of professional freedom, and resistance to the changes is understandably heightened by inadequate preparation for the introduction of such radical reform. Others point to the potential for greater ease of transfer between schools and the creation of standards against which parents, pupils and teachers can measure and agree progress.

Whether or not we basically welcome the National Curriculum, the danger exists that, in complying with its requirements, we lose sight of the fundamental purposes of education. These are restated in Clause 1 (2) of the Education Reform Act where it is said that:

> The curriculum for a maintained school satisfies the requirements of this section if it is a balanced and broadly-based curriculum which:
> (a) promotes the spiritual, moral, cultural, mental and physical development of pupils at the school and of society; and

(b) prepares pupils for the opportunities, responsibilities and experiences of adult life.

It will be a tragedy if ever schools lose sight of these aims through the pursuit of the detail of the National Curriculum.

Fears have been expressed that project work and inter-disciplinary work will suffer as a result of the new requirements. However, while schools may need to re-focus some of their efforts in order to ensure that mundane yet necessary skills (e.g. spelling) are acquired, early work in primary schools suggests that there should be no problem in meeting most of the demands of the National Curriculum through the more imaginative approaches that have been developed.

Meeting the needs of tomorrow's citizens

One of the more certain things about the world in which today's schoolchildren will spend their lives is that the pace of change is likely to continue or even increase. We may expect therefore that:

(1) Any 'vocational' knowledge and skills acquired may well be out of date by the time the pupil seeks a job. Indeed, in scientific or technical subjects, what is being taught in the schools and universities has already been superseded as it is being taught.

(2) The future for children holds fewer 'careers' of a structured kind. Those who are to succeed will have to jump from raft to raft of new skills as their existing skills and knowledge become redundant. This applies as much to the shop assistant or the typist as to the technologist or the teacher, or the lawyer or industrial manager.

(3) Employment seems to be shifting back into the small business. (Remember that the large enterprise is a phenomenon of the years following the industrial revolution.) A lot of children will have to set up their own businesses to succeed.

It follows that the most essential needs of tomorrow's citizens (as, indeed, of today's) will be those skills which are of general application (e.g. problem-solving, creativity, communication, numeracy) together with positive and flexible attitudes. Above all, they will need the ability to learn. While 'work'-oriented skills are of some value in preparing pupils for their first job, that is probably the limit of their usefulness.

Industry has often been accused of being reactionary in the demands it makes of education (e.g. in insisting on correct spelling, punctuation and clear, concise English expression as opposed to 'creative writing'). However, the interim report of the CBI Vocational Education and Training Task Force *Towards a Skills Revolution – a Youth Charter* (CBI, 1989) contains the following statements:

> All education and training provision should be designed to develop self-reliance, as well as specific skills.
>
> Lifetime learning must be promoted.
>
> Young people must be motivated to want to learn... promote a self-development ethic.
>
> Occupational competence includes adaptability, management of roles, respect for standards, creativity, flexibility, language skill.
>
> The outcomes at 19 should include the following core elements: values and integrity, effective communication, applications of numeracy, applications of technology, understanding of work, personal and inter-personal skills, problem-solving, positive attitudes to change.
>
> Re the National Curriculum: 'Employers are not sanguine that cross-curricular themes and skills will have the prominence and standing they deserve.'

Creating positive attitudes

The positive manager (see p. 136), whether a head or head of department, will recognize that his role is to steer his school, college or department on a positive course through the sea of change. Furthermore, he will need the support of the 'stakeholders' – parents, potential employers, local authority and pupils.

If we look at the 'force field' acting on the curriculum it appears as in Figure 11.1.

In a negative environment, the school staff may be so preoccupied by legislative demands, cutbacks, lack of resources, 'difficult' pupils and the varying demands of the other stakeholders that an atmosphere of hopelessness develops among both pupils and staff. No one is happy in an organization which has lost its sense of direction and in which the constraints seem overbearing. Energy is directed against the constraints instead of towards a purpose (see Figure 11.2).

The first problem is to develop within the staff the attitude advocated by Reinhold Niebuhr:

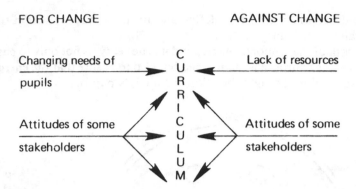

Figure 11.1 Curriculum force field

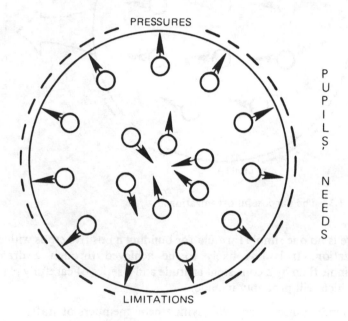

Figure 11.2 The frustrated organization

The courage to change what I can;
The patience to accept what I cannot change;
The wisdom to distinguish what I can change from what I cannot change.

The positive organization is one in which the constraints are defined and accepted but which tries to redefine and fulfil its purpose within those constraints (see Figure 11.3).

The task of the school manager, and it is not easy, is not only to ensure that a sense of purpose is maintained but also to ensure that the energy is being focused in the right direction for today's pupils.

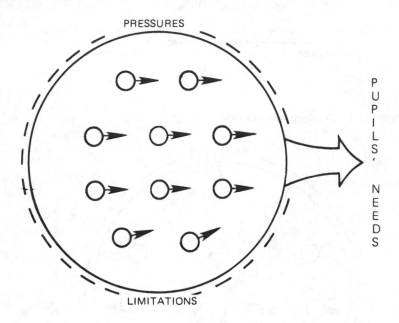

Figure 11.3   The purposeful organization

There is no one simple formula for building a positive ethos within the organization. It is less likely to be achieved through a dramatic programme than by a consistent attitude and a series of carefully planned steps which will probably include:

(1)   Sounding discussions with sympathetic members of staff.
(2)   Sounding discussions with influential members of staff, especially the most frustrated and recalcitrant. (Listen and note their responses and, however negative the replies, do not argue but keep asking their views on what should be done.)
(3)   Establishment of a small curriculum advisory committee (possibly heads of department, but this is also a good chance to develop some up-and-coming staff). Such a committee should be clear about its

duty to sound out all members of staff systematically, to recommend ways of taking into account the views of the other stakeholders, and to report its findings regularly for discussion by the total staff.

(4) Well-structured discussion at staff meetings, based on an understanding that the aim of the discussion is to suggest what can be done within the constraints rather than to complain about them. (A realistic suggestion about how to overcome an apparent constraint is always to be encouraged.)

Involving the stakeholders

The basic principles involved in curriculum development are no different from those set out in the chapter on decision-taking. While the ultimate decision rests with the school and ultimately the head, the wise head or head of department will take every opportunity to ensure that, on such a vital issue as curriculum, not only the staff but also the other stakeholders are actively involved. PTA meetings, meetings with industrialists, governors' meetings, and especially discussions with older pupils, all present opportunities for involvement. Suggestions can be invited, recorded and used. Education is not alone in having to adapt to the pressures of economic, technical, social and political change. Some widely accepted structures have evolved for 'corporate planning' and these can be adapted as well to education as to any other profession, to government or to industry. They provide a sound framework for thought, and discussion at meetings with staff and others.

Corporate planning

The main questions to which stakeholders should be invited to respond are:

(1) What are our aims and values as a school or college?
(2) In what order of priority do we rank our aims?
(3) What economic, technical and social changes do we anticipate over the coming years?
(4) What are the implications for the lives of the children in our schools? What are the threats and what are the opportunities? (The maık of a healthy organization or individual is a focus on the opportunities in change rather than the threats.)

(5) How do we need to adapt the curriculum?
(6) Given the needs which we have identified, how do our resources match these? What are the strengths and weaknesses of our resources?
(7) How do we need to develop or adapt our resources?
(8) What should be our action plan?

While it is useful to begin by discussing the questions in sequence, we should be prepared to amend our response to an earlier question (e.g. question 1) as a result of our analysis in response to a later question (e.g. question 3 or 4).

Aims and value systems

Few would disagree that the overall purpose of an educational insitution is to prepare its pupils for life. However, as soon as we ask what this entails we find a variety of deeply held convictions, including our own. These convictions are the product of 'values', i.e. our perception of what is important, right or good. People do not justify their values in logical terms, they are the fundamental beliefs or premises from which other arguments are deduced.

Our values are conditioned by upbringing and by the group or groups to which we belong: many schoolteachers are therefore likely to have certain values in common which will be different from the common values of many industrialists or pupils. However, while there may on occasion be fundamental disagreement about a particular value (some will believe that children should be taught to conform; others will not), the real problem comes with priorities. How do we rank in order of importance, for example, the ability to get employment, the ability to set up and run one's own business, the achievement of an academic qualification, a career in a profession, the use of leisure, an appreciation of the arts, the acquisition of knowledge, the acquisition of skills? The question is less one of individual educational values than of value *systems*.

Reconciliation of value systems is a need which is specially important to the educational and training role. Schools and colleges share the problem with churches, industrial training organizations and political parties. However, in the last three cases, a 'client' who is troubled by incompatibilities has the option of going elsewhere. Despite parental choice, this may not be such an easy option with schools.

For educational managers, particularly headteachers, an understanding of the value systems which affect his or her school is fundamental. How do staff see their priorities, how do pupils see priorities, how do parents see priorities, how do local industrialists see priorities? Are there important discrepancies which will produce tensions, a feeling that what the school is doing may not be 'relevant' and, consequently, discontent and misbehaviour in pupils, whose lack of faith may be reinforced by parental attitudes?

Though value systems are the underlying 'beliefs' on which arguments and actions are based, this does not mean that they are incapable of modification or even radical change. People are converted to and from religions, change philosophies radically, can move from idealistic to cynical systems, from spiritually based to materially based attitudes, and vice versa. Such shifts often occur because experience of life calls one's assumptions into question.

The important task for the educational institution is the reconciliation of value systems so as to achieve a clear statement of aims and beliefs to which a large majority of the stakeholders can subscribe and to which they feel commitment because they are satisfied that the process through which the aims have been defined has taken account of the main streams of fact and opinion. The statement of aims and beliefs should not of course be a watered-down compromise trying to be all things to all men, but one which clearly states priorities and commits itself to behavioural objectives of the form: 'A person who has been educated at this school should... .'

Curriculum development in practice

As in all decision-making processes the objective in curriculum development is to collect and use positive inputs while reserving the right to decide.

As we have indicated, the sequence of input will normally begin with the staff and should probably end with the staff. Useful techniques which can be used with the staff or any other of the interested groups are:

(1) Brainstorming on each of the first five corporate planning questions followed by a period in which subgroups respond to questions 1, 2 and 5.

(2) A curriculum representative committee to include representatives of staff, governors, parents and older pupils. Such a committee can

stimulate, co-ordinate and use the findings of a wider circle of meetings.

(3) Questionnaires (possibly based on 'ideas' meetings) which contain a mixture of structured questions (e.g. the request to list a number of possibilities in order of priority) and open questions. These can be sent to staff, parents, governors, pupils and possibly a local employers' panel. They are particularly valuable in ensuring that a proper sample is taken, and the analysed answers show the weight of opinion in various directions.

(4) Classroom discussions with pupils from which the results are systematically collected. Such discussions are usually very fruitful and are motivating for the pupils, who may arrive at a better understanding of the possible purposes of education.

Whatever the method, it is important that results and findings are openly available to those who contribute. Transparency is the name of the game.

At the end of the process, it is up to the head, with the help of the staff curriculum group, to put together a final document which summarizes:

(1) the aims, values and priorities of the school;
(2) the curriculum towards which the school will move;
(3) the rationale behind these.

Though the head is the final arbiter it goes without saying that the decisions should reflect the inputs rather than personal or staff prejudices. If this is not the case, credibility and motivation will be lost.

The whole process should have been carried out in the framework of the resource constraints and legislative requirements of which the school is aware. Hopefully the force field has now changed shape to Figure 11.4.

The procedure should have lined up the attitudes of a majority of stakeholders, though some will always remain opposed. However, the problem which still remains is that of adapting our resources. (See Chapter 13.)

Further reading

Galton, M. and Moon, R. (1983) *Changing Schools... Changing Curriculum*, Paul Chapman Publishing, London.

Hargreaves, D. (1982) *The Challenge for the Comprehensive School*, Routledge and Kegan Paul, London.

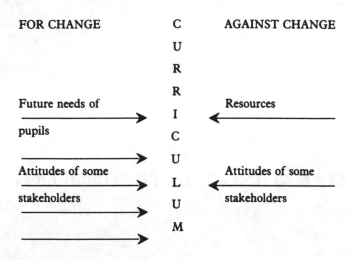

Figure 11.4 Revised curriculum force field

12
MANAGING THE TECHNOLOGY

Keeping pace with change

A key aim in curriculum development is to help the pupils cope with a world of rapidly changing technology. However, a separate challenge is to use the rapidly developing technology which is on offer to help the school staff in both its teaching and administrative commitments.

Language laboratories, video recorders, tape recorders, slide projectors and overhead projectors are with most of us as teaching aids. Photocopiers, electronic calculators, electronic typewriters and fax machines are in many of our offices. The computer, which has for some years been present as a subject for study, is now accepted as an important administrative and educational 'tool' - hopefully no school office will ever again waste money on a typewriter! Video recorders are being supplemented by video cameras.

The problems are:

(1) how to distinguish the truly useful from the gimmick;
(2) when and how to purchase, in an era when each new development is both better and cheaper;
(3) how to use the equipment effectively.

There are no easy answers to these problems.

Equipment appraisal

A possible solution is a properly controlled research project, in itself an excellent opportunity to develop staff. Such projects should be targeted to ask the questions:

(1) What are the features of the technology on offer?
(2) How might it contribute to the aims and efficiency of the school?
(3) What present resource could it replace?
(4) What new benefit does it offer?
(5) How does it compare in cost and effectiveness with the resource it would replace or an alternative way of providing the new benefit?
(6) What is the experience of those already using this technology?
(7) What problems would be posed by the introduction of the equipment (staff training, attitudes, redundancies?) and how could we overcome them?
(8) How reliable is the equipment? What would be the consequences of breakdown and the costs of maintenance?
(9) Will better and cheaper equipment shortly appear on the market?
(10) Will there be problems of compatibility with future equipment?
(11) Will the manufacturer/supplier stay in business and be able to support the equipment?
(12) Will there be ongoing development of software and add-on hardware?

Remember, in the case of new technology, that it takes time for a standard to emerge. Electronic equipment tends to become cheaper but will not go below the cost of the mechanical and non-electronic parts, e.g. the keyboard, the display unit, the housing, and the disk drives of a computer. Also remember that manufacturers may disappear from the market, causing problems with servicing, repairs and spare parts.

Trends in computing

In the case of the range of equipment which comes under the general heading of 'computers', some trends have emerged which point the way for some years ahead and which should guide the school manager in his or her approach to the technology. These are:

(1) the integration of office technology;

(2)   the 'add-on' concept;
(3)   user-friendly packages.

Office technology
Before 1980 we thought of the various pieces of office equipment as separate units: typewriter, calculator, computer, telephone, telex, filing system, duplicating machine, etc. Now, however, these are increasingly being seen as parts of one system, so that:

(1)   Letters can be created on a word processor which will automatically create a 'copy' in the computerized filing system while dispatching the letter over the telephone system or via a satellite so that it arrives in the computer of the addressee where he may view it and store it, printing out a 'hard' copy (i.e. on paper) if he so wishes.

(2)   Fax machines already digitize documents for transmission and it is only a matter of time before it becomes the norm to store this data directly in the computer either of the receiver or sender. One supplier has been offering an integrated computer and fax since early 1989 and many faxes incorporate limited photocopying facilities.

(3)   Voice messages will be digitized and transmitted from one computer to await the addressee in his or her computer.

Offices already exist in which all these facilities are available, and British Telecom have their Telecom Gold system whereby anyone with a computer, however small, can, through his normal telephone, leave a message for another subscriber in a central computer where it can be collected whenever the addressee dials in with his own computer. The network is connected to European and US systems and the cost of sending a 'package' of mail to anywhere in the world is that of a local telephone call, plus a small charge based on volume.

All this may seem futuristic to the head who is still struggling to get his or her first microcomputer for administrative use. However, the head should be thinking in terms of the future and considering how easily that microcomputer will fit into a future system. Will it, for example, be compatible with the local authority's system or planned system? It is, incidentally, quite realistic to expect (as sales people will tell you) that any computer hardware or software can be interfaced with any other. The question is 'At what cost?' A microcomputer which, as an isolated unit, is the 'best value for money', can be the worst value for money in the long term if it will not 'talk' to other systems and therefore has to be scrapped.

A situation to be avoided is that of cluttering your desk with multiple equipment when you could, and should, have a work station (computer jargon for a desk with a computer on it!) configured as in Figure 12.1.

The 'add-on' concept

A computer is not a standard piece of equipment but is, and always has been, a 'configuration' made up of a number of variables. Thus with even the simplest of home computers there may be a choice between cassette input or disk drives, between printers of various kinds, and between a colour monitor and a black and white monitor, as well as the possibility of various extras, such as a 'mouse' or a 'turtle'.

More important, however, is the possibility of enhancing the central unit by adding for example:

(1) machine memory;
(2) a clock;
(3) a graphics card;
(4) a colour card;
(5) a 'part' of one kind or another to allow, for example, a tele-communication link.

(Any of the above may or may not be standard on the equipment initially purchased.)

As the price of the electronic components reduces to the point where it is significantly less than that of the technologically more static components (keyboard, disk drives, housing, VDU, etc.), it is increasingly important to have the ability to modify the central unit as bigger (in capacity), smaller (in size) and cheaper (relative to capacity) 'chips' appear on the market. It may be feared that manufacturers will not wish, for commercial reasons, continuously to develop add-on features for their machines, preferring to encourage new sales of their basic hardware. However, in the case of the best-selling machines, there are already other smaller manufacturers who will supply suitable enhancements and this may help both to keep prices down and to ensure that 'add-ons' for a particular model will continue for many years after its purchase.

User-friendly packages

The development of computer programming is shown in Figure 12.2.

In the earliest days of computing, programs were set up by literally operating switches on the machine. A first step on from this was to program the computer in such a way that it would respond to

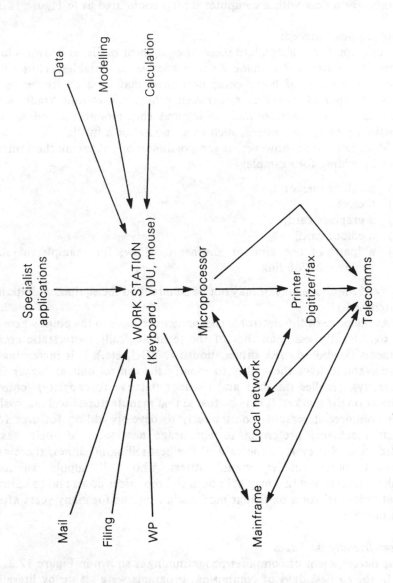

Figure 12.1 Work station configuration

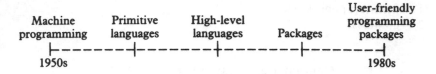

Figure 12.2 The development of computer programming

'commands' in the 'machine language' input via a keyboard directly or through tape. Subsequently, increasingly advanced languages were used. Then, it was realized that certain programs could be of value to other people with a similar need (e.g. accountants). Increasingly, standard programs were provided, but with the capability built in for these programs or 'packages' to be 'customized' to allow for variations of need.

Each development has been made possible by putting a larger program into the machine. Often layers of programs have been used one on top of another (e.g. the machine is programmed to accept machine language); this capacity is programmed to understand BASIC; BASIC is used to create a program package which is programmed to the needs of the user. All this consumes more and more machine memory (and disk space), and it is a happy coincidence that memory has become cheaper at the same time as human ingenuity has been developing these longer programs.

User-friendly packages aim to make it possible for non-experts to adapt the package to their own needs and to use it with minimal training. As well as packages geared to specific applications, there are now more general packages which enable a non-specialist to set up on the computer almost any operation that would previously have been done with paper. The three main uses that we have for paper in the office are:

(1)   communicating (reports, letters, memos, minutes, etc.);
(2)   calculating (budgets, cash accounts, etc.);
(3)   data storage (filing systems containing records, reports, etc.);

For each of these there is a corresponding computer application, as follows:

(1)   communicating = word processing (+ communications link);
(2)   calculating = spreadsheet;
(3)   data storage = database.

More recent developments in user-friendly packages are:

206   *Managing the Organization*

(1) desk-top publishing;
(2) graphics.

Computer applications in the office

Word processing
This is the application which really opened up the path to personal computing. It enables the secretary to type into the computer, so that she or her manager can amend at will without the need to retype more than the inserted or amended passage. Packages of this type will also normally automatically lay out the work as instructed, organize the pages, and, in the case of more recent packages, interface with databases and communication networks so that the report or letter which is prepared can be stored and retrieved or sent directly to the 'mailing list' via the Telecom or local authority network.

Spreadsheets
Most paperwork involving calculations organizes information into columns or rows. Spreadsheet packages, of which there are now many at varying degrees of sophistication, initially present the user with a 'spreadsheet' or 'worksheet', as shown in Figure 12.3.

	A	B	C	D	E	F
1						
2						
3						
4						
5						
6						

Figure 12.3 A blank spreadsheet

Into this 'sheet' the users can type whatever headings they wish, and tell the computer what calculations are to be performed by inserting formulae showing which 'cells' are to be added together, subtracted, etc. A 'cell' is the intersection of a row and a column and is numbered accordingly. Cells may be adjusted to whatever width is required. (See Figure 12.4.)
Facilities exist for manipulating data in many ways. For example,

	A	B	C	D	E	F	G
1			Form Register 4A				Week beginning
2	Name	M	T	W	Th	F	Total
3	. . . . .						sum(B3.F3)
4	. . . . .						sum(B4.F4)
5	. . . . .						sum(B5.F5)
.							
.							
35							

Total sum(B3.B34) sum(C3.C34)

Figure 12.4 A spreadsheet with cell entries and calculation formulae

spreadsheets may be combined so that, taking the example in Figure 12.4, it would be possible at a touch of a key to add together the weekly register for each form so as to have the school total by day.

Any formula can be put into any cell and the formula can then be copied to other cells which will receive a 'relative' formula, e.g. in Figure 12.4 the formula at cell G3, which is 'sum(B3.F3)' is copied to G4 where it appears as 'sum(B4.F4)'.

Databases
Database programs enable the user to enter records (e.g. the names, addresses and other details of all pupils) and then to update them, to sort them (e.g. into alphabetical order or by form), and to extract at will any which meet given criteria (e.g. all girls aged 14+ on 1 January 1985), or, indeed, the names and addresses of a set of children's parents for automatic envelope labelling.

On more advanced databases an entry to one record (e.g. a child's record card) will update one or more other records automatically (e.g. a school statistics record).

Desk-top publishing, graphics
Desk-top publishing packages have proved a boon to many schools, since they enable text and images to be laid out in a form that could previously only be achieved through professional typesetting and plate-making. Fonts can be chosen and mixed at will and text inserted, compressed or expanded to fill a pre-set column-format on the page. The result is that camera-ready artwork can be produced for printing to a standard that is indistinguishable from a professional product. DTP also enables the

rapid production of masters for overhead projector transparencies. To achieve the best results a laser printer is needed. DTP packages will include some graphics capability – at least a library of standard shapes that can be used to frame text and the ability to draw and place lines. However, if the prime aim is to produce illustrations rather than to prepare materials for publication, a full-scale graphics package may be more appropriate.

Combined packages, enhancements, transferability

There are packages which combine two or more of the word-processing, database and spreadsheet capabilities. There are also in-built programs for transmitting data and turning data into graphs of whatever type is desired.

Furthermore, just as some hardware can be enhanced, it is increasingly becoming possible to add on a new feature to your software package without having to re-enter all your data.

Finally, those who are creating new software for special applications are increasingly realizing that it must be compatible with the better-known packages.

Advantages of personal computing

'Personal computing', based on the use by non-experts of user-friendly packages, has many advantages over traditional computing. Among these are:

(1) Cheap software: because they have such a wide application, and therefore sell many thousands of copies, user-friendly packages are relatively cheap (about £500 buys a very comprehensive package covering all the facilities mentioned above).

(2) Trouble-free software: again because of the large market, user-friendly packages are written to high standards by the very best of computer programmers, and are tried and tested.

(3) No waiting for the professionals to produce programs: you do it yourself.

(4) Easy adaptation: you write your own program and you adapt it as and when you wish.

However, it must be borne in mind that:

(1) The programs should be sufficiently documented for someone else to use them.

(2) There are advantages in having some programs in common from school to school and certainly you want to have the best possible interface with the local authority. Co-operation is needed.

(3) While, on a good personal computer with a good package, you will be able to set up most administrative programs yourself, it is useful to have someone to whom you can turn for help if you wish to do something more advanced with what are now extremely powerful packages.

(4) You will need at least two intensive days of training in microcomputing.

Educational administration packages

The packages described above are of very wide application and can be used for many different purposes and by users ranking from major industry, to schools, to small shopkeepers and to local and central government.

There also exist a number of off-the-shelf packages dedicated to specific applications (e.g. bookkeeping) or to specific sectors. Among these are an increasing number of educational administration packages within which will be found ready-made applications to cover, for example:

(1) school roll;
(2) school reports;
(3) standard forms;
(4) examination entries;
(5) school finance;
(6) staff records.

Most of these could easily be created from the generic packages that we have listed, but the buying of a 'dedicated' package takes some of the work out of it and ensures greater standardization across the users of the package. The only problem is whether the user has sufficient freedom to adapt the package to meet exactly his or her specific needs.

One of the great demands of schools is for timetabling packages. These too can be bought 'off the shelf', but will vary considerably in the degree of help they give. There should be no problem in finding a package that can check for inconsistencies and can extract form, staff or individual timetables. However, there are so many variables involved in creating timetables that we do not yet know of any package that will automate the total task, though 'expert systems' and 'artificial intelligence' may bring us eventually nearer to perfection.

Educational 'author' packages

Turning from the use of computers for administration, it is also worth noting the appearance of user-friendly 'author' packages which enable teachers to prepare their own programs for classroom use.

Budgetary restrictions are such that education tends to want purpose-built programs on the cheap, and teachers are not the world's greatest respecters of copyright. The educational market does not therefore on the whole attract the best programs, and many teachers are put off by the fact that, for example, modern languages software has been known to contain grammatical errors. Some programs are written by teachers themselves in BASIC, and here the programming problems have been known to produce either 'bugs' or, on the other hand, very unsophisticated programs.

'Author' programs are designed to enable the lay teacher to design his or her own question-and-answer or branching programs following a series of 'prompts' from a menu. The answers to questions posed may take the form of multiple choice, yes or no, or data, though this last form has the drawback that computers are stupid and, unless specifically told, will only accept exact answers. A response may either provoke the comment 'correct' or 'incorrect', or take the pupil to a prescribed 'page' in the program which contains whatever information and/or further questions the program writer wishes. Finally the computer will report on right and wrong answers, and the time taken.

New technology and the educational manager

New technology affects - or should affect - the thinking and actions of the educational manager in at least the five ways listed below. Of these, the last two are the least obvious but arguably the most important.

An administrative aid. The benefits are obvious given the funds.

A curriculum subject. How the subject should be taught is a vexed question, since the one thing of which we can be sure is that any specific knowledge or skill (e.g. a programming language) will be quickly out of date. Approach is therefore more important than content.

A teaching aid. Here we are thinking in terms of the more conventional learning programs which may be purchased by schools or colleges, obtained from a central resource or created by teachers themselves. Such programs help pupils to acquire a defined body of knowledge or set of skills and rely on immediate feedback to pupil responses. Authoring packages enable teachers without specialist computing knowledge to create their own aids.

Part of the learning environment. The potential of new technology in this area is only beginning to emerge. However, our own work and that of associates leads us to believe that the computer can become an important part of the learning environment not only in allowing 'what if' options or hitherto impractical calculations to be tried as a part of business studies, physics or other courses, but also in developing discovery learning, creative thinking and social co-operation. Seven-year-old primary school children, originally introduced to the use of the computer through teaching packages, were introduced to features of the computer on a 'cafeteria' basis, i.e. they were shown graphic and other capabilities and given the choice of learning about those features which interested them. They then used these features much as they use the contents of a 'creativity corner' (sundry boxes, bobbins, etc.) in order to create something of use or of interest – a 'benefit'. This is clearly a critical skill for the future.

Groups of children have worked together co-operatively on such projects and in a 'Family Computer Weekend' we found that exploring together – again on a 'cafeteria' basis – the possibilities of micro-computers ranging from small home computers to the largest of the business models (and programs) provided a stimulating common learning experience and social experience for people ranging in age from eight to sixty-eight years of age.

A stimulus to change. The speed of developments in technology has focused attention as never before on the need for schools and colleges to see not only the threats but also the opportunities for change.

Further reading

Kelly, A. V. (1984) *Microcomputers and the Curriculum*, Paul Chapman Publishing, London.

13
MANAGING RESOURCES

Resource-driven or need-driven?

Our ability to develop the curriculum in the way that we wish to achieve our objectives as a college, school or department will, of course, depend on the resources that are available to us. However, it is extremely important that we ensure that the tail does not wag the dog, that the content of the education that we offer is not determined by the resources most easily available to us, as opposed to by the needs of our pupils.

Unfortunately, resources always seem to be most freely available in the areas where they are least needed. This is particularly true of teaching staff, who are most readily available for those subjects of which commercial employers have the least need. If we advertise for historians or English specialists we probably have a number of applicants of high calibre, but to recruit a computer specialist, mathematician, linguist, physicist or engineer may not prove so easy. In consequence the best teachers in many staff-rooms are those whose subjects are least useful commercially. These teachers are likely to be the most persuasive both in curriculum discussions and in influencing pupils' choice of options. Does a pupil choose a subject because he or she has an innate bent for it, or because the subject has been well taught, has been made interesting and is likely to be taught in such a way as to achieve exam success? The risk in such a situation is that we produce more and more people with the least-needed skills.

A similar phenomenon occurs with equipment, and schools can easily become the repositories for cheap junk or, even worse, expensive junk sold to education authorities at 'bargain' prices. A powerful, high-quality computer whose manufacturer has gone out of business and for which there is very limited software may be of doubtful benefit even at a knock-down price.

We must therefore be clear in our resolve to define the needs of our pupils and therefore our educational goals. Though resources may mean that the swing towards these goals has to be moderate, we must nevertheless attempt to make the transition and develop our resources very deliberately in the desired direction. When staff or equipment have to be replaced, we should see an opportunity for change and question whether we really wish to replace like with like.

Investing money

Resources are usually classified as:

(1) human;
(2) material;
(3) financial.

As far as educational establishments are concerned, the prime concern is how we share limited finance between the human and material in order to achieve our goals more effectively. The investment can take the form of maintaining or developing existing resources or of acquiring new resources. Investment may also take the form of buying in goods or services from contractors. The question is, or should be, how do we invest limited financial resources so as to maximize the benefit to the school.

Local management in schools

The 'Local Management in Schools Initiative' (LMS) at last gives to maintained schools the freedom to apply financial resources in the way that the governors and head believe to be most appropriate, and they will be able to switch expenditure according to need.

Under LMS schools will control:

(1) costs of teaching and non-teaching staffs;
(2) heating, cleaning and decorating of premises;
(3) supplies, services, books and equipment;
(4) the use of any income they can raise;

(5)   relative spending under each of the above headings.

They will be able to carry a limited amount of overspending or underspending forward to the next year, and will be able to modify their spending plans to deal with unforeseen problems such as staff sickness *provided that* they stay within their cash limits.

LEAs may decide whether or not to delegate additional responsibilities including those for:

(1)   school meals (unless the school can show that it can provide these more cheaply);
(2)   particular services (e.g. psychologists);
(3)   major repairs and maintenance of premises;
(4)   special staff costs (e.g. long-term supply cover).

What LEAs will not be able to delegate are:

(1)   'capital' expenditure (i.e. major investments with a life of more than one year, for example in land and buildings);
(2)   LEA administration, advice and inspection;
(3)   home-to-school transport;
(4)   government or EEC grant-aided project costs.

While the introduction of LMS gives schools freedom, the exercise of this freedom means that heads and senior staff *must* master the techniques of costing, budgeting, negotiating, contracting and financial control. While the support of a bursar or other specialist administrator may well be of help, all the experience of independent schools, industry and small business goes to show that to leave finance completely to the specialist is a recipe for frustration, conflict and disaster.

Cost/benefit analysis

The effective manager of resources will constantly be asking two questions:

(1)   Looking at the present and past, am I making effective use of the resources available to me?
(2)   Looking at the future, what is the most cost-effective way of achieving my goals?

While 'benefit' in education will not usually be measurable in financial terms, it is usually possible, and convenient, to reduce the resources used to a common denominator of money.

Some areas in which cost/benefit analysis can pay off in a school or college are:

(1)   the use of time;
(2)   teaching staff/equipment/ancillary staff choices;
(3)   training decisions.

The cost of time
Calculating the cost of time is a salutary exercise for most organizations. A person does not simply cost the organization his or her salary but also:

(1)   employer's contribution to National Insurance;
(2)   employer's contribution to superannuation;
(3)   a proportion of common-room costs (furnishings, heating, lighting, etc.);
(4)   stationery, textbooks, etc., for personal use;
(5)   meals (if supplied), etc.
(6)   INSET including supply cover.

These costs, if aggregated, mean that the real annual cost of a teacher is something between $1\frac{1}{2}$ and 2 times his or her salary. Allowing for holidays and weekends, teachers work something under 200 days per year and between a six- and eight-hour day depending on the time we allow for out-of-school activities.

If we assume a salary of £15,000 a year, therefore, some simple arithmetic tells us that the cost of an hour's time is something between £15 and £20. A two-hour staff meeting of twenty people, therefore, costs between £600 and £800. This may, of course, be money well spent, and it may be argued that some staff would not be doing anything else if they were not at the meeting. However, we should constantly be aware that we are using a valuable resource and ask whether we are getting the benefit which should flow from the investment.

Teaching staff/equipment/ancillary staff choices
Once we start to cost time we may begin to ask some pertinent questions about any 'office' tasks which are undertaken by teachers, comparing, say, the cost of the slow typing of an examination paper by a teacher with that of having a skilled secretary do the same job on a word processor. Incidentally, the most cost-effective method may well not be the secretarial solution, given that the teacher may spend time in hand writing and correcting, time which must be added to the secretary's. The best solution may be self-operated word processing for which it may pay

to train teachers in keyboard skills, perhaps using a skilled operator to key in original manuscripts quickly.

In choosing equipment for the office or classroom, cost/benefit analysis should be a normal routine. Will a word processor really bring savings in staff time and/or some benefit that we can use in terms of our goals? If we get a video recorder, how will it improve the quality of our teaching, either directly or by freeing staff time? In the case of equpiment, it should not be forgotten that the true figure for comparison will usually be the cost over a period of, say, a year. This will be a 'depreciation' cost (usually about a quarter of the capital cost) plus a maintenance cost.

There is, of course, no justification for saving staff time, unless that time can be put to other productive use or unless the net result is that we can cut staff numbers. Turning the argument the other way, of course, if staff cuts are imposed, an investment in equipment may be needed to maintain the quality of teaching.

Training decisions
Training should be seen as an investment and it should be remembered that the greatest cost element in training someone is his or her time, or that of the equivalent supply teacher. On this basis it is false economy to save money on course fees if staff will then be taught less efficiently.

In all the above examples, the point is not that cost/benefit analysis will yield a result one way or the other. What matters is that we get into the habit of assessing proposals in terms of their cost and benefits, however difficult it may be to estimate the latter.

Budgeting and financial control

Fundamental to the success of investment decisions is that they are planned through the process of budgeting.

Budgeting should start with the corporate plan (see Chapter 11):

(1)   What do we wish to achieve?
(2)   What are our priorities?
(3)   What do we need to do in order to reach our objectives?

What we then need to do is to see how we can best use the 'budgets' available to us. This process is an ideal application for a spreadsheet computer model with headings of cost down the side, months of the year across the top and, of course, the appropriate formulae to total by type of cost and by month.

Last year's costs will be a good starting point, but it is dangerous to simply extrapolate, and real value comes from challenging every item of cost to see whether it is really appropriate at that level for the coming year or whether a better result may be achieved by cutting one item and increasing another.

Assumptions made should be written down in a plan, e.g. 'We shall reduce the cost of cleaning by employing Easisweep Contractors.' 'The maintenance budget is increased by £X to allow for the re-painting of... .'

In going through the budget, thought should be given also to increasing revenue through, for example:

(1) fund raising;
(2) selling off unwanted equipment;
(3) hiring out the school premises (not, of course, forgetting any additional costs).

All this effort in drawing up a budget is, of course, then to no avail unless actual expenditure is monitored against it on a periodic basis, normally a calendar or lunar month. The latter concept (i.e. 13×4-week periods) often gives a better comparison since we are comparing like with like.

Figure 13.1 gives a typical spreadsheet for budgetary control. For some of the main headings you may need to have subsidiary spreadsheets (e.g. teaching salaries by department).

In order to help control, the figures used should be those for costs which are *incurred* for that period, i.e. though we may not have paid a bill or indeed received a bill, we must include any money that we have used for that period. This latter process is known as 'accruing', and we do it because the last thing that we want is a nasty shock when the bills catch up with us as they inevitably will.

Most crucial of all is that at the end of each period the head should review variances with the governors and senior staff and decide what action, if any, needs to be taken.

Resource control

We have dealt with the control of human resources at some length in Chapters 1, 6 and 13. The control of our material resources must also be considered. It involves:

	Period 1			Period 2			Cumulative to date		
	Budget	Actual	Variance	Budget	Actual	Variance	Budget	Actual	Variance
Teaching staff salaries									
Employment costs									
Other salaries									
Employment costs									
Heating									
Lighting									
Maintenance									
Total									

Figure 13.1 Budget monitoring

(1) Making sure that our material resources are actually present by keeping up-to-date inventories which are periodically checked.
(2) Ensuring that someone is clearly responsible for the control and maintenance of each piece of equipment.
(3) Reviewing the use to which resources are being put. This procedure has the benefits of:
    (a) making us realize where equipment or space is available for some other use;
    (b) causing us to think about clearing out (preferably selling) redundant equipment;
    (c) sometimes reminding staff that there is a resource available about whose potential they have forgotten.

Adapting existing resources to fit the need

A problem faced by schools is that resources in which we have previously invested may not fit the needs that have now been defined for the year ahead. Whether we actually achieve our aim depends on an ability to match our resources to it. Cost/benefit analysis, budgeting and resource control are tools which help us to invest money wisely and to avoid waste. However, in times of limited resources, success calls for helicopter thinking and imagination. Necessity is the mother of invention. Again commitment will depend on involving staff via techniques which have been discussed in Part I of this book, but every attempt should be made to avoid conventional thinking.

The basis for discussion should be a factual analysis of what exists and how the resources are being used. We need:

(1) A profile of staff against subjects taught and numbers of pupils.
(2) An inventory of all staff skills including those which are not currently being used. Such an inventory should not only include subjects but also teaching approaches.
(3) An inventory of equipment and how it is used.
(4) A review of available space and how it is being used.
(5) An assessment of available and potential sources of finance.

Against the view of the present, we can usefully set a view of the curriculum three years ahead with corresponding profiles and inventories.

These analyses are excellent development projects for younger members of staff.

Finally, we need to look at how we can possibly move from the present to the future. The widest 'gaps' can be identified and brainstorming used to consider how these may be bridged.

As a preliminary to the 'gap-bridging' brainstorm it may be useful to state some previously held assumptions about education and ask that these and others are deliberately set aside during the session. Typical such assumptions may be:

(1) That teachers can only teach subjects that they know. (Can they not guide their pupils in learning about what is unknown to both?)
(2) That knowledge is more important than mental skills. (Perhaps we can achieve school aims through any subject, if thinking skills are better understood.)
(3) That classes should be of uniform size and consist of regular groups. (Should we develop the principle of large groups for 'input' sessions – possibly using films and other aids rather than a teacher – with smaller discussion sessions?)

At the end of such a session the curriculum group will, of course, have to reconcile their bright ideas with the realities of staff attitudes and what can be done in one year. The outcome will be a compromise, but it should take the form of an action plan to decide in which direction the 'push' should go, with practical steps for moving in that direction and clear responsibility within the school for making the moves and reporting back.

Typical actions could be:

(1) to explore the possibilities of selling/buying unused/necessary equipment;
(2) to make approaches for funds for a defined purpose;
(3) to ask a member of staff to consider how he or she might help pupils to learn a new subject or to learn in a different way.

Further reading

The Local Management in Schools Initiative (1988) *The LMS Initiative: A Practical Guide*, London.

14
MANAGING THE ENVIRONMENT

External relations

In Chapter 9 we emphasized the importance of thinking of schools in the context of their environment (Figure 9.3) and said that heads are having to spend more time managing transactions across the boundary between their school and its environment. Recent legislation has intensified this need. Governing bodies have new powers and parents more rights. Although LEAs now wield less political influence over schools, they are still significant stakeholders, except for independent and opted-out schools. Employers are also an important constituency and can influence education both directly and through bodies such as Training and Enterprise Councils. It is therefore incumbent on heads actively to shape community expectations of schools, to solicit co-operation and support for their activities and to build a public image.

For many heads, dealing with these outsiders is among the least enjoyable aspects of their jobs. In her headteacher survey Anne Jones (1987) found that external relations (especially with employers) sometimes received scant attention, that governors were a source of even more exasperation than LEAs and that parents were tolerated rather than esteemed. Yet so far from wanting help in managing their boundary, most heads wanted simply to defend it against intruders. This, however, is a recipe for disaster. Schools are not, and cannot be, closed systems; their boundaries must be semi-permeable if they are to thrive and respond to environmental change. The aim of heads and senior managers should be to direct traffic across the boundary and to forge interdependent partnerships and understandings across it.

To assert this is not to deny the uneasy relationships that sometimes exist with some parents, some governors and some elected LEA members. All can interfere, disrupt and consume time and energy. But the coin has two sides: they can also offer support, contribute and argue the school's case. The question is what heads can do to engender helpful behaviour, discourage unhelpful and, where there is conflict, to manage it constructively.

Ignorance often lies at the root of conflict and misunderstanding; parents, employers and teachers harbour myths about each other. The more we retreat behind our boundaries, the less we comprehend each others' worlds. Schools, like industry, have to project an image and actively manage their public relations; otherwise outsiders will form their own (probably mistaken) impression of what they are like inside. The school that ran a seminar for local employers, 'Comprehending the Comprehensive', had the right idea. Where adults other than teachers are involved in the curriculum, they can be advocates for the school. A school where visitors feel welcome and comfortable is less likely to engender antagonistic attitudes.

The angry parent

Even so, angry parents or neighbours will cross the boundary and heads will be faced with managing conflict. The guidelines in Chapter 7 (which dealt with internal conflict) still generally apply to conflict across the boundary: thus heads should aim to lower the emotional temperature, steer away from a win–lose situation towards a problem-solving approach and not start arguing or driving parents into feeling that they have to make a stand for the sake of honour. Self-control, listening skills and empathy are vital. Pause to think about and then reflect back what has been said, to show you have listened, and summarize at the end, including whatever action is agreed.

Always respect the position and feelings of parents; even if tempted to think them stupid, show them the opposite, remembering that you would probably feel the same way if you started from the same imperfect knowledge base. For instance, some parents have been conditioned by their experience of others in authority to tar heads with the same brush. Animosity should therefore not be taken personally, but seen as directed towards the authority role.

Parents as partners

Running through the legislation is the notion of parents and teachers jointly involved in children's education. 'pupils are to be educated in accordance with the wishes of their parents' (1944 Education Act). The 1981 Act and circular 1/83 see professionals and parents as partners in decision-making about pupils with special educational needs (20 per cent according to the Warnock Report). The 1988 act requires parents to be involved in decisions about departures from the national curriculum.

Quite apart from the law, good practice requires heads to cultivate fruitful relationships with the parent body. Problems are more easily resolved by parents and teachers together than by either alone. Parents' attitudes strongly influence their children's progress; so schools that set out to educate parents can enhance the classroom experience. Moreover, reservoirs of talent and goodwill exist among parents, and many surveys suggest that they would like to be more involved with the life of the school. At primary level it is known that parental involvement is a determinant of school effectiveness (Mortimore *et al.*, 1988). The Sussex Project showed that parents who gained access to the classroom showed increased confidence in teachers. Joan Sallis talks of 'collaborative equality': there should be consensus about objectives, exchange of information about methods and dialogue to discuss the success of what has been done (Glatter *et al.*, 1988, p. 150). Such involvement works; Everard witnessed in a project aimed at improving special needs provision impressive contributions of 'ordinary' parents not only at the technical level but in the management of change. While teachers may have the edge over parents in pedagogy, in management many parents can contribute on more equal terms.

Joan Dean (1985) of the Surrey Inspectorate offers useful advice and check-lists to heads wishing to build a more productive relationship with parents, and the Hargreaves Report (1984) suggests two structural devices to the same end: (1) using a form group as a parental group to discuss with the form teacher and head of year/house common problems and ways of dealing with them; and (2) a home/school council consisting of representative parents from each year group, their heads, a governor, the head and a teacher in charge of pastoral care, with responsibility for fostering home/school relationships.

The same goes for local employers: the aim is for schools to foster the kind of collaborative relationship that Marks and Spencer have with their suppliers.

Governors

Much the same also applies to the governing body as to the parent body. Again there is a legislative framework (especially the 1986 and 1988 Acts). 'In a well-managed school, the head and governing body will work in a close and balanced partnership.' (DES 1988a.) The necessary changes in role relationships will take some time to work through. The transfer of power and responsibility within the LEA-governing body–school system is a good example of strategic change, and several of the techniques described in Part III are relevant to building a healthy working relationship.

Heads have a duty to advise and assist the governing body to discharge its functions and many new governors pay tribute to the help they receive. However, some heads try to keep governing bodies at arms' length. Governors can only help to the extent that they understand what the head is trying to do and how he is doing it. This means sharing problems and concerns as well as achievements, and soliciting help and advice. Reports to governors should not be confined to factual reports of past activities; they should also deal with philosophy, strategy and forward planning.

A common complaint from businessmen who become involved in education is that the papers they get are prolix and not user-friendly. Since schools are in the communication business by definition, they need to set high standards in communicating with busy people unfamiliar with teachers' jargon. Another complaint is that meetings with educationists are unproductive and inconclusive; although it is the responsibility of the chair to conduct meetings, heads can offer valuable guidance, avoiding the traps of over-long agendas and ill-prepared items (Chapter 5).

It is in the management of change that governors can be particularly helpful, acting as sounding boards and evaluating the effects. Governors are a potential resource for change and because of their position in the local community may be more powerful advocates of the school and its needs than the head himself. Hence it pays to cultivate the friendship and support of governors and to involve them in the work of the school. Unfortunately, as Anne Jones (1987) found in her survey, this is seldom done well: 'what appears to be lacking between heads and governors is professional respect and any sense of working together in a common cause'.

Skills required for dealing with parents, governors and employers

At the skills level, heads have much to learn from the methods used by reputable sales representatives in industry for fostering beneficial relationships with customers and getting them to buy products and ideas – sometimes called the skills of persuasion. They are not as alien to the school culture as might be supposed, for they are firmly based on consideration for others.

The key principle is empathy with the other party. Show respect for him and his opinions. Present your ideas and proposals from his standpoint. Understand his world. Consider his self-interest and what he is trying to achieve by relating to the school (you may have to ask questions to find out). Ask yourself how acceptance of your proposal can help him. Think of the benefits to him, rather than letting him infer them from the features of your proposal; you can turn a feature into a benefit by answering his question 'so what?'. Also list the drawbacks to him of rejecting your proposal. Avoid, however, a long monologue; instead, use questions to establish in his mind the problems and drawbacks which your proposal will help to mitigate. Give time for points to sink in. Test reactions with questions and watch non-verbal behaviour.

Since both emotion and logic influence decision-making, try to get the other party into the right mood. Ascertain mood with a friendly question. Establish enduring rapport and create an emotional bond. Look for ways of offering a small service.

If you need a decision (e.g. agreement to provide resources), never end an encounter without one, even if it is only agreement to make one at a specified future meeting. Timing is of the essence in moving people towards agreement. They may need nudging. Once there, sum up what has been agreed.

If the other party raises obstacles and difficulties, handle the situation as you would manage conflict (see above and Chapter 7). The awkward or antagonistic customer who always raises difficulties presents a special challenge. Try to soften your attitude towards him. Understand his mood, use tact and work through his objectives. Such negative people tend to lack friends, so if you can get through to him emotionally, you are home and dry.

Follow these precepts with sincerity and you will acquire a reputation as firm, considerate and 'someone I can do business with'. Your propositions and ideas will become more 'yes-able', though you may not clinch them all.

Personal application (an exercise in empathy). List some adjectives and phrases or draw some cartoons that you think governors would use to caricature your school. Then construct in the same way your image of the governing body. How do you want each image to change? What should be your first steps in bringing about the change?

Further reading

Dean, J. (1985) *Managing the Secondary School*, Croom Helm, Beckenham (especially Chapter 12).
Jones, A. (1987) *Leadership for Tomorrow's Schools*, Blackwell, Oxford.

PART III
MANAGING CHANGE

Organizations are dynamically conservative: that is to say, they fight like mad to remain the same. Only when an organization cannot repel, ignore, contain or transform the threat, it responds to it. But the characteristic is that of least change: nominal or token change.

(Donald Schon, 1971 Reith Lecture)

15
CHANGE DESCRIBED

The nature of change

How often we are aware that something is crying out to be changed, yet somehow the sheer inertia of 'the system' proves too great to overcome! Since managers are there to get things to happen, how is it that they so often fail to achieve significant, timely or orderly change?

Industry, like education, has faced this problem for many years, and not only is it now more clearly understood, but it is also one that has become the focus of a good deal of management training, with considerable success. In the past, most training has been aimed at helping managers to manage the *status quo* more efficiently but, as the environment becomes more turbulent, so it becomes more important to develop their skill in coping with change, and indeed in steering it. GCSE and the Education Reform Act have now put change at the top of the agenda in schools.

The main thrust in raising managers' capacity to manage change has come from a set of behavioural science theories and approaches called 'organization development', usually abbreviated to 'OD'. Schmuck *et al.* (1977) is one of its leading proponents in the context of education. Fullan *et al.* (1980), also a proponent, has defined it thus:

> OD in school districts is a coherent, systematically planned, sustained effort at system self-study and improvement, focusing explicitly on change in formal and informal procedures, processes, norms or structures, using behavioural science concepts. The goals of OD include improving *both* the quality of life of individuals as well as

organizational functioning and performance, with a direct or indirect focus on educational issues.

The meaning of the phrase has been changing somewhat over the years (Everard, 1989b), and the corpus of knowledge is now more popularly described as 'the management of change' or, outside the United Kingdom, 'school improvement' (Weindling, 1989).

Unsuccessful attempts to change organizations have been made throughout history: Caius Petronius, for example, a Roman consul, recorded his experience thus:

> We trained hard, but it seemed that every time we were beginning to form up into teams we would be reorganized. I was to learn later in life that we tend to meet any new situation by reorganizing; and a wonderful method it can be for creating the illusion of progress while producing confusion, inefficiency and demoralisation.

By contrast, major changes have been successfully introduced, using behavioural science, in such companies as ICI (Pettigrew, 1985), whose former chairman, Sir John Harvey-Jones, said at the 1984 annual general meeting: 'Management of change is a key task at this time. One of ICI's most precious assets is a climate in which reasonable and necessary change can occur.' ICI is one of a number of companies that have been involved in helping school heads to develop such a climate and to implement change (Heller, 1982 and Everard, 1984).

What are among the causes of success? Do the same factors account for success in educational change? Is it possible to make useful generalizations about effecting major change which can be applied to any new situation, and thus produce a 'tool-kit' for managers in schools to carry around with them? Unfortunately the subject is more complex than it might appear. In any case there is no way of learning how to manage change solely from a book: real proficiency comes from practical experience accompanied by reflective learning. Nevertheless, we can set out the important principles, offer useful techniques and give some practical guidance on systematic approaches to change.

Since one of the main difficulties in managing change is conceptualizing the process, we need to start by asking what we mean by 'change' and by related words such as 'innovation' and 'development'. For practical purposes we can ignore the semantic differences between these words.

Let us take some concrete examples of changes currently in progress in many schools:

(1) introducing local management (LMS);

(2) improving the quality of school management or leadership;
(3) setting and implementing educational objectives for the school;
(4) developing a whole-school policy;
(5) introducing a formal system of staff appraisal and development;
(6) amalgamating two schools;
(7) opting out;
(8) building closer links with the community;
(9) bringing computers and information technology into school administration and the curriculum;
(10) handling the Training and Vocational Education Initiative (TVEI).

Why are such changes apt to be so fraught, and only rarely turn out to surpass our reasonable expectations of the benefits to result from them? The problem with change is that it is far more difficult to manage than people with limited experience of managing organizations think it should be. Those with particularly rational minds have major problems in encompassing the complexities of implementing change; the more obvious the need for it, in their view, the more exasperatingly obtuse are those responsible for failing to carry it out. However, to grasp the nature of change one has to understand the more subtle ingredients in human and organizational behaviour. Beckhard and Harris (1987, p. 116), from their wealth of experience of consulting with managers on their change efforts, conclude:

> One of the biggest traps... is the failure of organizational leaders to resist the temptation to rush through the planning process to get to the 'action stage'... it has been our experience that a great portion of large-system change efforts failed because of lack of understanding on the part of the organizational leadership of what the process of intervention and change involves. When the manager lacks an appreciation for and understanding of the complexity of the intervention process, it is predictable that the emphasis will be on 'action' or results.

Although this book aims to be practical and skills-oriented, we cannot escape having a section on problems and concepts of the change process, before coming down to practical guidance. The nature of change is not well explained in many management books, nor in many management courses. Perhaps this is caused by failure to distinguish between theories of education (what we ought to be doing in schools), theories of organization (how we should be set up to do it), theories of change (what causes progress towards where we want to be) and theories of chang*ing* (what has to be done to influence those causes). Let us therefore try to unpick the problem.

The call for change may spring from outside the school or educational system, or from within. The growth of ethnic minorities in the population, the alleged failure of education to prepare young people for working life and the erosion of the country's capacity to afford escalating public expenditure have all been cited as reasons for making changes in schools. But within schools themselves situations arise that cry out for change: a failure of discipline, dissatisfaction with exam results, or a member of staff (including the head) wanting something done differently. In the discussion that follows we shall have in mind mainly change stemming from outside the school, but regardless of the source there are some fairly common factors:

(1) The individuals involved will start with different feelings about the desirability of the change, some seeing it as a threat or a source of insecurity and of concern about personal exposure and possible weakness. The change may involve having to learn new skills and attitudes and unlearning old ones and the 'not invented here' syndrome may apply. The co-operation of all cannot be assumed, yet it may be essential if the change is to be successful.

(2) It will not be clear at the beginning how things will look when the change has been implemented: there will be many unknowns and fear of the unknown. Even the few people around with a clear vision may find themselves confronted by a number of different visions and fantasies among their colleagues.

(3) Institutional politics will become important: individuals will align around common interest groups, both informal (e.g. a staff-room coalition) and formal (e.g. a union).

(4) There will be a number of internal consequences of the change: it will impinge on various systems and interests inside the school (e.g. the exam system and pupils' interests).

(5) The school in which the change occurs is not isolated: the change itself may stem from, and the results impinge on, a part of the environment, such as the local education authority.

(6) The change is complex, or at least by no means straightforward, in that the correct action may be counter-intuitive: it involves many people's behaviour over a period of time.

(7) There are a number of obstacles to the change: some are obvious, others latent. Examples are organizational impedimenta like status, demarcation, authority; lack of support and commitment, or of resources; the psychological or legal contract between the teacher and the school; all kinds of personal motives. In any organization there are always people who can be relied on to think of 101 reasons why something can't be done!

(8) Several ways of implementing the change can be envisaged: there are, for example, degrees of freedom in the order in which necessary tasks are tackled, who does them, who is consulted and who is told – all of which may generate conflict.

(9) Those in managerial positions will sense that the change will involve them in a lot of conflict, bother and hard work. This they may dread, especially if they feel hard-pressed already.

In other words, change of the kind we are describing engages both our intellect and our emotions; it may impinge on people's value systems; it not only affects individuals but also the organization, its structures, its norms and its environment. Consequently, it will not happen successfully unless it is promoted, steered or facilitated with all these crucial factors being taken into account.

Personal application. Think of some example of actual or needed change in your school. Do they match this general description? How would you like to amplify it? Do you recognize all the factors listed above? How far are they taken into account in managing the change?

Appreciating the complexity of change

Dynamic conservatism is a social phenomenon. It stems more from the propensity of social systems to protect their integrity and thus to continue to provide a familiar framework within which individuals can order and make sense of their lives, than from the apparent stupidity of individuals who can't see what is good for them.

Few individuals in organizations appreciate how multidimensional change really is; we tend to espouse a comfortably simplistic notion of it. Sometimes this helps; we might not so readily accept some changes if we could foresee all the implications. But usually it hinders change, because it diverts us from dealing with reality. Once we apprehend that it is the *social system* that withstands change, we begin to realize some of the complexity; for there exist within such systems innumerable relationships, unwritten norms, vested interests and other characteristics that will probably be disturbed by a proposed change.

Heads and senior staff who want to implement change therefore have a sizeable educational task on their hands: they have to help everyone concerned to discover and conceptualize the true nature of change and how it impinges upon us all. (This is separate from the equally important need to develop the skills for coping with change.) Change will affect beliefs, assumptions and values, and be affected by them. Change will alter the way we are expected to do things. And change will alter the things we need to do them with.

This attempt to help people to conceptualize change is like tilling the ground before planting the seed; or to use another metaphor, it is like tuning the receiver to the carrier wave before the message of change is transmitted. It involves both helping people to understand change – *any* change – in the abstract, and helping them to apprehend the nature of the particular change being introduced. These matters have to be discussed face-to-face; it is insufficient to read about them – they must be tossed around and savoured. There must be a suitable outlet for the fears that the prospect of change evokes in everybody (however robust) – fears that one will not be able to cope, that one's sense of competence will be eroded and one's occupational identity will be dented.

It is no use pretending, in stiff upper lip fashion, that these feelings do not occur when we confront the need for behavioural or conceptual adjustment: they do, and we might as well come to terms with it. Change usually leads to temporary incompetence, and that is uncomfortable. Some changes (TVEI and ERA for example) challenge the core values we hold about the purpose of education, a purpose in which we have invested our careers. They may also shake vague, unarticulated beliefs which we have never quite understood, or discussed with professional colleagues. Fear of tampering with something unknown but still perceived as important can only be assuaged by trying to clarify what it is we are really worried about. So it helps to hammer out a set of beliefs that are shared with colleagues and regularly subjected to review and revision in the light of experience: beliefs about *both* education *and* change.

Why plans for implementing change fail

The best laid schemes o' mice an' men Gang aft a-gley.

The first reason why those who initiate change often fail to secure a successful conclusion to their dreams is that they tend to be too rational. They develop in their minds a clear, coherent vision of where they want to be at, and they assume that all they have to do is to spell out the logic to the world in words of one syllable, and then everyone will be immediately motivated to follow the lead. The more vivid their mental picture of the goal, and the more conviction they have that it is the right goal, the more likely they are to stir up opposition, and the less successful they are likely to be in managing a process of change. As George Bernard Shaw once observed: 'Reformers have the idea that change can be achieved by brute sanity.'

Another reason is that reformers are operating at a different level of thought from that of the people to be affected by the change. Take, for instance, the implementation of the 1981 Education Act, for which there could be six levels:

(1) Philosophy   Integration of children with special educational needs in mainstream schools
(2) Principle   Education to be in least restrictive environment
(3) Concept   Locational, social, functional integration
(4) Strategy   Provide support staff and systems to achieve integration
(5) Design   Set up multiskilled force of peripatetic professionals
(6) Action   Establish new posts according to plan and eliminate some existing posts.

If the head of a special school, having been exposed by an education officer to the higher levels of thinking and having agreed to the strategy, were to spring straight into action with his staff, without first engaging at their level of thinking, they would undoubtedly resist.

Effecting change calls for open-mindedness and a readiness to understand the feelings and position of others. Truth and reality are multifaceted, and the reality of other people's worlds is different from yours. Most people act rationally and sensibly within the reality of the world *as they see it*. They make assumptions about the world, and about the causes of things, which differ from yours, because their experiences are different, and they even experience the same event in different ways. Hence innovators have to address themselves not just to the world they see, but also to the world other people see, however misguided, perverse and distorted they may think the outlook of others to be.

Therefore, implementing change is not a question of defining an end and letting others get on with it: it is a process of interaction, dialogue, feedback, modifying objectives, recycling plans, coping with mixed feelings and values, pragmatism, micropolitics, frustration, patience and muddle. Yet, messy though the process is, adopting a objective, rational, systematic, scientific approach to implementing change is far more likely to be crowned with success than relying simply on intuition (though that has its part to play too). The point is that rationality has to be applied not only to defining the *end* of change, but also the *means*.

Another fallacy is that those who have the positional power to inflict change on an organization will be successful in implementing enduring change: seldom are their sanctions adequate to do so, especially in the educational system above the level of pupil. They have to take into account the feelings, values, ideas and experiences of those affected by the change. This is not an ideological argument for democratic decision-making so much as a pragmatic one for managerial effectiveness: successful managers are observed to do this. The so-called scientific-rational mode of management has long been discredited and supplanted in successful organizations. (Failure by academics to appreciate this is usually at the heart of objections to schools learning anything from industry about management.)

Another trap in implementing change is to ascribe the problems that necessitate change to the shortcomings of individuals. Not only is personalization of the problems likely to lead to defensiveness, but it is often a misdiagnosis of the true cause. Most organizational defects are attributable to methods and systems.

The next reason why some plans for implementing change fail is that they are addressed to insoluble problems. However uncomfortable it may be for legislators and managers to admit to impotence, it has to be acknowledged that some undesirable conditions of society are so little understood or so complex to explain causally that in the present state of knowledge and expertise there is no solution to hand. Even if someone of outstanding conceptual ability could fully grasp the problem, it would be an impossible task to transfer that understanding to others who have a significant and indispensible part to play in solving the problem. *Felix qui potuit rerum cognoscere causas*, quoth Virgil ('happy is he who can find out the causes of things'); but we live in an unhappy world.

However, on a happier note, not all problems are intractable, and as time goes by we do learn how to improve our methods of solving problems and introducing change: think of the Schools Council, for instance. Even tackling seemingly intractable problems is not impossible: the best way to eat an elephant is one bite at a time.

16
ANTECEDENTS OF SUCCESSFUL CHANGE

Organizational conditions conducive to successful change

Fortunately, enough surveys have been made of organizations that *do* implement change successfully, for us to give some useful guidelines to heads and senior staff wishing to bring their schools into this category.

Some of the surveys have focused on commercial organizations, others on schools. Some schools have tried to apply the results of the former surveys to themselves, and found that many of the criteria are transferable. Her Majesty's Inspectorate's *Ten Good Schools* (1977), Peters and Waterman's *In Search of Excellence* (1982) and Goldsmith and Clutterbuck's *The Winning Streak* (1984) are examples of such surveys; no doubt the growing databank of good practice run by the Centre for the Study of Comprehensive Schools will lead to more.

Peters and Waterman believe (p. 110) that a major reason for excellence in the seventy-five most highly regarded American companies is the habitual acceptance of change, or 'intentionally seeded evolution': the excellent companies are *learning organizations*, which have developed a whole host of devices and management routines to stave off ossification. They experiment more with change, and encourage more tries. Likewise Goldsmith and Clutterbuck (p. 10) identify this as one of the eight distinctive characteristics of successful British companies: 'These companies have a continuous interest and commitment to things new, to the process of change.'

Professor Beckhard, of MIT, has stressed the critical importance of managerial strategy in keeping an organization healthy, and quick on its feet. The top managers need to have a model or a philosophy of how the organization should work, and how it can be changed; then they must constantly update this in the light of hard experience. They should strive to build an organization with distinctive approaches to purpose, structure, process, people, realism and the environment.

Purpose

Effective organizations tend to be purposeful and goal-directed. Their managers, departments and the individual members work towards explicit goals and have a clear sense of direction. The development of purpose is a continuing activity providing a focus and a framework for understanding the whole and linking it together. Thus schools without explicit aims and a whole-school policy would not meet this criterion of effectiveness.

Structure

The structure is determined by work requirements, not by authority, power or conformity. Form follows function. Different departments may be differently organized, according to the nature of their work. Procedures may not be standardized: people can do things their way if it works. Thus, in a school, some learning would not be subject to the norm of a 45-minute period. Power to do things is dispersed to where it is needed; for instance, the power to get a defective pottery kiln repaired would reside in the department, rather than be invested in a deputy head.

Process

Decisions are made near to where the requisite information is, rather than referred up the hierarchy. Authority is delegated accordingly, as is happening in LMS. Communications are frank, open and relatively undistorted. Ideas are considered on their intrinsic merits, rather than according to their source in the hierarchy. Conflict and clash of ideas (not personalities) is encouraged, not suppressed or avoided, and everyone manages conflict constructively, using problem-solving methods. Collaboration is rewarded, where it is in the organization's best interests. Competition is minimized, but when it occurs it is because people are vying with one another to contribute to the organization's success.

People

Each individual's identity, integrity and freedom are respected, and work is organized as far as possible to this end. Attention is paid to intrinsic rewards. Everyone's work is valued (e.g. including that of the non-teaching staff in a school). People's interdependence is stressed. Individuals evaluate their performance by comparing themselves to others; they review one another's work, and celebrate achievement.

As Peters and Waterman report (1982, p. 277): 'The excellent companies have a deeply ingrained philosophy that says, in effect, "respect the individual", "make people winners", "let them stand out", "treat people as adults".' At the same time, central direction co-exists with individual autonomy:

> Autonomy is a product of discipline. The discipline (a few shared values) provides the framework. It gives people confidence to experiment, for instance, stemming from stable expectations about what really counts. Thus a set of shared values and rules about discipline, details and execution can provide the framework in which practical autonomy takes place routinely.
>
> Peters and Waterman (1982, p. 322)

Goldsmith and Clutterbuck (1984) also identify the balance between autonomy and control as crucial. Without this discipline, teachers' autonomy in the classroom, or 'academic freedom', soon degenerates into licence. Lavelle (1984) also places autonomy in context: quoting Stenhouse: 'Teacher autonomy is seen as the ethical base of professionalism and a cornerstone of tradition', he points out that this can lead to gross disjunctions of practice unless that autonomy is set within the framework of the school and its value system. Mant (1983) makes a similar point.

Realism
People deal with things as they are, with a minimum of 'game playing'. An 'action research' mode of management predominates: i.e. the organization has in-built feedback mechanisms to tell it how it is doing. Then it uses this valid and factual information about how things are in order to plan improvements. There is widespread awareness of the 'health' of the organization and its parts, just as the human body knows when it feels well or poorly.

Environment
The organization is seen as an open system embedded in a complex environment with which it constantly interacts. The changing demands of the environment are regularly tracked, and an appropriate response made. A school would have its eyes and ears open, alertly sensing what was going on in the community and in County Hall. In turn, the

environment would inject a sense of reality and proportion into what might otherwise be a claustrophobic system.

Balance
All these factors are interdependent, and have to be balanced. For example, Everard was involved with a major change initiative in ICI, the 'Staff Development Programme'. Its objectives were:

(1) in the short term, the achievement of an exceptional and demonstrable improvement in organizational effectiveness; and
(2) in the longer term, the development of an environment in which major improvements occur naturally and continuously, without being enforced or imposed.

In conducting the programme it was essential to link the benefits to the organization in terms of improved effectiveness with benefits to the individual in terms of personal and professional development.

In educational settings, Fullan (1982, p. 97 and 112) makes the same point, applauding leaders who not only plan the organization development associated with the change, but simultaneously foster staff or professional development. He argues that effective educational change cannot occur without improvements to the teachers' working life. Change must not simply aggravate teachers' problems.

Collegiate culture
There is one condition of successful change which seems more prevalent in industry than in schools: industrial managers and professional staff get together more often, whereas the cellular organization in schools means that teachers struggle privately with their problems and anxieties. It is unusual for teachers to observe and discuss their colleague's work, and there is little attempt to build what Fullan (1982, p. 108) calls 'a common collegiate technical culture or analytic orientation' towards their work. The processes of teaching and learning are inadequately explored compared with the processes of manufacturing, marketing and management in industry.

One of Everard's most vivid experiences in the management of change was bringing together ten senior managers off-site to meet Professor Trist, an organizational consultant, with the request to come prepared to talk for five minutes each on 'the problems of the division'. For the first time, ten very different people, from different departments, shared their concerns, only to find that they were essentially the same. But they also shared a vision of how things could be, and the professor explained why things were as they were, and how they could be changed. The new, deeper understanding provided an immense store of energy for beneficial change, which was steered into channels that enabled organizational improvements to occur.

In schools that wish to change, regular opportunities for such encounters must be created, and the negative energy of disaffection must be transformed into a positive will to make a difference to the way things are, to the benefit of the teachers and the organization. You may not be able to get hold of a professor, but it helps to invite someone from outside the system who knows something about organizational, managerial or pedagogical processes.

Fullan *et al.* (1980), in their research on North American schools, report similar findings. The schools good at change are characterized by openness of communication, a high level of communication skills, a widespread desire for collaborative work, a supportive administration, good agreement on educational goals, and previous experience of successful change.

Let the last words of this section be taken from *Ten Good Schools* (HMI, 1977). Her Majesty's Inspectors concluded:

> The schools see themselves as places designed for learning; they take trouble to make their philosophies explicit for themselves and to explain them to parents and pupils; the foundation of their work and corporate life is an acceptance of shared values.
>
> Emphasis is laid on consultation, team work and participation, but without exception the most important single factor in the success of these schools is the quality of leadership at the head. Without exception, the heads have the qualities of imagination and vision, tempered by realism, which have enabled them to sum up not only their present situation but also attainable future goals. They appreciate the need for specific educational aims, both social and intellectual, and have the capacity to communicate these to the staff, pupils and parents, to win their assent and to put their own policies into practice. Their sympathetic understanding of staff and pupils, their acceptability, good humour and sense of proportion and their dedication to their task have won them the respect of parents, teachers and taught. Conscious of the corruption of power, and though ready to take final responsibility, they have made power-sharing the keynote of their organization and administration. Such leadership is crucial for success and these schools are what their heads and staff have made them.

Personal application. Rate the conditions in your school along the dimensions listed in this section, using a 5-point scale (1 = favourable, 5 = unfavourable):

Philosophy	Realism
Purpose	Environment
Structure	Collegiate culture
Process	Quality of leadership
People	Balance

Pick out the three least favourable conditions. What practical things can you do by the end of (next?) term to make these conditions in your school more conducive to the implementation of successful change?

Managerial qualities needed to handle change

'The ability to create and manage the future in the way that we wish is what differentiates the good manager from the bad' (Harvey-Jones, 1988, p. 96).

Observation of people who are more successful than others at managing complex organizations in which major changes have to be implemented shows that they tend to have a distinctive mix of knowledge, skills, personal attitudes and values, and the capacity to orchestrate these as they make a host of personal decisions that lie at the heart of organization management. By the very nature of their competence as educators, heads are well endowed with some of the qualities that are required – more so, perhaps, than their counterparts in industry. Other qualities, however, are more commonly found to flourish in a business environment. Few people in schools or industry are such paragons as to possess all the requisite qualities in full measure. However, an understanding of the kind of person who is good at handling change is helpful both in selecting senior staff and project leaders and in assessing what qualities we need to develop.

Before describing the key qualities that seem to be needed to implement change effectively, it is instructive to examine the characteristics that Peters and Waterman (1982) found in the leaders of successful companies. The two are related.

Such leaders listened to their employees and treated them as adults. They saw that leadership, unlike naked power-wielding, was inseparable from followers' needs and goals. Caring ran in the veins of managers of the 'excellent' companies. They did not allow intellect to overpower wisdom. They set and demanded high standards of excellence. As Henry Kissinger said: 'Leaders must invoke an alchemy of great vision.' But they had to combine visionary ideas at the highest level of abstraction with actions at the most mundane level of detail. They had the capacity to generate enthusiasm and excitement, to harness the social forces in the organization and to shape and guide its values: 'Clarifying the value system and breathing life into it are the greatest contribution a leader can make. Moreover, that's what the top people in excellent companies seem to worry about most.'

Yet success in instilling values appeared to have little to do with charismatic personality. None of the men studied relied on personal magnetism. All *made* themselves into effective leaders by persistent behaviour and high visibility.

How different these characteristics are from the teacher's stereotype of the business tycoon! And how similar to those of many a highly respected head! The heartening conclusion is that these people *make themselves* effective, although Mant argues in *The Leaders We Deserve* (1983) that there has to be in an effective leader a basic orientation that enables him to see himself as part of a higher purpose external to himself.

Valerie Stewart (1983), a British psychologist and business consultant, has listed the following characteristics of people who are good at managing change:

(1) They know clearly what they want to achieve.
(2) They can translate desires into practical action.
(3) They can see proposed changes not only from their own viewpoint but also from that of others.
(4) They don't mind being out on a limb.
(5) They show irreverence for tradition but respect for experience.
(6) They plan flexibly, matching constancy of ends against a repertoire of available means.
(7) They are not discouraged by setbacks.
(8) They harness circumstances to enable change to be implemented.
(9) They clearly explain change.
(10) They involve their staff in the management of change and protect their security.
(11) They don't pile one change on top of another, but await assimilation.
(12) They present change as a rational decision.
(13) They make change personally rewarding for people, wherever possible.
(14) They share maximum information about possible outcomes.
(15) They show that change is 'related to the business'.
(16) They have a history of successful change behind them.

We have used for training purposes (with minor modifications) a list of qualities supplied by Beckhard in identifying successful managers of change and indicating what further development was required. The qualities themselves range from those that are usually regarded as intrinsic in the personality to those – the majority – that are capable of being systematically developed. The most easily assimilated qualities are those of knowledge and comprehension.

Figure 16.1 lists some important categories of knowledge, with a column for self-rating (use a five-point scale, with 5 indicating deep knowledge and 1 superficial).

	Rating
Knowledge of	
(1) people and their motivational systems – what makes them tick;	
(2) organizations as social systems – what makes them healthy and effective, able to achieve objectives;	
(3) the environment surrounding the organization – the systems that impinge on and make demands of it;	
(4) managerial styles and their effects on work;	
(5) one's own personal managerial style and proclivities;	
(6) organizational processes such as decision-making, planning, control, communication, conflict management and reward systems;	
(7) the process of change;	
(8) educational and training methods and theory.	

Figure 16.1 Knowledge required for managing change

Figure 16.2 lists some of the skills that are important in managing change; all of them can be systematically learned, and some develop of their own accord, albeit patchily, as the manager gains experience of the job.

Various personality characteristics, attitudes and values are also important, and these are listed in Figure 16.3. They have been arranged roughly in order of decreasing inherence; i.e. those towards the bottom of the list respond best to training.

Caution is needed in rating oneself against these characteristics because of the possibilities of self-delusion. More reliable ratings can be obtained in a management group that agrees to assess each other candidly and discuss the results.

It is, of course, not these dissected qualities of knowledge, skills and

Rating

Skills in

(1) analysing large complex systems;

(2) collecting and processing large amounts of information and simplifying it for action;

(3) goal-setting and planning;

(4) getting consensus decisions;

(5) conflict management;

(6) empathy;

(7) political behaviour;

(8) public relations;

(9) consulting and counselling;

(10) training and teaching.

Figure 16.2 Skills required for managing change

Rating

(1) a strong sense of personal ethics which helps to ensure consistent behaviour;

(2) something of an intellectual by both training and temperament;

(3) a strong penchant towards optimism;

(4) enjoyment of the intrinsic rewards of effectiveness, without the need for public approval;

(5) high willingness to take calculated risks and live with the consequences without experiencing undue stress.

(6) a capacity to accept conflict and enjoyment in managing it;

(7) a soft voice and low-key manner;

(8) a high degree of self-awareness – knowledge of self;

(9) a high tolerance of ambiguity and complexity;

(10) a tendency to avoid polarizing issues into black and white, right and wrong.

(11) high ability to listen.

Figure 16.3 Personality characteristics required for managing change

other characteristics that alone determine whether a manager will prove effective: it is the way in which he is able to synthesize them into a synergistic whole, and call them forth in response to particular situations. 'Style' is a word sometimes used to describe how he does this, and is assessed by observing his behaviour (Chapter 2).

Personal application. Pick out from the ratings you have given yourself in the three figures those qualities that you most need to develop. What can you do to start a change process in yourself, leading to a greater capacity on your part to manage change?

17
A SYSTEMATIC APPROACH TO CHANGE

Introduction to the approach

So far we have considered the nature of change, its complexity, the conditions that help an organization to cope with change, and the qualities that managers need to bring about specific changes.

In no way can the management of change be reduced to something like the checklist that an airline pilot runs through prior to take-off. It is, and will remain, an art, though the 'artist' has at his disposal some tools and technology to help him, and it is gradually becoming more of a science than an art.

We shall describe a general approach to major change, which has been found by experience to be effective in industrial, health service and educational settings, and is underpinned by theories of organizational behaviour. The value of this approach is in helping to identify all the bits of work that need doing in order to effect the change; unless a systematic approach is followed, it is almost inevitable that one will be caught unawares by snags that one has totally overlooked.

The approach described is largely based on the work of Beckhard and Harris (1987), modified by long experience of its use in ICI (and by ICI staff working with school heads), and amplified in the educational context by Fullan (1982). Everard has used it to produce a practical training guide to the implementation of the 1981 Education Act, 'Decision-making for Special Educational Needs' (Evans *et al.*, 1989), which was piloted in four local authorities in 1988-9. Although the examples relate to SEN, the core material (instructions, handouts, slides, worked examples, etc.) can readily be adapted for other change programmes.

The approach is mapped out in Figure 17.1. There are six key stages that have to be carried out sequentially, though some recycling may be needed in the later stages of the process. These stages are:

(1) A preliminary *diagnosis* or reconnaissance, leading to a *decision* to undertake a change programme: is the change sound? Is it inherently likely to succeed?
(2) Determining the *future*: what do we want to happen? What will happen if we do nothing?
(3) Characterizing the *present*: what are we here for? What are the demands on us? What is stopping us? What is working for us?
(4) Identifying the *gaps* between present and future to determine the work to be done to close them: who is resistant? Who can help the change? Who should manage it?
(5) Managing the *transition* from present to future: who does what by when? How do we gain commitment?
(6) *Evaluating* and monitoring the change: was success achieved? will the change endure? What has been learned?

A word of warning about using this approach is needed. It must not become a shackled approach. It needs to be used flexibly and with careful thought. A golfer may complete a successful round without using all his clubs. So do not worry if some of the elements in the approach do not speak to your situation. Do not labour any of the stages if common sense and intuition provide you with a short cut, especially if the scale of the change is relatively modest. But do be wary of skipping an essential step in the logic. Equally, if you have tried other approaches successfully, or have read authors like Bolam *et al.* (1978), Havelock (1973), Plant (1987), Schmuck *el al.* (1977) and Stewart (1983), by all means adopt whatever approach works for you.

Assessing the soundness of a proposed change

It should not be assumed that changes proposed from within or without the organization should be adopted without question: they may be unsound on educational grounds or on grounds of practicality, as judged by those who will have to bear the brunt of the change. After all, an unsuccessful change, however progressive the idea seemed, does not necessarily benefit the pupils; and it may harm them. A succession of

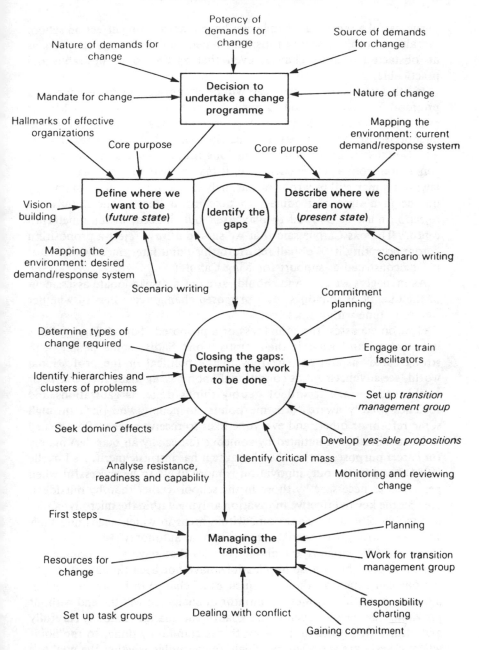

Figure 17.1 Stages in the process of change

unsuccessful attempts at change can have a devastating effect on school morale and evoke a sense of disillusionment and impotence that acts as an obstacle to future change, even that agreed to be desirable and practicable.

In other words the shrewd head will be circumspect in his response to a proposal for change (including one to which he is personally attached, or even one enshrined in legislation). A proposal may seem eminently well-intentioned, so that to reject it seems churlish and scarcely defensible; its adoption may seem inevitable in the long run; it may emanate with great conviction from a respected source; it may appear to carry the force of law: but it may still be wrong or untimely to adopt it, for the system may not be in a state of readiness to take in on board. The impulse of rejection must be allowed to play itself out; indeed, in the nineteenth century Thomas Carlyle said that we should *always* reject a proposition before accepting it. We shall return to this point later; meanwhile, let it not be construed as support for King Canute!

As managers we can, and should, attempt a dispassionate assessment of the quality or soundness of a proposed change regardless of whether we are in tune with it ourselves.

How do we assess the soundness of a proposed change? First, who is initiating it, and what is their motivation? Sadly, some people with strong career aspirations, be they in the political or the professional world, see advancement as conditional upon having made their mark, or established a track record of getting things done. Organizations and societies usually award 'brownie points' to people who push through some reform or other; and everyone likes to receive esteem. So we need to beware of change initiated by someone (especially an outsider) mainly for career purposes, rather than because it has intrinsic merit. As Lavelle (1984) has pointed out, innovation is more likely to be successful when perceived as necessary by those in the school, rather than by outsiders. He sees the key to effective innovation as lying within the microdynamics of the school and the classroom, within areas in which heads and their staff wish strongly to exercise their personal autonomy.

We must be circumspect about changes that have some popular or topical appeal, but whose implications have not been thought through. No one can expect all the consequences of change to be worked out in advance, but it ill becomes an initiator of change to will the end without providing the means. Even if the goal of the change has been carefully and clearly defined (and not even this is commonly done, to the point where criteria are specified by which we can judge whether the goal has been attained: see Chapter 10), the means of implementation may be vague in the extreme. Or again, the magnitude of change may not be appreciated, so that the whole system stands to be overwhelmed.

Another point to consider before adopting change is the extent to which it is supported within the power system. Has it been initiated from the Department of Education and Science? Does the local education authority support it? It is especially important to check the degree of political backing if additional resources will need to be negotiated at the implementation stage. Support may be needed from several levels in the hierarchy.

The teachers' unions' attitudes, the governors' support, the parents' attitudes and of course those of the teachers themselves, all need to be taken into account in judging the extent of demand or support for the change.

Government grants in support of a change, such as the 1983 initiative on school management training in England and Wales, may give the change a fair wind, and indeed may be vital for success, but the ingenuity with which people can gain access to funds yet divert them to other purposes is well-known in all walks of life. As many teachers know, TVEI is a case in point. Government legislation may also indicate support and even appear to mandate adoption of a change, but again the propensity of a complex system for outwitting the intentions of the legislators (as in parts of the Butler Education Act of 1944) is well documented. Accordingly, we should be careful not to read too much into grants, circulars and even legislation.

These are some of the factors that wise heads will take into consideration in deciding what stance they will take to a change instigated by another part of the education system. It is neither necessary nor practicable for all conditions to be ideal before a proposed change is adopted; but some judgement has to be made about the probable success of a decision to adopt, and if the head is convinced that the change, however well-intentioned, is doomed to failure, then it may well be that he is right to resist that particular change at least for the time being. His school may not be ready for it. This is not to suggest that all changes should be resisted, nor that resistance invariably succeeds in fending off the attempt to change, nor that some token response may not be prudent.

Personal application. Think of some educational changes you have experienced in your career, which have produced the least successful outcomes. Were any basically unsound? Why? How could they have resisted?

The reconnaissance

Having decided that a proposed change is sound, we have to conduct a reconnaissance. Much educational change is technically simple but socially complex, and the complexity arises not so much from dogged, mindless opposition of narrow-minded staff as from the difficulty of planning and organizing a multidimensional process involving many people, all with different perceptions and outlooks. The factors affecting implementation cannot be dealt with in isolation from each other, because they form a set of interacting variables which has to be seen as an entity. What are the factors?

First, there are the characteristics of the change itself: is it needed? Is it relevant to the particular school at this time? Has the relevance to be established? Is it complex? Is it feasible? Can it be presented as practical in the short run, not too costly and potentially helpful to the teachers?

The question of need is not an absolute one. We have to ask if it is needed more than other changes, the implementation of which will use the same (usually scarce) resources. It is quite possible to overload any system or organization with change, so the issue of priorities and sequencing changes is a vital strategic decision for any manager. When some LEAs saddled their schools with four major simultaneous changes – for example multicultural education, mixed-ability teaching, helping the under-achiever and avoidance of gender discrimination – at a time when there were already unavoidable changes brought about by contraction, reorganization, etc., they could not expect all these changes to be enthusiastically or successfully handled. The changes required by the 1988 Education Reform Act have also overloaded the system. So the effect of all the changes already taking place on the school's capacity to cope with yet another change will have important implications for the rate at which plans for implementation can be put into effect.

Lack of clarity about the goals and means of effecting change is a common problem which we addressed in preceding chapters. All who are affected by the change need a clear picture of what it will mean for them: what will they be doing differently, after the change has been implemented? They want to know specifically what it means *in practice* for them. Nor will they be content to be fobbed off with false clarity, in which the commanding heights of the future scenario are sketched starkly and boldly, but the terrain in their neck of the woods is left totally vague. Clarity is not something which can be pre-packaged in some sort of blueprint; it is something that grows through dialogue and questioning. We must judge how long it will take to achieve clarity, and incorporate this process into the time planning. The provisions of ERA for religious education and worship that is 'broadly Christian' exemplify this difficulty.

Complexity is an unwelcome but usually unavoidable factor, because worthwhile change often requires the bringing together of a set of interlocking conditions into a critical mass powerful enough to break through a log-jam of problems. However, much more care is needed in complex change, to ensure that there is proper co-ordination of all the activities needed to implement the change successfully. Leadership is called for, in addition to tactical skills.

Then there is feasibility. If a new syllabus is to be introduced, are there opportunities and funds for any necessary in-service training? If physically handicapped pupils are to be integrated into an ordinary school, is it possible to equip the buildings accordingly, other than at inordinate cost? Is the time-scale of the change realistic? You do not have to have the solution to every problem at hand before you accept that a change is feasible, but you do have to assess how imaginable solutions are.

The second set of factors affecting the implementation of change concerns the particular locality where the change is to take place. History is the first such factor: has the LEA a track-record of introducing or facilitating change successfully on previous occasions, or has a succession of bad experiences built up a negative climate of cynicism, disillusionment and apathy? Are there people there who can facilitate change, such as well-respected advisers with time available? Are there any local problems that would be helped incidentally by tackling the larger change?

Thirdly, what is special about the school? Does it have a track record of innovation? Are there problems that could be simultaneously helped by implementing the change? For instance, there may be a deputy head who has not been really stretched, and for whom the responsibility for carrying out a complex change programme would offer considerable career advantage. What is the head's attitude to change? This is an important question, because research shows that the head in any organization plays a disproportionate part in determining whether change is successful or unsuccessful. Active support is almost indispensible. Then there are the teacher interrelationships: it is difficult to bring about successful change without a lot of human interaction. Professional discussion in a positive, supportive atmosphere helps change, whereas retreating to the familiar surroundings of one's classroom or office hinders it. Are the teachers relatively confident in their own ability, yet open to suggestions from colleagues on further improvement? If so, the school has fertile soil for implanting a programme for change.

Last, there are the factors deriving from the external environment. Is the change against the grain of parental outlooks, or of local or national government policies? Would future employers of the pupils think well of it? Would they even understand its significance? What will the chair of governors think?

If, after all this, it is decided to undertake a change programme, someone with the necessary authority should formally mandate it and a 'prime mover' should be appointed to take the next steps.

Describing the future

The next piece of work to be done is to answer, with some precision, the question: 'What do we want to happen?' Later, we shall answer a related question: 'What will happen if we let matters drift?'

We need to define where we want the organization and its constituent elements (see Chapter 9) to be, how it should behave, or what it would look like, as though viewed from a helicopter or through a wide-angled lens, when the process of change has been fully completed. The jargon for such a word picture, probably projecting several years ahead, depicting exactly what shall have been achieved, is 'the future scenario'. When this vision is shared, it can become a powerhouse for change.

Ignore, for the moment, detailed questions of feasibility (dealing with obstacles comes later); otherwise the mind gets entrapped by the constraints of the present, and creative thought is impaired. As Churchill once said: 'Don't argue the difficulties; the difficulties will argue for themselves.'

On the other hand, it pays to think operationally, so as to build a self-consistent picture that has a ring of reality about it, rather than to fantasise about a dream world in which unlimited resources are available and the laws of logic and arithmetic are repealed.

Take everything relevant into the scenario – finance, parents, governors, unions, local education authority, employers, etc., and decide how these will be behaving differently in the desired future. What different demands will they be making on the school? How will the school ideally respond? Let your reach exceed your grasp. If there is a suggestion of cloud-cuckoo-land in your scenario, never mind: the object of the exercise is to find out what you value and want, and unless you know this you will not have a clear idea of the direction and goal of the desired change. To stimulate your thinking, read a few accounts by well-known forward thinkers of where schools are going, e.g. Anne Jones's *Leadership for Tomorrow's Schools* (1987).

Try to be specific: will each child have a computer in the classroom? What kinds of INSET will be done? Will the influence of TVEI, GCSE and Education for Capability have transformed classroom teaching? Will schools have enough young, creative teachers in shortage subjects? What will the universities be demanding? Don't forget that it is not just the schools that are changing: they are trying to track moving targets.

It is invariably necessary to take time off from the daily round in order to give oneself the opportunity to reflect and to muse about the future; there is no way in which scenario-building can be slotted into a busy, fragmented day. Some managers never actually get round to starting a change process until they have learned to manage their time better, and that may have to be a preliminary personal task in the total process.

Where there is a close-knit team at the top of an organization (e.g. the head and his or her deputies), the scenario-building is often most effectively carried out together off-site, say at a residential weekend event in a relaxed but workmanlike atmosphere, perhaps with the help of an experienced outsider to guide the process.

Having constructed the 'ideal' scenario, without too much additional work we can also project a second scenario which describes the situation that we think would probably come about if no steps were taken to change direction. This is sometimes dubbed the 'doom' scenario.

Comparing 'where we want to be' with 'where we shall end up' if we let things go on as they are, is a helpful way of pinpointing what has to be done.

More is said about what to include in a scenario in the next section.

Personal application. Without filling in all the detail, outline on a sheet of paper the desired scenario for your school five years hence. Then construct your 'doom' scenario.

Describing the present

The next stage is to articulate the salient features of the present situation *in the context of the future*. Sometimes the order of stages 2 and 3 on p. 248 is reversed, but the future context is always important. The advantage of building the future scenario first is to free the imagination from the constraints of the present, then to allow the present to be viewed against some clear goals. Three questions should be answered:

(1) Where is the system now?
(2) What work is needed to move it?
(3) Where are we, the initiators, in all this?

The answers provide us with a list of *what has to be done*.

The core mission

In this stage we have to go right back to fundamentals: the starting point is a definition of the organization's reason for being. Why does it exist? What is its central *raison d'être* or 'core mission'? It is not as easy to answer this question as might at first be thought; it is still less easy to get unanimous agreement on what the answer should be. The reason for being is generally assumed rather than debated and defined explicitly. It might be, for a school:

(1) to educate children; or
(2) to prepare children for life, citizenship and work; or
(3) to be a lively centre for effective learning and development for the young; or even
(4) to provide rewarding jobs for the staff teaching the children.

There may be several elements in a statement of core mission: if so, the order of priorities is important.

Environmental mapping

No organization exists in total isolation: it can only thrive if it interacts dynamically with its environment. Environments are never static and have proved for schools, as for industry, remarkably turbulent in recent years; this necessitates a process of continual adaptation to the changing demands of the environment if the organization is to survive. Those managing change, therefore, have to cultivate an outward-looking mentality (see Chapter 9). The more complex and turbulent the environment, the more important it is that those who run the organization should perceive what is going on 'out there' and understand the problems and opportunities it presents. Local management, the national curriculum and pressures for vocational orientation are obvious factors to take into account in recording where the system is now (1989): there may well be other factors round the corner to recognize in building the scenarios.

Pressures emanate from different sectors of the total environment, so it is helpful to map these various sectors or 'domains' and identify the main demands, or changes in demand, stemming from each of them. Figure 17.2 is part of such a 'domainal map' for a mathematics department contemplating a major reorganization based on the introduction of computer-aided learning.

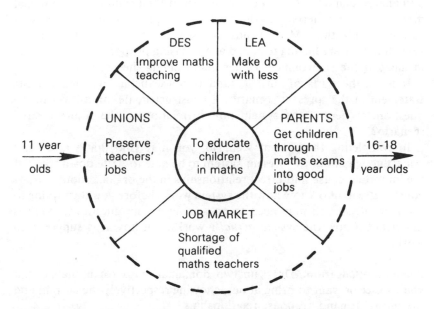

Figure 17.2   Domainal map for a mathematics department

Concentrate on those domains, and the associated demands, that are most relevant and important to the change being planned. Then, for each demand, write down the organization's typical response pattern: what does the school do at present to cope with these demands?

Thus the response to the LEA in the example given might be not to solicit additional resources. The future scenario, however, might call for a more assertive response, and hence a set of goals and actions might emerge in order to bring about the desired state. At the same time, the demand from parents may be thought likely to intensify, as they gain more power on governing bodies, and the school's response may have to be a faster development of new teaching methods.

It may become apparent that, if nothing is done, the system is heading for conflict or even disaster (the 'doom' scenario). But no one wants to submit to the future: we want to shape it! So something must be done to alter the demand–response system. Either we have to ask what future demand we would *like* to be made by each domain, and then plan to influence it; or we have to adjust our response. Often it turns out that influencing a domainal demand to fit an organization's response capability is a more attractive proposition than submitting to an unmanaged demand. An important aspect of the technique of domainal mapping is that it alerts us to the need to manage the environment as well as the organization. Many heads have been finding over the last few years that they are having to spend an increasing proportion of their time influencing the environment rather than running their school.

It is on the basis of this demand–response behaviour that a basic statement of the 'present scenario' is constructed, i.e. an answer to the question: 'Where is the system now in relation to the future desired scenario?'

In completing the present scenario, you may find that you do not know enough about the present system to be able to write down some of the important cause-and-effect relationships in the organization. It is, of course, essential to know how the system works before you start trying to influence it, so you may need to go around asking questions. What is important is how the system *actually* works, not how it is supposed to work.

Personal application. Draw up two domainal maps for a change that you foresee or want to bring about, showing respectively the current and the future demand–response relationships.

Readiness and capability

Further definition of the present scenario is needed under the heading 'readiness and capability to change'. Any organizational change will encounter resistance from people, forces and systems and will depend on finding countervailing influences that will help to promote the desired change. In the previous example of the maths department, the children, with their predilection for computer games, may be one such influence. Other key factors may be the head, staff-room opinion, Phyllis, the recruitment system, the exam system, etc. Remember that some of the factors that need to be influenced will be external to the school, because organizations are always embedded in an environment with which they interact.

Having identified the key individuals, groups, forces or systems that might influence the change, positively or negatively, we next consider:

(1) How *ready* is he/she/it to change in the desired direction (high, medium, low)? Readiness is to do with willingness, motives and aims.

(2) Irrespective of readiness, how *capable* is he/she/it of making or helping the change? Capability is about power, influence, authority and resources like equipment and skills.

Figure 17.3 is sometimes useful in categorizing people or departments confronted with change. It indicates a distribution along the spectrum of resistance to or enthusiasm for change, with most people following the herd. This is fortunate, because it means a smaller 'critical mass' who have to be persuaded to accept change. It is seldom profitable to concentrate on the 'total resisters' or those who 'try anything'; given some choice in the matter, aim for the 'early change drivers', that is, people who have developed a reputation for being in the van of change, and who already have a track-record of successful innovation.

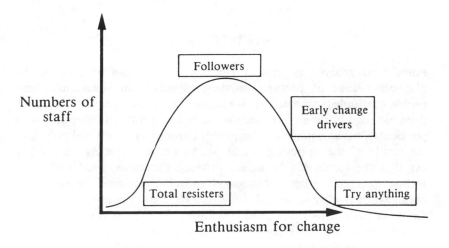

Figure 17.3 Distribution of resistance/enthusiasm

Personal application. Fill in the chart in Figure 17.4 for any change that you have in mind. Enter key people, etc., in the left-hand column.

This exercise helps you to focus on what work you will need to do to create the critical energy for change. Other techniques that are helpful in

	Readiness			Capability		
	H	M	L	H	M	L
1						
2						
3						
4						
5						
6						

Figure 17.4 Readiness and capability chart

this context are 'force field analysis' (see below) and the Gleicher formula (Chapter 18).

Force field analysis

Force field analysis is another technique which can be used at the diagnostic stage of problem solving, especially in situations where people's attitudes and reactions are important. It uses Lewin's concept of dynamic equilibrium (familiar in another form to chemists and physicists), which explains the apparent immobility of a social system as the result of the opposing forces acting on it balancing each other exactly. The forces can be needs, drives, aspirations, fears and other feelings generated either within oneself or in interpersonal, intergroup or organizational-environmental situations affected by a proposed change from the present to the desired condition. Not all the forces impeding change are inertial; they could be political or ideological forces.

Some of the forces tend to drive the point of equilibrium towards the desired condition; others restrain such movement. Force field analysis is the identification of the forces, their direction and their strength. Relative strength can be shown by the length of an arrow, in a diagram such as Figure 17.5. In using the diagram, each arrow is labelled with the force it represents.

It is implicit in the theory underlying the model that, in general, movement towards the desired condition can most readily be achieved by

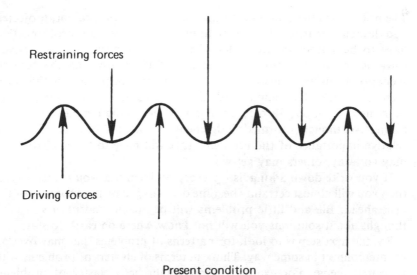

Figure 17.5 Force field analysis

reducing or removing the restraining forces. Intensifying the driving forces before reducing the restrained forces tends to build up a counter-reaction which increases the tension without moving the point of equilibrium.

The technique is usually used in groups, with the diagram drawn on a flipchart. The steps in the process are:

(1) Define specifically the change that is desired and ensure mutual understanding.
(2) Consider all the forces at work in the present situation; do not consider possible or hoped for events or solutions. Try to understand the forces felt by the people or groups affected by the change – not by the group doing the analysis.
(3) Draw arrows of length proportional to the strength of the forces and label them. If insufficient information is available to estimate the strength, decide how it can be obtained.

Personal application. Draw a force field diagram for a change needed to move your school towards a desired future scenario.

Problems to be tackled

The next step in the process is to examine carefully the present, projected and desired scenarios with a view to pinpointing the main problems that have to be solved, in order that the present scenario may be shaped towards the desired future, instead of drifting towards the 'doom' scenario. Consider the different demands and responses in the three scenarios. Are the people and the systems likely to change (e.g. retirement of head, reform of A-levels, less union militancy, etc.)? Subjective, though informed, judgements will have to be made about the relative importance of the problems that will have to be tackled: some may go away, others may get worse.

If you write down a long list of every problem that you can conceive, then you will almost certainly become discouraged by the enormity of the task ahead. Big and little problems will be mixed, and until you have thought about solutions you will not know where on earth to start.

So, the next step is to look for patterns of problems that may overlap or interconnect in some way. Think in terms of clusters of problems with a related theme. For example, there might be a cluster of problems connected with 'internal communication', or with 'maintaining everyone's commitment to their jobs while the change is being effected'. Sometimes you will come across a 'domino effect': when one problem in a cluster has been solved, the solution to all the others will fall into place fairly easily. For instance, if the English department shows that mixed ability teaching actually produces better exam results, it may be easier for other departments to follow suit.

Another helpful sorting technique is to identify and write down the types of change that you need to make, e.g.

(1) changes in policy;
(2) changes in working procedures;
(3) changes in staff training;
(4) changes in equipment and layout.

Some problems will have to be tackled before others; some will take longer to solve: so set some priorities. Whittle down the list to a manageable number of problem clusters, logically arranged and ranked in order of priority. Set the less urgent problems on one side, to tackle later.

Personal application. If you are some way down the road of tackling an organizational change, write down each problem on 'Post-it' adhesive slips (for easy sorting). Choose and label a problem cluster; arrange the problems on a flipchart in order of priority; identify any domino effects and important interactions.

Resources for change

If you have followed through the approach so far, you will have a clearer idea of what has to be done to effect the change you want, but possibly some misgivings about your ability to achieve it, and only a hazy idea of how to go about solving the problems that you have identified as important. To be clear about what the problems are, however, is to point yourself down the right road to solving them. A vague appreciation of the problems is liable to divert you and others down false trails.

Some introspection is now needed to find out what is going for you. The manager initiating change brings several things to the change effort. His qualities have already been mentioned (Chapter 15), i.e. knowledge, skills, personality characteristics, situational awareness, style, etc. His practical experience, and success or failure in past change efforts, are relevant. His position in the organization brings some influence. His motivation is of key importance. Questions to ask oneself are:

(1)   Do I need to seek additional training to help me make the change?
(2)   Which key people have I the power to influence directly?
(3)   Can I influence others through indirect leverage, e.g. through the chair of governors?
(4)   Have I any control over the reward system (e.g. career opportunities)?
(5)   What can I offer in return for support?
(6)   What are my real reasons for wanting change:
  (a)   Organizational
       to improve effectiveness?
       to reduce cost?
       to improve the teachers' lot?
       to educate the pupils better?
  (b)   Personal
       to impress others?
       to advance my career?
       to reduce pressures on me?
       to foster my professional interests?

The balance between these last two sets of motives, (a) and (b), is

always assessed by others and if it is perceived (however unfairly) as tilted towards personal interests, it can lead to a rejection of the change.
And the final question:

(7) Am I really determined to bring about the change, irrespective of other demands on my time? If not, why not? What would clinch my determination? If not me, who else would take the lead?

Personal application. Put these questions to yourself in relation to the change you want to bring about.

Individuals or task groups unfamiliar with problem solving may need special help from people particularly skilled as 'facilitators'. These can be internal, such as trained TVEI co-ordinators, or external consultants, such as industrial training managers (see p. 268 and the Westfield School case study in Chapter 19). The sort of things they do are shown in Figure 17.6.

Further reading

Gray, H.L. (ed.) 1985 *Organization Development (O.D.) in Education*, Deanhouse, Betley.
Heller, H. (1985) *Helping Schools Change*, CSCS, Nene College, Northampton.
Plant, R. (1987) *Managing Change and Making it Stick*, Fontana, London.

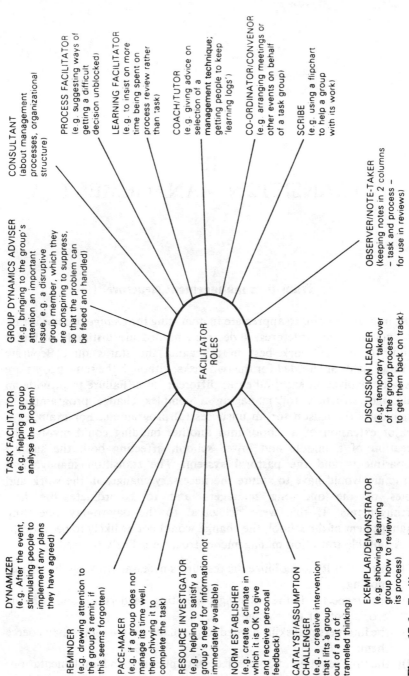

Figure 17.6 Facilitator roles

DYNAMIZER
(e.g. After the event, stimulating people to implement any plans they have agreed)

REMINDER
(e.g. drawing attention to the group's remit, if this seems forgotten)

PACE-MAKER
(e.g. if a group does not manage its time well, then chivvying it to complete the task)

RESOURCE INVESTIGATOR
(e.g. helping to satisfy a group's need for information not immediately available)

NORM ESTABLISHER
(e.g. create a climate in which it is OK to give and receive personal feedback)

CATALYST/ASSUMPTION CHALLENGER
(e.g. a creative intervention that lifts a group out of a rut of tramelled thinking)

EXEMPLAR/DEMONSTRATOR
(e.g. showing a learning group how to review its process)

TASK FACILITATOR
(e.g. helping a group analyse the problem)

GROUP DYNAMICS ADVISER
(e.g. bringing to the group's attention an important issue, e.g. a disruptive group member, which they are conspiring to suppress, so that the problem can be faced and handled)

FACILITATOR ROLES

CONSULTANT
(about management processes, organizational structure)

PROCESS FACILITATOR
(e.g. suggesting ways of getting a difficult decision unblocked)

LEARNING FACILITATOR
(e.g. to insist on more time being spent on process review rather than :ask)

COACH/TUTOR
(e.g. giving advice on a selection of a management technique; getting people to keep 'learning logs')

CO-ORDINATOR/CONVENOR
(e.g. arranging meetings or other events on behalf of a task group)

SCRIBE
(e.g. using a flipchart to help a group with its work)

OBSERVER/NOTE-TAKER
(keeping notes in 2 columns – task and process – for use in reviews)

DISCUSSION LEADER
(e.g. temporary take-over of the group process to get them back on track)

18

TRANSITION MANAGEMENT

Transition management structure

The important point to appreciate in managing the *change* process is that the management structures, style, etc., needed are distinctly different from those that work best in managing the status quo. Separate arrangements are needed for the two tasks, although the same people are usually involved in each, albeit in different roles. Failure to provide an adequate structure for managing a complex change programme is frequently the reason for an unsuccessful programme. For example, a major extension of a school into another building could involve the creation of a middle and lower school, affecting both the subject departments and the pastoral system. The transition management structure would have to secure the necessary changes in the work and roles of the operating managers and to co-ordinate the new arrangements. If this were delegated to the day-to-day operating management of the school, the change would not be likely to be smooth.

A suitable transition management structure is likely to need:

(1) the authority to mobilize the resources necessary to keep the change moving;
(2) the respect of the existing operating leadership and of the proponents of the change;
(3) the interpersonal skills needed to persuade people rather than coerce them;
(4) the time required to do the necessary planning and implementation.

The choice of a suitable structure depends on the nature of the change to be managed. Some of the possibilities for managing the transition state are:

(1) The head himself could become the project manager, possibly assisted by an external adviser or consultant. This may be particularly helpful if the change will have an impact on many external boundaries, since it is usually the head who manages the school boundaries. On the other hand, he may not have the time to invest in managing the current state, preparing to manage the future state, and managing the transition which could easily take 50-100 hours out of his working year.

(2) A project manager could be appointed, such as a deputy head. This is appropriate when there are many internal boundaries to be managed.

(3) An existing group of managers, such as a committee of heads of house, can be given the transition management task, in addition to their normal operational roles. This is only likely to be effective if they operate as a well-knit team.

(4) A group of representatives of constituencies could be chosen, such as representatives of unions and management. This may be useful for changes that are politically charged.

(5) A group of natural leaders could be selected. This might be done, for example, if the formal leadership was lacking in credibility, and it provides an excellent opportunity for staff development. However, they would need to be assured of the necessary clout and to earn the respect of the operating leadership.

(6) A diagonal slice of people at different hierachical levels in different departments could be used. This structure might be chosen, for example, in cases where the existing hierarchy was the main source of resistance to the change.

(7) A special task force can be set up, selected from staff whom the head feels he can trust – a sort of 'kitchen cabinet', responding to him informally and candidly. This may be the best structure when it is important for the head to exert direct control, but is unable to devote the necessary time himself to the transition management. However, it may give rise to political problems.

Sometimes a combination of these possibilities is best, with the structure changing at various stages in the change programme. For example, an inter-service group formed at a local conference called to improve implementation of the 1981 Education Act considered its own composition at its first meeting and changed it, bringing in two parents. Interestingly, it was chaired not by the most senior official in the group, or even someone from the education service, but by a social worker with good process skills.

A sure recipe for failure in a school is for the head to exclude himself by failing to display active interest and support: he must maintain a close working partnership with the transition management team, if he is not a member of it.

One general point is that it is very difficult for a stable organization to change itself, i.e. for the regular structures of the organization to be the structures used to manage the change. The creation of temporary systems using novel approaches is more likely to be effective. Examples are given in Chapter 19.

By the same token it can be enormously helpful to bring in an external consultant or 'facilitator' to the transition management structure, such as an LEA adviser, a local training manager or a college lecturer with appropriate experience (Gray, 1988; Holmes, 1985; Weindling, 1989); few major organizational changes in ICI were ever accomplished by divisions pulling themselves up by their own bootstraps. More and more LEAs are using consultants (e.g. Cheshire, Cleveland, Newham and Sheffield: see Heller, 1982; Taylor, 1984; and Lavelle, 1984). Even if a consultant is used, it is also important to provide training for people in the transition management structure. Fullan (1982) recommends no less than 27 days of training per staff member per year, and warns that too little training can be dangerous, because it brings problems to the surface without solving them. This may be a counsel of perfection, but industrial experience would suggest that a lead operator in the management of change should have about a month's training. Unfortunately, current provision of such training in the public sector is far from adequate in quality or quantity.

Whatever option is chosen for setting up a transition management structure, there needs to be some system for informing, consulting and involving people affected by the change. Any change creates anxieties, and the transition managers have to explain fully what is happening, in order to build up wide 'ownership' of the change and to motivate people to let it happen and make it work. The communication must be two-way, so that the managers are provided with reliable information about the real impact of the change. At one school visited by one of the authors, an otherwise very capable transition manager (a new deputy head) seemed to be short of intelligence about how the change was really perceived by the scale 1 and 2 teachers, so he assumed an unrealistic degree of commitment to the change. The shrewd manager pokes 'climate thermometers' into the organization at several levels, since he wants to deal with things as they really are, and not as they are intended to be.

Personal application. Consider a potential major change problem involving your school. What transition management structure would you set up to handle it? What problems would your choice create? How would you handle them?

Tasks for the transition management

The kind of tasks that will fall to the transition management structure will depend on the nature of the change. Consider, for example, the amalgamation of two schools, with representatives of each school and of the LEA managing it.

(1) Plans need to be developed to manage:
   (a) the period of the change;
   (b) any unaffected systems (e.g. a youth wing on one site);
   (c) organizational integration and operational effectiveness during the change (i.e. managing the 'present state');
   (d) the future situation, when amalgamation is complete.
(2) Because change can be unsettling to people, their apprehension has to be recognized and assuaged as far as possible. Rumours may spread, so clear information about the future state and its effect on people inside and outside the school must be supplied.
(3) Planning needs to cover changes in structures, roles, tasks, people and formal and informal systems. Many attempts at change go wrong when these elements are treated in isolation, so make sure that there is consistency and integration.
(4) The person leading the change needs to be visible, and available to give guidance and support, especially in connection with any conflicts that arise. Any negative energy (frustration, anxiety, threat) needs to be managed so as to encourage constructive behaviour.
(5) People need help in understanding the nature of change. There will always be uncertainty, since at the outset only broad outlines can be set, and the details usually require the involvement of many people.
(6) Communications and information systems need to be effective and to operate in both directions, since: (a) role expectations will need clarifying; (b) norms and assumptions need to be brought into the

open and examined; (c) implications for work-loads and job satisfaction need to be understood. Especially important are sensitive areas such as job security and rewards.

(7) Empathy with those affected by the change is important: the 'death' of one of the schools in an amalgamation may induce a sensation akin to mourning, and people need time to disengage from the present state and adjust to the future. In these circumstances some counselling may be needed.

These needs can place a high demand on management and lead to emotional strain if they are not planned for in advance. Admittedly, the amalgamation of two schools is a somewhat extreme example of change, but it is surprising how people can be disturbed and upset by even relatively modest changes, if they feel threatened or disadvantaged in any way. As Fullan says (1982, p. 120), you have to understand the subjective world of the role incumbents as a necessary pre-condition for engaging in any change effort with them: you must understand what reality is to those in each role. To do this, personal contact is essential, with time for discussion and reassurance.

It is therefore of critical importance that organizational arrangements to provide the time and skill required are carefully thought out and designed. These arrangements then need to be communicated so that everyone concerned understands how the change is being managed.

Developing a plan

Using a 'crisis management' approach to cope with change is not to be recommended, as it is extremely stressful for all concerned. It is far better to draw up a strategic plan to deal with the process of change. Effective planning does not come naturally to many teachers, although anyone who has constructed a school timetable will obviously have valuable expertise. In the authors' experience teachers tend to confuse decisions or intentions with plans, so that specificity is lacking.

A process plan is like a road map for the change effort. It contains detailed statements on who is to do what by when; it clarifies objectives and sets mileposts along the path to their achievement. It unambiguously specifies the means of its own implementation, and it incorporates ways of checking and monitoring progress. The characteristics of an effective plan can be summarized as follows:

(1) It is *purposeful*: the activities are clearly linked to the change goals and priorities.
(2) It is *task-specific*: the types of activities involved are clearly identified rather than broadly generalized, and responsibility for carrying them out is unambiguously assigned.
(3) It is *temporal*: target dates are specified and achievement is monitored.
(4) It is *integrated*: the discrete activities are linked to show inter-dependencies and sequencing networks.
(5) It is *adaptable*: there are contingency plans and ways of adapting to unexpected problems, such as time slippage and unforeseen resistance.
(6) It is *cost-effective*: in terms of the investment of both time and people.

There is one further point. The people who are assigned responsibility for implementing the various activities in the plan usually have their normal work to perform as well: the change activities are an added extra. Management may see the additional responsibilities as an enrichment of their normal work. However, if the change activities do not bring with them a pressure to achieve targets equal to that which applies to operational work, then they will not be regarded as fundamental to the job. So if change activities are inadequately recognized or rewarded, those involved will give a higher priority, in the direction of their energy, to the area which provides the intrinsic rewards, e.g. classroom teaching. Therefore management should be explicit in regarding work on change as part of the primary work of the people concerned, and attempt to recognize, reward or punish it accordingly. In some circumstances this may involve negotiation and the temporary transfer, curtailment or postponement of operational work.

Personal application. Reflect carefully on the adequacy of any plans for major change or other projects with which you have been associated. What went wrong? Which of the characteristics of an effective plan were wanting? Can you generalize about the shortcomings that most often recur? What can you resolve to do about it?

Hierarchy of objectives

There are two main approaches to the development of tension and energy in organizations. The first is the use of controls and the second is the use of purpose, goals and objectives. Controls are effective only if they are backed by a rigorously used reward and punishment system, which can lead to the development of negative energy if mishandled. Purpose, goals and objectives generate tension by developing hope for achievement and of a better condition in the future. However, once a goal is achieved, tension is relaxed and there is no further generation of energy. In order to maintain tension continuously, it is necessary to establish a hierarchy of objectives and to update them regularly.

It is possible to identify four levels of objectives:

Aspirations. These tend to be very long term, bordering on the idealistic. Such gleams in the eye generate little energy or excitement. Replacement of O-levels and CSE by a single exam was for years such an aspiration, before they merged into GCSE.

Strategic. These are time-bound and are expressions of what has to be done by year X (say, five or more years away) if we are to reach our aspirations. A school faced with falling rolls and a drift of population away from the area might well set a strategic objective to become a community school catering for a wider age range, in order to survive.

Tactical. These focus on a point in time, usually not more than half-way between the present and the time when the strategic objective is to be attained. Agreement on a tactical goal seen as realistic is the main device for generating tension and energy. It has to make clear where the responsibility lies for the achievement of the goal.

First steps. These are immediate things that have to be done in order to make further action legitimate, such as an announcement that a working party will be set up to initiate the change process.

It is important to consider objectives at one level in the context of those at other levels to ensure coherence and consistency of approach. Diagrams are often helpful in showing how the various objectives interlink.

Gaining commitment

Experience in organizational change has shown that in addition to developing the plan for carrying out the change, the planners must determine who in the organization must be committed to the change and to carrying it out, if the change is actually to take place. Traditionally, managements consider this from a political stance, talking of the need to 'get a few people on board', 'get the governors' approval', 'have the unions' agreement' or 'have the majority of the teachers going along'. We would like to suggest, however, that in addition to these intuitive political judgements about who needs to be committed, there should be a systematic analysis of the system to determine those subsystems, individuals and groups whose commitment to the idea, to providing resources (e.g. money and time) and to carrying out and persevering with the change is necessary. Then the manager has to develop a plan to gain the necessary commitment; this is sometimes called 'responsible scheming', which sounds better than 'manipulation'.

The steps in developing a commitment plan are as follows:

(1) Identify target individuals whose commitment is needed.
(2) Define the 'critical mass' needed to ensure the effectiveness of the change, i.e. the minimum number of people who must be committed.
(3) Assess the present level of commitment, of each individual in the critical mass, to the change.
(4) Develop a plan for getting the necessary commitment from the critical mass.
(5) Develop a monitoring plan to assess progress.

Step 3 can be helped by judging where each individual is on a scale of commitment such as:

(1) ready to *oppose* the change;
(2) willing to *let* it happen;
(3) willing to *help* it happen;
(4) willing to *make* it happen.

Secondly, a judgement can be made on the same scale of where each individual needs to be for success. Plotting the position on a chart helps (Figure 18.1).

Step 4 is a crucial one to which there are various approaches. Force field analysis (Chapter 17) can help. Another way is to apply the Gleicher formula, which can also be useful in assessing any system's readiness to change:

Individual	Oppose	Let	Help	Make
Head			O ——— X	
First deputy head		X ———————————— O		
Union representative	X ——— O			
LEA adviser		XO		

X = present position
O = desired position

Figure 18.1 Commitment chart

$$C = f(ABD) > X$$

where

C = change, which is a function (f) of:

A = extent of dissatisfaction with the status quo (present state)

B = clarity of vision of where we want to be (future state)

D = feasibility of the first practical steps for getting there

X = cost of the change, in both financial and psychological terms.

Sometimes managers can gain commitment to change by fanning dissatisfaction with the *status quo*, or with the 'doom' scenario to which this will lead if nothing is done. Or they can paint an attractive and enticing picture of the future state, convincing people that it is something worth striving for. Often, however, it is the practical steps involved in the change which need spelling out, so that people can see just how it will work for them. The net cost of the change can be reduced by trying to ensure that it gives ultimate personal advantage to those affected by it, to offset the extra efforts required in breaking the old mould. Enlightened self-interest always helps. Professional development, or an improved chance of career advancement, are two such benefits.

Other approaches to gaining commitment are:

(1) Use of power: although there are still heads who rule with a rod of iron, coercive power is a decreasingly effective strategy for gaining real commitment. But there are times when it helps to overcome initial resistance, enough to give way to more acceptable and enduring methods of winning hearts and minds.

(2) Involvement: a participative style of management helps, but

sometimes takes a long time to produce results. A way round this dilemma is to think of involvement as applying to three distinct levels – shaping the decision, shaping the implementation and shaping the pace of change. Significant commitment can be obtained at the second and third levels.

(3) Problem-solving activities: significant parts of the system are not always aware that there is a problem. By involving them in trying to identify and clarify a problem or need, one can increase their appreciation of the problem and, often, gain their commitment to change.

(4) Educational activities: sometimes a training course or educational event will provide the kind of awareness and commitment which policy statements or directives cannot accomplish.

(5) Treating 'hurting' systems: one way of moving the process forward is to begin work with those subsystems that are 'hurting'. Change is more likely to occur, and the 'critical mass' is more likely to develop, with such subsystems.

(6) Change the reward system to value different behaviour: consider both extrinsic and intrinsic rewards; they need not be financial.

(7) Functioning as a role model: changed behaviour by the leader is sometimes required in order to get others to change theirs.

(8) Forced collaboration mechanisms: in order to get commitment, it is sometimes necessary to require people to work together and to take on certain managerial roles.

(9) Persuasion: the techniques used by reputable salesmen are worth considering; these are described on page 225.

The process of selecting a mechanism to involve those whose commitment is essential is often best helped by analysing the forces that get in the way of change. Thus if one can find an activity that unfreezes frozen attitudes, one may be helping the process of creating the conditions necessary for allowing new attitudes to form, with a consequent increase in energy and commitment. This is better than forcing the change on those who are resistant to it.

Finally, when it comes down to dealing with particular individuals, you may have to be ready to spar with the negative thinkers who habitually resist change. Derek Waters, who has trained many ILEA primary school heads, has a useful list of common objections (Figure 18.2) which he gets his courses to role-play. There are effective rejoinders to all these snipers' bullets. Try thinking of some and keep them up your sleeve!

(1) I can't see that working with the teachers here.

(2) I can just hear what our parents would say about that – especially after the trouble with the mathematics work last summer.

(3) It won't work in a large (small... county/voluntary... urban/rural) school.

(4) I'm sure we haven't got the space (resources/materials/time) for that.

(5) You realize the French (Germans) abandoned that idea five years ago?

(6) How do you think the new governing body are going to react? You remember what they said about the sex education programme!

(7) I wouldn't want the local newspaper to get a hold of this one.

(8) Isn't that an untested theory?

(9) Isn't that an American idea?

(10) You're not putting that idea forward seriously, are you?

(11) Yes, it does sound as though it would work. But you do realize what it would do to the language work programme, don't you?

(12) Isn't that the approach they used to advocate that environmental studies should be tackled back in the sixties?

(13) I can see it would be a good idea, but why change – for so small a gain?

(14) It's a fine plan – but I wonder if it is just a little too advanced for us at this point in our development?

(15) We're different here.

(16) It sounds like a very fashionable thing to do.

(17) If it's so good, why hasn't someone else tried it?

(18) From a practical point of view it does seem all right; but what about the wider implications?

(19) Hardly what I would call a professional approach to our problems.

(20) Is this your own idea?

(21) I'm sorry, but I don't see the connection with what you are suggesting and what most of us perceive as our real needs.

(22) I can think of some much better ways to spend the money.

(23) Perhaps we ought to wait for a more opportune time.

(24) With respect, I don't think you have been here long enough to understand our set-up and how we prefer to work.

(25) I hope you don't expect the infants (juniors) to join in this new scheme.

(26) We have tried this before.

(27) The caretaker will have some very definite views about these plans.

(28) I really can't keep wasting my time like this.

(29) Wasn't that something Keith Joseph tried to introduce?

(30) Well, we would like to do that, but the Education Reform Act makes it impossible!

(31) And how are we going to do this with two teachers short in that department?

(32) What?

(33) You must have stayed up half the night thinking that one out. (Consider your reply most carefully, if you actually did stay up half the night.)

Figure 18.2 Verbal barriers to change (used with permission of Derek Waters)

Responsibility charting

In carrying out any plan, or determining how the future state is to be managed, it is vital to ensure that the key people (or 'actors') understand how they are going to be involved. The allocation of work responsibilities can be assisted by a technique called 'responsibility charting'. It aims to clarify role relationships, as a means of reducing ambiguity, wasted energy and adverse emotional reactions. The basic process is as follows:

1. The vertical axis
Using a form designed as shown in Figure 18.3, two or more people whose roles interrelate or who manage groups that have some interdependence (e.g. a head of year and a head of department) develop a list of actions, decisions or activities (e.g. disciplining pupils, recording disciplinary incidents, using common equipment) and record them on the vertical axis of the form.

2. The horizontal axis
Then, *working individually*, each person identifies the 'actors' who have some kind of behaviour towards each action or decision, and lists these actors on the horizontal axis of the form. Actors can include:

(1) those directly involved;
(2) those immediately above them in the hierarchy;
(3) groups as well as individuals (e.g. the senior management team);
(4) people outside as well as inside the organization (e.g. the chairman of governors, the divisional inspector).

CODE: R – Responsibility (initiates)
A – Approval (right to veto)
S – Support (put resources against)
I – Inform (to be informed)

ACTORS → DECISIONS ↓														

Figure 18.3 Responsibility chart

3. Charting behaviours individually

Still working individually, the required behaviour of each actor towards a particular activity is charted, using the following categories:

> R = *Responsibility* for seeing that decisions or actions occur;
>
> A = *Approval* of actions, with a right to veto them;
>
> S = *Support* of actions or decisions by provision of resources, but with no right of veto;
>
> I = *Informed* of action or decisions, but with no right to veto.

4. Reaching a consensus

Now working as a group, all the actors (or as many as possible) share their individual perceptions, possibly by circulating the form or by using flipchart displays. Where there is agreement, the only further work is to agree the nature of any support action. The purpose of the meeting is to produce an agreed version of the responsibility chart by a consensus decision. A majority vote will not do: differences have to be ironed out and resolved. The end result must be that each actor treats the decision as though it were ideal.

True clarity will not be achieved if more than one R exists for an activity. Agreement on where the R should be assigned for any activity is the first step in the discussion, and the actor concerned (who will be an individual) will certainly have to agree with subsequent categorizations. There are three approaches which may help, if agreement cannot be reached on who has the R:

(1) Break the problem down into smaller parts.
(2) Move the R up one level in the organization by including a new actor.
(3) Move the decision about the allocation of the R up one level.

Once the R has been placed, other letters can be agreed. A ground rule is that a decision must be made on which *single* letter goes into the box.

Another problem that will occur is that agreement may only be reached on some activity by assigning a large number of As. This, however, is unrealistic, because it leads to a situation in which there is great difficulty in getting decisions that allow progress on the work. Discussion is then needed on how to change some As into Ss or Is.

5. Circulating the chart

Having developed the chart, the group then tests it out with any actors not present at the meeting (indeed no major actor should have been absent) and circulates it to colleagues as a vehicle for communicating operating practice.

6. Using the chart

The actors use the chart to check what their appropriate behaviour is and to call the attention of other actors to behaviour that is out of line with what was agreed.

The usefulness of responsibility-charting lies not only in the end product of an agreed chart, but also in developing understanding of people's different roles, and a better appreciation of different feelings and attitudes towards the operation.

Personal application. With the help of one or two colleagues with whom you have to work on some operation, draw up a responsibility chart following these guidelines. Afterwards, review how the process worked and in what other contexts it could be applied with advantage.

Monitoring and evaluating change

One of the problems with change is ensuring that it is followed through. With something as discrete as the amalgamation of two schools, it is relatively easy to know when the change is complete. However, some changes, such as 'improving school leadership' are ill-defined. To move from the present to the future state, the system has to be unfrozen, changed and fully stabilized in the new state. We need, therefore, to have yardsticks by which we can recognize when the organization has got to where it wants to be, and which we can use to set a ratchet to prevent backsliding. The last thing we want is a façade of change, followed by the system gradually sinking back into its old ways of working. As Sir John Harvey-Jones has observed (1988, p. 114):

> Ultimately change is only anchored firmly when individuals have changed their perceptions and values, and it is important to be realistic about the time that this may take. Five years is absolute par for the course of changing attitudes and even that is only achievable if one is moving well within the establishment grain of thinking.

To help stabilize the system in the new state, we need to develop success criteria or measures that will tell us that the change has been effective and has become truly assimilated. The 'future scenario' description may yield some useful clues to the measures that might be adopted, if it is specific enough. Some means of gathering reliable information and analysing it should be set up as part of the overall plan for change (not as an afterthought), and may have to extend beyond the point when the change can be said to be complete, so as to make sure that it endures. The means of measuring success might take the form of a checklist of procedures, a questionnaire about role responsibilities, an analysis of exam results or an attitude survey to be completed by those most likely to know if the change has been successful – perhaps the pupils. It will focus on the actual outcomes of the change.

It is necessary to assign responsibility to named individuals for monitoring the critical factors that measure success and for managing the processes needed to take corrective action in case of a shortfall. Responsibility charting is useful for this. Processes that influence several of the success criteria and are known to have been inadquate in the past merit particular attention.

The existence and purpose of the evaluation or review plan, and the intention to use it for correcting any tendency for the system to regress, should be communicated to those involved, because this will help in the process of stabilization of the change. It will signal the completion of the transition stage and the arrival of the 'future state'. Success makes obsolete the behaviour that led to success: new behaviour is now needed, appropriate to the future state having been attained.

A further reason for this review is to check on unforeseen consequences of the change, so that any new problems thrown up are properly managed, and new opportunities made the subject of further change.

The results of the review should be carefully studied so that the management knows what activities have been successful. Organizations can consciously learn how to manage change more effectively, but only if they review the process, consolidate the successful practices and plan to overcome any difficulties next time round.

The whole organization is entitled to receive some kind of report from management about the success of the change, and this may well be linked with expressions of thanks for their co-operation. This is all part of the attempt to mould the reward system so that change efforts and development are valued and recognized as much as operational work.

Finally, there is the possibility that other schools will be able to benefit from your experience, e.g. through the databank operated by the Centre for the Study of Comprehensive Schools (access is not limited to

comprehensives) at Nene College, Northampton. This can only be done
if the actual outcomes of the change are well documented.

19
SOME CASE STUDIES OF CHANGE

In this chapter we give case studies of three schools that are consciously managing change of a complex nature. These particular schools were chosen from twenty-one visited by one of the authors in a research study on the problems of secondary school management. They were selected for this chapter because they bring out a number of interesting comparisons between school and industrial management practice. In order to preserve confidentiality, the schools have been given fictitious names.

Each school was revisited four years later to find out whether the changes had endured successfully and whether the momentum had been sustained.

Westfield School

The head of Westfield School was familiar with much of the material in this part of the book and was using a systematic approach with considerable success. As the change programme was still in progress, it was too early to assess the full results, but there were clear signs of impressive progress in 1984. The approach was also being followed by schools in the LEA which formerly employed him.

Westfield School is a co-educational 11–18 comprehensive school in a rural area of England. Its origins lie in an old grammar school. There are 1,200 children and 60–70 staff.

The head was educated in the independent sector and had been a lecturer at a teacher training college. In this latter capacity, his duties required him to place students for teaching practice, in the course of which he had visited many schools. Later he had been deputy head of a grammar school and more recently head of a comprehensive school. This last was in an LEA area which had been active in bringing about change, with help from managers of a large industrial firm in the locality. By contrast, his current LEA had a reputation for being conservative.

Among the formative influences in his development were a strong liberal streak, a fascination for administration, the anti-model of a 'workoholic' head to whom he had been deputy, and above all the experience of working in his former LEA along with other heads under the guidance and support of a very able LEA adviser, an industrial chaplain and a group of local industrial managers. This had convinced him that change needs actively managing, and that training managers from industry can be very helpful in facilitating this process. Indeed, at his current school he had struck up a relationship with a local industrial firm whose management training manager paid periodic visits to consult with the school on the changes that were being implemented.

His predecessor at the school had epitomized much that was traditional in a headmaster: it was said that he was an autocrat who kept knowledge to himself, who was held in awe and latterly had introduced few changes of a management nature, although he had undoubted qualities in a number of areas. It was surprising to find at so many of the schools that the author visited, how often the previous head was described in similar terms. Although entitled to have three deputies, the previous head had only appointed two, one of whom had died shortly after the present head took over; hence the new head was able soon after arrival to appoint two new deputies, one an existing senior member of staff, the other a young outsider.

The head's account of the changes he was trying to bring about was as follows:

(1) He wanted to change the image of the school head to one who was devolutionary and participative in management style.

(2) He wanted to get the whole ethos of the school to be participative: some departments had not met together for twenty years, and if staff encountered disciplinary problems they would not share them with colleagues but sent the miscreant straight up to the head for punishment.

(3) He wanted to be seen to delegate and to encourage this in others. (Indeed, so successful had he already been with one member of

staff that he had been hauled over the coals by an LEA officer because this member of staff had personally lodged an official complaint with the authority's planning department without passing it up through the line.)

(4) He wanted to introduce a modern concept of careers education, moving away from the existing idea of providing job information into the area of life and social skills; this was a move encouraged by the governors.

(5) He was trying to introduce a clearly defined system for taking key decisions, such as in allocating funds and scale points. He had not inherited such a system from his predecessor.

(6) He had already transformed a block which had been built separately from the rest of the school as the 'ROSLA Block', and which had taken on something of a poor image. He had now integrated the occupants with the rest of the school.

(7) He had introduced a regular staff meeting, the first of which was followed by a visit to the local pub for informal exchanges; and he had consitituted a 'Senior Planning Group' (SPG), consisting of himself, the three deputies and the heads of the lower school, the middle school and the sixth form. This met fortnightly. There was also a regular meeting of heads of department, and the pastoral heads met informally.

(8) He was inviting staff regularly to his house for an evening meal, and hoped that eventually all would be able to come; so far only one had refused. By this and other means he had been able to get on Christian-name terms with most staff.

(9) He was looking at the possibility of introducing a staff appraisal system.

(10) He had discontinued corporal punishment in practice, although it was still there as an ultimate sanction.

He said that his three main problems were: (1) those caused by a small number of unsatisfactory staff; (2) too little control of the time available for training staff; and (3) lack of financial control. As an example of the latter, he said that the buildings had been allowed to run down and looked tatty, but he was not allowed to use local odd-job men to get things put right: everything had to be submitted as part of the authority's overall programme. The authority then decided priorities, putting items out to competitive tender at greater cost than if he were able to organize the improvements himself. He had been well trained in good husbandry - how to acquire money and spend it wisely - at the public school where he had taught. He also felt his staff could be trusted to spend more money. In fact, his budget was only £35,000.

Summing up, his 'future scenario' was distinctly different from the 'present state' which he inherited. His vision was of a school characterized by excellence in terms of the ethos, the quality of the teaching and the effectiveness of its organizational processes.

The new deputy head

The head's vision was substantially shared by, and much discussed with, the new arrival, the deputy head, who was playing a key role in transition management. He had proved a very happy choice: despite his clear commitment to helping the head to make major changes in the way the school was run, with all the apprehension that this caused among the established staff, he had quickly gained the confidence of the staff, most of whom had been at the school for many years. A young geographer, he had started his career in commerce, with a firm of accountants which had given him a good training in work organization. This had been followed by a spell at a very different firm, with American roots. He had had no formal training in management, however.

The differences in management style between his first school and his original employers were extreme. The latter were open with information, which everybody shared, while in the school his colleagues kept their ideas secret. In commerce his training had been systematic; in school he had just been told: 'Here is a course, there is a class, do it!' However, it worked, and the head, a priest, used to come into his class to see him teach and to offer suggestions.

A subsequent post had been head of humanities in an urban comprehensive school where the culture was very open, and his staff of fifteen to eighteen worked very much as a close-knit team totally committed to doing their best for the children. Here he had learned the value of exposing one's problems in a supportive group.

At Westfield School, he was responsible for curriculum and staff development, but he described himself as a change agent in the school. The following is his own account of his work in this role.

Many teachers had been in the school for twenty years and it was quite a problem to persuade them that change was needed. There were few young staff in the school (only two probationers), and the older ones had become inured to the previous head's autocratic style, so that they could not readily adjust to the present head's participative style. There was a big block of resistance at head of department level, which he was trying to overcome in discussion. He had held four 2-hour meetings with heads of department on a voluntary attendance basis, but not all had come. There were no defined objectives for the departments, nor had there been job descriptions, though now at least there was a check-list of duties.

This check-list had come about as a result of four meetings. He was well aware that not all HoDs adhered to the list, nor would he expect them to. But things were changing: he was now involved in individual discussion to see how some of the suggestions that had come out of the four meetings might be implemented. The whole process was ongoing, and the four sessions represented a starting point; a discussion document for further negotiation.

Originally, the HoDs did not consult with their departments, this being seen as a 'management game'; everyone expected to be told what to do and saw no point in consultation. The mere fact of HoDs being assembled to discuss their roles was seen as frightening: 'Does this mean I am no good?' This kind of fear, which one of the HoDs subsequently confirmed as having been present, needed counteracting. After a long tradition of 'just getting on with the job', the concept of any kind of review was quite new.

The deputy head's job, however, was to be helpful, and he seemed to have gained the confidence of a good many staff in spite of his innovations. A curriculum review every four years had been imposed on the school, but it did not involve staff below HoD level. Although he had been hoping to introduce some form of staff appraisal, it was not possible for the time being.

His key objective was to get teaching methods changed from an authoritarian style to something more student-centred. He was using discussion as the main vehicle, asking such questions as: 'What have you done that's good?' Teaching loads, however, slowed down progress. Other approaches were to bring in outsiders to talk to staff, and to use the changes imposed by falling rolls to modify and combine jobs. Very few staff moved of their own accord, but happily two who were particularly set in their ways were taking early retirement.

An important activity had been an open weekend conference, attended by about half the staff (others feeling too threatened to come, or else not wanting to give up a weekend). The conference identified a few issues as needing particular attention:

(1) the sixth form, and how it could be helped to learn;
(2) the pastoral curriculum, in relation to the world of work or unemployment;
(3) the future of the school at a time of falling rolls.

The pastoral curriculum discussion group was stimulated by the head's wish to introduce a life and social skills programme, with a 'You and Your World' course for all third, fourth and fifth years (with a common core curriculum). Staff from all departments had taken part in its planning.

There were still many cynics and much to be done. Many more staff now attended courses, compared with five years before, but they only brought back minor ideas which they shared informally with their colleagues.

As mentioned above, one of the outsiders who was working with the school on an ongoing basis was the management training manager of a large local firm, well skilled in the practice of management development. He had introduced useful check cards headed 'To Do Today', which helped sort priorities, highlight objectives and improve personal organization. He had also helped staff to give and receive personal feedback, which had a rub-off effect on school teaching. At first his experiential techniques had been regarded as game-playing, but were now becoming more acceptable. Flipcharts, the appearance of which in industrial managers' offices often indicates a systematic approach to change, had become commonly used in the school by now, so much so that one child had recently been heard to exclaim: 'What, not *another* flipchart!' Some classes had been introduced to small group work. All this had started with the outside manager offering voluntary sessions on helping staff to improve their management style. About thirty staff had come to all or some of his sessions. Though understandably somewhat suspicious at first of an outsider, all now felt he had a good influence. For example, his ideas had been incorporated in 'You and Your World' sessions, in which stimulation of commercial processes involving the use of computers had been used to teach pupils about unemployment and its causes. Some role-plays of 'haves' and 'have-nots' had been effective with pupils.

All in all, about half of the HoDs were beginning to change their teaching methods, and this could be partly ascribed to the skill of the management training manager in initiating style change.

Comments by other staff

Some of the comments made by other members of staff about the changes in train were as follows. The deputy head (administration), a long-serving fifty-three year old, clearly one of the pillars of local society, regarded the head as very good: compassionate, thoughtful and an excellent delegator. The deputy head (administration) said that some staff, not comprehending the head's role, thought he did not do anything, but they were mistaken. The head was well liked as a person, loyal to his staff and had created a climate in which they had a sense of all helping one another, though the change had been very gradual. The climate was also much more open now, and the head more accessible. His predecessor had called only six staff meetings in twenty years.

The deputy head (administration) also thought the new deputy head (the change agent) a very good acquisition and liked working with him.

Commenting on the contribution of the visiting management training manager, he said that the residential weekend he ran had demonstrated that there were such things as management skills, but that some staff still felt that though such skills might be relevant in industry, they certainly did not apply in schools. The manager had also helped in building interpersonal relationships and influencing people.

The other deputy, a woman in what was predominantly a man's world, had worked with four heads at the school. She generally approved of the new head's style, thinking he was a good organizer, though she had sometimes wished that he would step in and rule, as he did once in a conflict over school meals supervision.

She also approved of what the management training manager was trying to do. She liked his 'positive strokes', his diaries and his ordering of priorities. She had hoped that it would be possible to introduce staff appraisal, but so far it could not be achieved.

The head of sixth had worked in industry as a chemist at the same firm as the management training manager, and noticed that industry was very much more aware of structure than were schools. He had also been on an interviewing course with another firm and thought it very well and slickly presented. It had taught him the range and depth of questions that ought to be asked.

Reflecting on the changes introduced by the new head, the head of sixth was very aware that the latter expected staff to exert their own discipline, and not send children to him for a 'blasting'. He thought the head's open style was refreshing, and that the school's aims were now better understood.

Although the head and the new deputy were generally liked and well respected, there were some real misgivings about their supposed deviousness and a feeling that they ought to be more honest with the staff: 'We're not that stupid!' In the view of some staff, the way they played their roles was tantamount to manipulation. Moreover, the influence of the visiting industrial manager needed watching: what was he really trying to do?

Despite these concerns, it was the long-serving deputy head (administration) who saved the day: he at least was highly trusted for his integrity and could always be relied on to act as a mediator between the new brooms and the rest, if things got out of control.

Commentary

Although this is not a copybook example of every practice advocated in this book, Westfield School is an intriguing case study of how approaches to change used in industry are being successfully applied in a school, gradually but apparently to good effect.

A key to success was the general outlook and leadership of a head with a clear vision of what he wanted to achieve, ably supported by a deputy who had the interpersonal skills and resilience needed for the chief change-agent role. The older deputies had important roles, the administrator being seen as the one who would mediate when conflict occurred, and the pastoral deputy, signalling to the doubters by her being won over to the new regime that it might be acceptable after all.

The old habits of thought and teaching style were, however, deeply embedded in the staff, and were supported by the strong conservatism of the local authority, so the rate of change could only be gradual and sometimes painfully slow.

The opportunities for bringing in new members of staff were severely constrained, and retraining opportunities were limited by lack of free time.

Already, however, there were striking successes, not least those facilitated by the external consultant. Indeed, the new sixth-form induction course seemed to be a model of its kind, fully utilizing modern training approaches and looking very different from what one might expect to find in a school with conservative traditions.

The head's vision of the future state was not a rigid one: it allowed for plenty of dialogue among the staff. Both he and the change-agent deputy were well aware of staff attitudes and feelings, and had come to terms with the fact that they could only be modified slowly. However, it seemed that the staff were not yet fully tuned into what would happen in practice as a result of the decisions taken by the senior planning group.

It is perhaps surprising that the school's core mission and key aims were not articulated, and made the subject of vigorous discussion and debate, at an earlier stage of the change programme. Steps taken to build and share a common understanding can act as a valuable focus for a school's work. However, to fill the gap, the head, his deputies and the management consultant had recently spent a working weekend at a study centre planning the long-term aims, and shorter-term targets and strategies of the school.

The 'present state' that the head took over fell well short of fulfilling the antecedent conditions for successful change listed in Chapter 16: the school was not managed against goals and objectives; its structure and climate were authoritarian; there was inadequate communication flow; there was little collegiate culture; and the links with the environment, though strong at the social level in the community, were poorly developed in the increasingly important domain of employment. The conservative LEA environment was generally hostile to change and to devolution of power. The very low turnover of staff and their insulation from the outside world combined to produce a school settled in its ways. These conditions presented a formidable challenge to the incoming head.

On the other hand, he would rate highly on many of the measures of managerial effectiveness (Chapter 16), especially in his familiarity with organizational processes; so he was a good match for the school and its problems.

The cornerstone of the transition management structure he set up was the new deputy head, who played a key change-agent role. However, the senior planning group also acted as part of the structure; by having in the group established members of the hierarchy, he was able to treat it as one of the 'critical masses', whose commitment to change had to be won.

Predictably, his motives for the change, and his 'devious' methods of achieving it, came in for suspicion. It is rare indeed to find innovative managers whose staff give them a totally clean bill of health as regards their integrity, even when their behaviour is impeccable.

The role of the external consultant (the industrial training manager) is particularly interesting. Though coming from a different culture, with all the suspicions that this is apt to arouse, he worked hard to establish credibility by introducing the staff to techniques that had short-run advantages to them, in a problem area that 'hurt' – how to make better use of their all-too-scarce time. It is from this kind of bridgehead that trust can be gradually extended. The consultant's experience of strategic planning of change in a large organization was very valuable to the head and new deputy in dealing with such practical issues at teacher level, and the three were able to hold fruitful strategic and tactical discussions in a high-level language of change. So effective was this partnership that the trio are in demand for providing inputs to school management training courses sponsored by a consortium of nearby local authorities.

The level of commitment to change in one of the important environmental domains, the local authority, fell short of ideal. While opposing some changes, in other directions they were prepared to 'let it happen', but did little to 'help it happen'. Because improved effectiveness depended on gaining their support (e.g. in relation to financial autonomy and control)), work to bring the LEA decision-makers on board would no doubt continue.

Altogether, there was much good practice to show at the school, which achieved not unimpressive (though not outstanding) academic results, in the way in which it was actively adapting to change. It will be interesting to see if and how it introduces a set of agreed school aims and objectives and a system of staff performance appraisal.

Four years on...

Although the same head is still in post, there are three new deputies and six new HoDs. Promotions have been mostly internal, with the school growing its own timber from strong rootstock, leading to a competent staff who work together well. Interdepartmental co-operation is much improved and the introduction of TVEI in 1989 is expected to improve it further. Glasnost now prevails. The curriculum has been maintained with fewer staff and children (a demographic fall from 1,300 to 850). The new management team is very strong – a real team at both task and social level. The senior planning group meetings continue three-weekly, the HoDs' twice-termly and the staff meeting (none too productive) every half-term. Periodical weekend workshops are run, e.g. on counselling skills by the industrial management training manager, who still acts as a consultant, trying to diffuse his skills: one deputy called his contribution to the management team 'fantastic', and even the cynics value what he has done.

The school now has a set of aims, collaboratively evolved, displayed in the main corridor and elsewhere. These enshrine its values and are used as a touchstone for important decisions. Disappointingly, however, staff appraisal is still not in place, but the head himself is appraised by a local neighbouring head who gets the children to complete a questionnaire.

The first GCSE results were exceptionally good and the school has won a curriculum award. It has become more sought after by parents (15% of children come from outside the extensive catchment area) who, with the governors, are now accepted by staff as partners.

There is a more positive approach to the management of resources, which is well delegated. The school is into LMS and its budget has risen sharply to £1.25 million. The monitoring system has improved and there is effective forward planning three years ahead, with long-term aims linked to targets and timescales.

The head and the former change-agent deputy have both been active in disseminating good practice to other schools, through books and seminars. The overall picture is one of real attitudinal change; development is built into the system. The thrust comes mainly from the management team (rather than from the still conservative LEA), impressively supported by the industrial training manager as consultant.

Easterham School

Easterham School was situated in a metropolitan conurbation where the population was predominantly white and working class. It was a mixed comprehensive school with over 1100 pupils aged from 11 to 19, and was particularly affected by falling rolls. Although the buildings are modern and the school well equipped, it was the least sought-after of the four secondary schools in the same catchment area, and its reputation had been diminishing in recent years. Its academic achievements were poor. The school had the reputation of being tough, and many of the pupils arrived late, played truant or misbehaved.

There was little sense of community in the surrounding area, where attitudes ran against the tide of modern thinking on social issues, leaving the school to try alone to inculcate progressive values. The governors were somewhat suspicious of change, only the LEA being supportive, to the extent of giving the head a relatively free hand.

Standards of discipline and academic attainment had slipped somewhat during recent years. The former head had been much involved with professional activities outside the school, but his health had not been good, and when he left, there was a rather long interregnum while the future of the school was reviewed, and the first deputy head had to manage as best he could.

The school staff were strongly unionized, and there had been instances of unofficial industrial action. Certain staff appointments had been made at a time when it was difficult to attract able teachers in some subjects to an area such as this, and some of these teachers have not proved up to the job, which has given problems at head of department level. Comparatively little movement of staff to other posts had taken place, so the age structure was not ideal.

The staff espoused the principle of mixed-ability teaching on egalitarian grounds, but had not all adjusted their pedagogical approach to cope with the difficulties this presented, so that the very able pupil was apt to be disadvantaged.

The new head

The above, then, was the situation that confronted the new head when she took over the school some six months before the case study was written. However, by paying some visits to the school in the term before she was appointed, and by spending the summer holidays reflecting and preparing for the job, she was able to decide quite early on what she wanted to happen, and to lay plans for making it happen.

Her first priority was to establish good order and discipline among both the pupils and the staff. Second, she was determined to improve the image of the school in the public eye, in order to persuade more parents to send their children to the school and thereby assure its survival in the falling-roll situation. Third, she saw the need to exert firm leadership from the top and establish her own authority.

To these ends, she promulgated on her arrival a long paper describing the new organization structure, and wrote role-descriptions for the deputies and other staff. These left no room for ambiguity about the responsibilities of the management team and about the purpose and authority of the various committees that survived her arrival. She also wrote a school prospectus for issue as soon as she arrived. Among other things this set out what the school stood for and explained the school's organization structure (Figure 19.1).

She wanted the organizational arrangements to be based on a sound consultative system in the school, for several reasons:

(1) to make the best use of resources, especially teachers' knowledge and expertise;
(2) to increase job satisfaction by enabling teaching and non-teaching staff to influence their own working conditions and environment;
(3) to involve everyone (i.e. the stakeholders) in developing and owning a whole-school policy, which would form the basis of managerial authority in the school;
(4) to provide pupils with a model of how a good organization is run.

Such a consultative system, she explained in her paper, in no way removed the power, right or responsibility of the head to make decisions affecting the school, with or without consultation; nor did it mean rule by a proliferation of time-wasting committees. Some complexity was unavoidable, however, because of the number of stakeholders in the

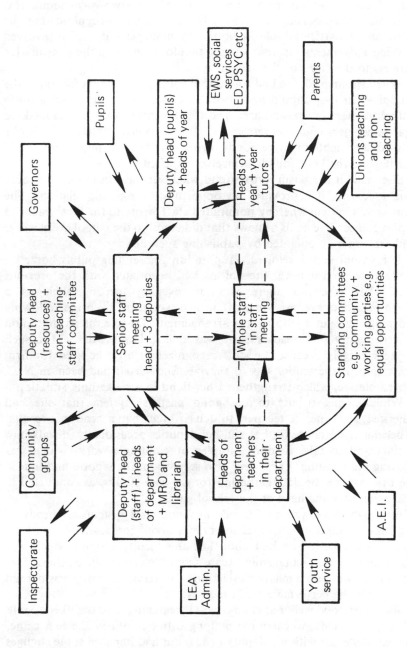

Figure 19.1 Organization structure for Easterham school

school, and it was important to maintain effective two-way communication with those outside the school boundary. She recognized that the head had a particular role in boundary management, which involved making judgements on what weight should be given in the consultative process to the views of the various groups.

When she arrived, she had found that some pupils wandered round the school when they should have been in class, so she instituted a duty-patrol-teacher system, and arranged for the entrances to be manned, so that latecomers could be reprimanded, and to ensure that the school's immediate neighbours were not disturbed. Six or seven pupils who tested her beyond the limit found themselves expelled.

She made it her business to attend whatever local meetings she could gain access to, if it provided an opportunity for public relations. She instituted a system whereby nominated staff wrote to the local paper to report four or five items of news that did credit to the school every week; and the paper co-operated by publishing such news.

The school had developed a reputation for sending pupils home on inadequate pretexts; e.g. the unions had negotiated with the previous head that whenever there was an evening meeting such as a parent–teachers evening, time off in lieu would be given the following morning. She put a stop to this arrangement. Despite the strong union presence among the teachers, she was able to impress her will in such matters, largely because the staff recognized clearly the need for firm leadership, if the school was to survive. She herself had been an NUT representative, which strengthened her hand in a bargaining situation.

While paying tribute to the good pastoral system that she had inherited, she expected teachers to deliver much better academic results. It became the practice for her and her deputies occasionally to walk into a class and to take random samples of children's work, which was proving illuminating. They were also seen about the school, and indeed the first part of the data-gathering for the case study was conducted in discussion with the head at the school gate.

Although there was no formal staff appraisal system, all heads of department underwent formal interviews about the academic work of their departments. She had abolished the faculty system, which was distancing the top management team from the classroom teachers. Her impression was that a massive injection of in-service training was needed to upgrade the performance of the staff.

She understood well that change was threatening, and she liked to talk to people affected, to carry them along with her. When she first came, she had done this with her deputy heads, but had imposed some changes down below because of their urgency. However, she felt that curriculum change was an important area for full consultation.

First deputy head

He had been at the school for sixteen years, having worked his way up through head of mathematics and head of sixth form. He had been a deputy for nine years. His particular brief was resourcing. He had found that there were frequent frustrating delays in delivery of goods and services. Although he had developed a reputation for persistence, and used all the authority his position gave him, a great deal of his time was spent in trouble-shooting.

As the acting head during the interregnum, he had experienced the arrival of the new head with particular relief, and although there had been some crossed wires, by and large he supported what she was trying to do. The fact that she was shaking things up was having a beneficial effect on staff motivation. She worked prodigious hours and gave up many evenings to school activities. He saw the capacity to work long hours as one of the chief qualities a head required; the others were physical resilience, the memory of an elephant, the ability to listen, then make up one's mind clearly and rapidly, and firm leadership. He said the staff wanted someone competent as head and they had got their wish.

Third deputy head (staff and timetable)

She was a relatively recent appointment, having responsibility for the timetable and curriculum, for managing the heads of departments and for the discipline and professional development of staff.

One of the problems she had to tackle was the under-achieving teacher, say at HoD level. She used most of the 'tricks of the trade', such as regular reviewing of work, establishing and agreeing overriding priorities which are then underscored and monitored, and showing a peristent interest in progress. With some staff, relentless pressure was needed, and she thought that sometimes early retirement was to be encouraged and the LEA inspectors' help should be sought.

She had found that a union representative could give management very helpful advice, especially in disciplinary matters.

Commenting on the interregnum, she said it had been a year of aggravation with no outcomes, which had been most dispiriting. Now the staff were becoming more happy and confident. She felt that the reasons for the new head's success were the way in which she had analysed the problem, and seen it not as a power issue but as one of establishing the accountability of staff for the outcomes of their work. She had improved the school's organization structure and thereby released time to think and talk, and had developed personal trust among staff. She had shown her preparedness to negotiate, but also her firmness in taking decisions. Above all she thought of the education of the children as the prime reason for the school's existence. Although there was still an undercurrent of non-acceptance from some teachers, she thought this was well under control. It partly arose from differences in values: there were those who thought that challenging children was not the way to care for them.

Among the obstacles to improved effectiveness, she cited the difficulty of raising teachers' expectations of children and vice versa, which partly arose because so many teachers had spent all their career at this school, and therefore knew no better. New teachers stimulate others by bringing in new expectations and new horizons. She was all for getting her teachers out and about, visiting other schools, going for interviews, visiting one another's lessons, receiving INSET – anything to stimulate them.

Commentary

The situation that the new head had faced on taking over the school had been one that called for major change. The stakes were high: survival, no less. The problems were formidable: time was not on her side. She was helped in her task by a supportive LEA and by a high degree of ability among her senior management team – not least, its ability to conceptualize the change process.

Her diagnosis of the problem was rapid and crisp. She enunciated the school's future philosophy and aims before she arrived, publishing them in a new school prospectus. On arrival she soon established her authority, and sought to get the whole authority system in the school on a proper footing. She set up not so much a power system as an authority structure, based on a sound consultative system. This was aimed at getting the staff's support and commitment, so that she could actively manage with their consent against an agreed set of standards and clear role responsibilities. Her document on how she intended to structure the school also made it clear what were the principal values she espoused and was a good way of starting to manage the culture of the school.

She took personal responsibility, though with some delegation, for boundary management, to produce a rapid improvement in the school's public image and, in the longer term, to influence the various stakeholders' demands on and expectations of the school, and thus to create a more benign environment.

She discovered at first hand what went on in the school, by walking about, manning the gate, visiting classes and sampling pupils' work. Then she ensured, mainly through one of the deputies, that the work of the various departments was regularly reviewed and action taken by the HoD if it was found to be below standard. The less competent staff were subject to objective-setting interviews and their performance was relentlessly monitored.

For important areas of change, such as the developing pastoral curriculum and the forging of closer links with the local community, she continued the use of task groups already in existence, closely linked into the new authority structure.

Bearing in mind that this case study was written only six months after the arrival of the new head, it is not surprising that there were gaps in the picture of the future scenario, and some of the elements of the systematic approach to change required further attention. However, the essential short-run actions had been taken, and had already given the organization a taste of success and a feeling of being on the move. It was not all plain sailing, but both the organizational conditions and the managerial qualities required for successful change seemed to be largely present in Easterham School.

Four years on...
The momentum of change since the original study has been breathtaking. From being the LEA's worst secondary school when the head took over, it reached average in two years and became over-subscribed in four. It has changed from three- to five-form entry and would be six if the LEA allowed. It no longer has problem staff or takes problem children from other schools; instead, a neighbouring comprehensive school is in its turn struggling to survive.

The current high reputation rests largely on good order and discipline, the quiet atmosphere and the pupils' motivation. Academic results have steadily improved, the first GCSE results being 'massively better', but there is further to go. As hardly any parent has been to a university, expectations are not high. All these improvements have been achieved against a background of prolonged and serious industrial action by teachers with a history of militancy.

There have been a number of staff changes and morale is much improved. The former acting head took early retirement and the other two deputies both got headships. The replacement third deputy is a change agent who has worked wonders in curriculum development and has now become the new head. The former head has become a director of education. The weak HoDs retired early; other staff left on promotion. Turnover has been high (the school is in an unattractive location), but Easterham has become a school where people now want to come and teach.

Some 60 to 70 per cent of the staff have been appointed by the departing head and told unmistakably what is expected of them. As a result there has developed a consistency of values. The organization structure has stood the test of time, as has the consultative system, the value of which was highlighted in an inspectors' report which noted how involved the staff felt in the running of the school and how praiseworthy their hard work in improving it.

The management team is well balanced and has been developed so as to avoid dependency on the departing head. More and more transient working parties have been set up and have worked well. HoDs' meetings have become more like workshops than formal meetings.

Staff appraisal awaits an LEA scheme, but the head interviews deputies and they the HoDs once a year to review progress and set targets. Although unions banned INSET for three years, some took place nevertheless. When the ban was lifted there was a real push; both external management courses and internal INSET were used. INSET allowed personal and social skills education to become well established and pupil profiles to be introduced, accompanied by portfolios of pupils' work recorded with a 'Polaroid' camera in each department. Major pedagogical progress has been made and development projects undertaken. A new system of silver and gold awards encourages positive pupil achievement and a computer is used to put together unique, very presentable reports for each child from teachers' proformas which are optically scanned; this pioneering system is being disseminated to other schools.

Industrial relations have been a tightrope in this LEA, with teachers vilifying heads unmercifully. This head contained the situation by remaining an NUT member and negotiating easements from local representatives. She kept role relationships separate from personal relationships, which never broke down, and succeeded in transforming the staff from unreasonably militant to among the most reasonable in the area.

An adventitious but pleasing development came about when a neighbouring special school for autistic children was closed for redecoration. Easterham offered temporary refuge as a two-month experiment in integration. The Easterham children were told about handicap and some volunteered to befriend the guests. Although the SEN teachers expected the disruption to exacerbate behaviour, the reverse happened. The staff of the two schools mixed freely and the Easterham staff asked the head if they could have the autistic children permanently; this is happening, and Easterham became the first school in the country to have an autistic unit. The experience proved very positive for both the children and their parents.

Easterham is a shining example of what can be achieved in four to five years by effective school management, turning an ailing school on the brink of closure into a centre of excellence, in conditions of industrial unrest that could hardly be less propitious. It is a case study that offers much food for thought.

St Swithin's College

This is a case study providing particular illustration of the personal stamp that a head can put on a school in effecting change, mainly by managing the culture and the people.

St Swithin's College is a Victorian private boarding school with 550 boys and 30 sixth-form day girls. The attractively presented prospectus clearly described the school's aims and what it stood for, with such phrases as 'to teach everyone how to work' 'to widen their minds', 'to excite their imaginations', 'to see change as an opportunity not a threat, to meet the needs of the future', 'everyone is motivated to develop his or her potential to the full', 'a civilized yet steely young person at least is the vision'.

The head seemed to epitomize and radiate these values, and himself held a clear vision of where he wanted the school to be. He was a man likely to generate high expectations. He had been a salesman in the City before he decided to teach, and tribute was paid to his salesmanship by the staff.

His only formal management training had been on an Industrial Society Action-Centred Leadership course, but he was an avid reader, and was able to apply to the running of the school principles from such books as *In Search of Excellence* (Peters and Waterman, 1982) and Hamilton's biography of Lord Montgomery (1981).

He conceived the most important aspect of a head's job to be the training of his staff, and he applied himself to this with energy. This aspect was one of a trio, stressed by Montgomery, of first picking your men, then training them well, then maintaining their morale. Clear directives and the setting of objectives were part of this, and very much a part of his practice. Some 70 per cent of the staff had been his appointments (the rest he inherited), and he had been at the school for only five years. Clearly, other staff had left.

His approach was not dissimilar from that which distinguishes the chief excecutives of the 'excellent' companies described by Peters and Waterman (1982): shaping the value system and concentrating on the people.

Selection was particularly important. He was quite clear about the criteria that should be used in appointing staff to positions of responsibility, such as housemaster or head. They needed to be good 'salesmen' with parents; they must be men held in respect by the boys; they must be good teachers, able to keep order; and they must be people with spare, unused capacity, backed by a wide variety of interests – not dreary men.

Heads of department, however, needed a different set of qualities. First and foremost, they must have the ability to lead adults and to educate their departments – not the boys. Then they needed to be men of ideas, so that their subjects would live; and they needed the ability to develop a clear, simple organization, with basic syllabuses, good reading lists, effective tests for identifying weak masters, etc.; also the determination to use and develop modern teaching resources, such as videos.

The selection process for internal promotion in the school consisted of the head sounding out views, especially those of the second master, but more interestingly those of the boys, whom he regarded as sound judges of form. He canvassed their views by asking them informally: 'Who do you think would make a good housemaster?' and by piecing together information culled from frequently posing the general question: 'Are you well taught?'

A further important input into appointment decisions came from the disciplined use of a staff appraisal system. Every member of the common room (fifty-six) was interviewed formally by the head once a year for at least an hour, in which past achievements and difficulties were reviewed, and future targets and aspirations discussed and agreed. A member of staff at middle management level said that the kind of questions asked were: 'What are you doing?', 'Are you overloaded?', 'What do you want to do?' It was not, apparently, experienced as threatening or prying.

The introduction of a staff appraisal system, soon after the head's arrival, had gone smoothly. Some of the longer-serving members of staff expressed suspicion and reluctance to take part, but the younger ones welcomed it and saw it as positive, supportive, constructive and helpful. The system had been imposed without consultation, but there had been an explanatory paper accompanying its introduction, summing up what it was intended to do. The emphasis was on setting objectives and monitoring progress towards them.

The need for staff appraisal and feedback on performance arose, in the head's view, partly from the capacity of teachers to delude themselves, unlike boys, whose self-knowledge was far greater and more accurate. Teachers tended to be inflexible and not to recognize their weaknesses, so this information needed drawing out.

Weak staff had to be moved; to do otherwise was to let down the boys. Weak HoDs were particularly serious problems; they had to be found jobs elsewhere in the school or, if none was available, they had to be helped to come to terms with their unsuitability and find another occupation.

At the other end of the scale, it was important to recognize and reward merit. The head always wrote letters to people who had performed well, telling them so, and said 'thank you' to them. Financial reward was also possible as there was enough flexibility to make one-off payments. There was, for example, a bonus system directed at rewarding contributions to various objectives, such as saving electricity.

The head's approach to the management of change was very positive. In the first place, he saw it as important for the boys to experience a changing environment, otherwise there would be an atmosphere of staleness rather than vitality. Second, it was his view that the head should lead change. This he did by writing a clear paper, which did not go into detail, then delegating to the second master the implementation phase. The second master was adept at picking up ideas and running with them. The boys' ideas should also be worked on: he regularly asked the prefects how they thought the school could be improved. He was afraid of the school running out of momentum, and was determined to have around him people who brought up ideas. To facilitate this, he had convened groups of eight people and given them the question to discuss: 'What do we do well and what do we do badly?' This had proved useful and productive.

The second master

There being no deputy head, the second master was the second in command. He had been in the job for twelve years. All staff responded to the head, not to him; it was the head who ran the school and he was accountable to him. His was a buffer role: he was responsible for 'keeping the common room sweet' and ironing out administrative problems.

Commenting on the head's style and his own relationship to him, he said that the head was good at innovations and assumed full responsibility for them. He did not impose them despotically; indeed he positively encouraged opposition and wanted the second master to speak out against the head's views, even in the staff-room, when he did not agree. He was also a marvellous salesman. He had a gift for public relations, and he was particularly good with parents and with the heads of preparatory schools. This quality was widely respected, and he expected other senior staff to do likewise. For example, he had encouraged the electronics department to design, manufacture and sell (with appropriate publicity) an electronics kit for feeder schools, which helped to cement the relationship with these schools. The head was also active in the local community, making the school's facilities available to deserving causes, in order to foster goodwill and a benign environment.

The head of department
This master had worked in the family hotel business before entering the teaching profession. He had been in the school for four years. Commenting on the differences between managing a business and running a school, he said that heads had despotic power, and their power of patronage was enormous by comparison with business. There should, in his view, be more encouragement of devolution.

As to how he experienced the head's management style, he said that some things, like timetable changes, were imposed, whereas other innovations were 'sold' to the staff. The staff appraisal scheme was 'sold', and some of the senior staff only acquiesced in its introduction, rather than supported it. He himself had found it very helpful; it was not an inquisition; it was aimed at the agreement of future targets which were set in broad terms.

The careers master
A modern linguist by background, this master had spent six years in the purchasing department of a well-known company, latterly as a purchasing manager, before deciding to become a teacher. Commenting on how he found the management system in the school compared with that in business, he said there was *no* management system until the present head arrived: the school was more like an unmanaged

community. The new head, however, gave himself a more managerial role, by introducing objective-setting and actively managing the boundary with the outside world. He also introduced a managerial structure, with individual tasks being identified and assigned to particular staff; roles were clarified and assigned. He placed considerable emphasis on change, made a five-year plan, and put in a new set of people to carry it out. Objective-setting had been the key to its implementation.

Asked about the management training that teachers should receive, this master was convinced of the importance of giving would-be teachers experience of the world outside education: a closed loop system was fatal. Teachers actually needed management skills. Not only that, but they ought to introduce the pupils to management processes and get them accustomed to working them.

The deputy bursar

Here again was a man with wide outside experience before he came to the school. He was a professional accountant with recent experience as a 'company doctor'. His predecessor, a naval victualler, had brought the school's financial administration from the nineteenth into the twentieth century; his job was to take it into the twenty-first. For example, he planned to introduce a computerized management control system, which would include a word-processing facility for the general office. Until the present head arrived, there was no management structure in the school, and very little commercial awareness; the latter was still regarded as new in the school community.

The bursar's role had developed over the years, thus releasing the head for more academic and pastoral acitivities. In a telling phrase, he described the two roles as like those of joint managing directors.

Commentary

In an independent school the head has more freedom than in the state sector – notably more freedom to hire and fire staff. Nevertheless, examples can be quoted from the state sector of the same managerial approaches being used to turn a school round from a downward slide to an upward path. Strong and determined leadership can be applied in any organization.

This head supplied the vision to the staff of the school of how things could be; he articulated its value system and himself lived by it. He harnessed the energy that would keep the school vital and on the move. He set up task groups to look for improvements. He set objectives and monitored them. He had a five-year plan. Not only did he look after the internal management of the school, delegating freely the administrative tasks, but he set about influencing the environment, ensuring that the stakeholders' demands on the school were conducive to its success – especially the demands of the feeder schools.

Whenever he found people not up to the job even after counselling and training, he replaced them, for the interests of the pupils and the school came first. His information system for acquiring the data he needed for key internal appointments was highly developed, and his selection criteria were sharp and clear. He set high store on breadth of interest and colourfulness in his staff: not for him the narrow-minded specialist. He encouraged people to stand up to him, for conflict of ideas was healthy, if constructively managed, and he did listen.

If there was a hint of despotism in his style, especially in comparison with what is acceptable in industry, it was at least leavened with benevolence, and it even secured enduring change in so sensitive an area as staff appraisal. If there was something of the salesman in his make-up, then at least it was characterized by integrity and the respect for the individual which is the mark of a good salesman anywhere. Schools need to sell themselves in a competitive world, whether in the state or the independent sector.

Could he have made even more of a mark by following the more systematic approach used by the head in the first case study? The authors naturally think so, since it is their experience that good managers are receptive to learning; and by comparison with many industrial firms that set their sights as high as this school had, the amount of formal management training that its senior staff had had was woefully little. There was still a long way to go.

Four years on...
The school's standing has continued to grow: more prep schools send boys; more teachers want to come and teach; courses have been greatly improved; five Designer Awards and a Young Engineer of Great Britain Award have been won.

The biggest changes have been in the use of computers. The bursar's office is fully computerized; so is timetabling; and pupil profiles will follow. Houses have their own computers and most staff use them. The business of producing electronic kits for prep schools is now run by the boys, using spreadsheets, etc., to give them experience of operating a trading company. Circuit boards are produced photographically and the three information technology centres design their own computers.

The head of *biology* is responsible for spreading the use of computers into teaching – an interesting choice, which avoids an over-technical approach and capitalizes on his penchant for problem-solving. The principles on which the innovation is managed are: (1) to concentrate on learning processes rather than content; (2) to start with staff who have problems on which they would value help; and (3) once the 'early adopters' are going well, to disseminate good practice elsewhere.

A new director of studies, steeped in industrial society methods (action-centred leadership), used a systematic approach to curriculum development, where there have been several significant changes over the four years. A prefects' course in leadership, a new personal and social skills course for fourth formers and of course pedagogical changes arising from GCSE are examples.

Management of the school is now a team effort; the carefully selected team consists of the head, the second master, the director of studies and the chaplain. This has proved effective and reduced the head's workload. Appraisal continues, with the academic part now being delegated to HoDs. The head himself is formally appraised by the chairman of governors.

Although many of the concepts in this book are used in managing the school, this has been more the result of careful selection of staff with a developmental approach rather than of training, coupled with the head's up-front leadership in which he proclaims his expectations of the staff and pupils. All new staff, for example, are told clearly that their main task is to change things for the better. A strategy for change which is largely based on selection obviously works best in schools whose reputations enable them to attract good teachers; schools other than St. Swithin's are more likely to depend on INSET for improving performance.

Further reading

Paisey, A. (1984) *School Management: A Case Approach*, Paul Chapman, London, contains several case studies involving major change – especially in Chapters 2, 3 and 7.

GLOSSARY

CNAA: the Council for National Academic Awards is the official validating body set up to grant higher academic awards to students who have successfully followed courses approved by CNAA as leading to those awards at institutions not authorized to grant their own degrees.

CPVE: Certificate of Pre-Vocational Education.

CSCS: the Centre for the Study of Comprehensive Schools, based at Nene College, Northampton (formerly at the University of York), is a national organization set up in 1980 with funds from industry, the Department of Trade and Industry and the Schools Council, to collect, study and disseminate good practice in comprehensive schools. The initiative for the Centre came from a group of headteachers with wide experience of running comprehensive schools and in-service management courses. Its extensive data bank of case studies, commissioned reports and research projects covers many topics dealt with in this book.

DES: the Department of Education and Science is the government department centrally responsible for education in England (but not Scotland, Wales or Northern Ireland).

DTP: Desk-top publishing.

ERA: the Education Reform Act of 1988. A major piece of legislation, introducing a National Curriculum, mandatory testing, local management of schools (LMS) and the right of schools to opt out of the local authority system.

HoD: head of department. Secondary schools are structured according to subject discipline, with the various departments headed by senior practising teachers. In Scotland the term 'principal teacher' is more common. Some schools also have faculties which group together related subjects. Where the context so requires, the term HoD should be taken to include also heads of faculties.

HMI: Her Majesty's Inspectors of Schools are responsible for visiting schools to monitor and advise upon the quality of the education provided. They publish reports of school visits, drawing attention to strengths and weaknesses, and occasionally produce general reports on contemporary curricular issues. Although attached to the DES (*q.v.*), SED (*q.v.*), etc., they enjoy a considerable measure of independence.

ICI: Imperial Chemical Industries plc is a British multinational chemical company (one of the largest organizations in the private sector) which for many years has had a reputation for progressive management. Through its schools liaison officers it helps science teachers to improve their teaching materials and has been active in transferring some of its management practices to schools.

ILEA: the Inner London Education Authority was an elected body responsible for providing and co-ordinating all the public sector education in inner London. Disbanded under ERA, its principal functions are now provided by the boroughs.

INSET: in-service education and training is provided mainly by public sector educational institutions, universities, LEAs (*q.v.*) and the DES (*q.v.*).

LEA: local education authorities are bodies of elected representatives responding to county, metropolitan district and borough councils. The permanent officials are headed by a director of education or chief education officer responsible for the administration of the authority. Their powers were curtailed by ERA. Most teachers are employees of an LEA.

LMS: local management of schools. A provision of ERA (*q.v.*), which devolves much power and authority from LEAs to individual schools.

MSC: see TA.

NAHT: the National Association of Head Teachers is the largest professional association of heads and deputies in the United Kingdom, covering both the primary and the secondary sector.

NTL: the National Training Laboratories are an American organization which has successfully pioneered the development and application to management and organization of the behavioural sciences, especially humanistic psychology, since World War II. Its nearest UK equivalent is the Tavistock Institute for Human Relations. Both are proponents of experiential, as distinct from didactic, learning methods.

NUT: the National Union of Teachers is the largest and most powerful teachers' union in the United Kingdom. It is affiliated to the TUC (Trades Union Congress).

OD: organization development has no satisfactory definition. It is used to denote an approach to the improvement of the effectiveness of organizations and of the individuals that staff them. This approach makes systematic use of the behavioural sciences (applied psychology, sociology, social anthropology, etc.) to diagnose situations and solve the problems that emerge. Although not synonymous with the management of change, OD is very much associated with it.

ROSLA: raising of the school leaving age. In UK schools compulsory education continues to the age of 16 – formerly 15, and before that, 14.

SED: the Scottish Education Department discharges the responsibilities which in England are handled by the DES (*q.v.*). The two education systems differ in some major respects, so it is often misleading to speak of 'British' education.

SEN: special educational needs. A phrase used to refer to the needs of children with handicap and disability, provision for whom is covered by the 1981 Education Act, which followed the Warnock Report on the subject.

SHA: the Secondary Heads Association is the main professional association for (specifically) secondary headteachers and their deputies.

TA: the Training Agency took over the training functions of the Manpower Services Commission (MSC) in 1988. It is an independent government agency responding to the Department of Employment. It is responsible for administering public training policy and is used by government to exert pressure (e.g. through TVEI) on the education system, in the hope that it will respond more effectively to their interpretation of the country's economic needs. One of its functions is to improve the partnership between education and training.

TVEI: the Training and Vocational Education Initiative is a government-funded scheme administered by the TA (*q.v.*) which is aimed at shifting the focus of secondary education towards practical and vocational activities, and thus to counter the 'academic drift' which followed the Fisher Education Act of 1917 making the universities responsible for the main examination system. It is intended to apply both to the so-called 'academic' and to the 'non-academic' pupil. An initiative with similar aims is the Education for Capability movement sponsored by the Royal Society of Arts.

REFERENCES

Adair, J. (1987) *Effective Teambuilding*, Pan, London.
Adair, J. (1988) *Developing Leaders*, Talbot Adair, Guildford.
Argyris, C. (1970) *Understanding Organizational Behaviour*, Dorsey Press, Homewood, Ill.

Baron, C. and Thomson, B. (1989) *Stress and You*, Gower, Aldershot.
Beckhard, R. and Harris, R.T. (1987) *Organizational Transitions: Managing Complex Change* (2nd edn), Addison-Wesley, Reading, Mass.
Beer, S. (1971) *Brain of the Firm*, Penguin, Harmondsworth.
Belbin, R.M. (1981) *Management Teams: Why They Succeed or Fail*, Heinemann, Oxford.
Berne, E. (1967) *Games People Play: The Psychology of Human Relationships*, Penguin, Harmondsworth.
Blake, R.R. and Mouton, J.S. (1964) *The Managerial Grid*, Gulf Publishing Co., Houston, Texas.
Bolam, T., Smith, G. and Cantor, H. (1978) *LEA Advisers and the Mechanisms of Innovation*, NFER, Slough.
Boyatzis, R.E. (1982) *The Competent Manager*, Wiley, New York.
Brown, W. (1971) *Organization*, Heinemann, Oxford.
Burgoyne, J.G. (1976) *A Taxonomy of Managerial Qualities as Learning Goals for Management Education: Development and Initial Testing*. Centre for the Study of Management Learning, Lancaster.
Burns, T. and Stalker, G.M. (1961) *The Management of Innovation*, Tavistock, London.
Bush, A., Glatter, R., Goodey, J. and Riches, C. (eds.) (1980) *Approaches to School Management*, Paul Chapman Publishing, London.
Buzan, A. (1974) *Use Your Head*, BBC Publications, London.

CBI (1989) *Towards a Skills Revolution: A Youth Charter*. Confederation of British Industry, London.

Child, J. (1984) *Organization: A Guide to Problems and Practice* (2nd edn), Paul Chapman Publishing, London.

Council for National Academic Awards (1984) *Handbook*, CNAA, London.

Cyert, R.M. and March, J.G. (1963) *A Behavioural Theory of the Firm*. Prentice-Hall, Englewood Cliffs, NJ.

Dean, J. (1985) *Managing the Secondary School*, Croom Helm, Beckenham.

DES (1988a) *School Governors: A Guide to the Law*, HMSO, London.

DES (1988b) *Schoolteachers' Pay and Conditions of Service Document*, HMSO, London.

Dunham, J. (1986) Helping with stress, in M. Marland (ed.) *School Management Skills*, Heinemann, Oxford.

Emery, F.E. (1969) *Systems Thinking*, Penguin, Harmondsworth.

Evans, J., Everard, K.B., Friend, J., Glaser, A., Norwich, B. and Welton, J. (1989) *Decision-making for Special Educational Needs*, Tecmedia, Loughborough.

Everard, K.B. (1980) The christian layman in management, *Industrial and Commercial Training*, vol. 12, no. 4, p. 140.

Everard, K.B. (1984) *Management in Comprehensive Schools - What Can Be Learned from Industry?* (2nd edn), Centre for the Study of Comprehensive Schools, Nene College, Northampton.

Everard, K.B. (1986) *Developing Management in Schools*, Blackwell, Oxford.

Everard, K.B. (1989a) Competences in education and education management, *Management in Education*, vol. 3, no. 3, pp. 14–20.

Everard, K.B. (1989b) Organisation development in educational institutions, in N. Entwistle (ed.) *Handbook of Educational Ideas and Practices*, Routledge, London.

Fayol, H. (1930) *Industrial and General Administration*, Pitman, New York.

Fullan, M., Miles, M.B. and Taylor, B. (1980) Organization development in schools: the state of the art, *Review of Educational Research*, vol. 50, no. 1, pp. 121–184.

Fullan, M. (1982) *The Meaning of Educational Change*, Teachers College Press, New York and Ontario Institute for Studies in Education.

Galton, M. and Moon, R. (eds.) (1983) *Changing Schools... Changing Curriculum*. Paul Chapman Publishing, London.

Garratt, B. (1987) *The Learning Organization*, Fontana, London.

Glatter, R., Preedy, M., Riches, C. and Masterton, M. (eds.) (1988) *Understanding School Management*, Open University Press, Milton Keynes.

Goldsmith, W. and Clutterbuck, D. (1984) *The Winning Streak: Britain's Top Companies Reveal Their Formulas for Success*, Weidenfeld and Nicolson,

London.

Graham, D.G. (1985) *Those Having Torches - Teacher Appraisal*; also *In the Light of Torches* and *On from Torches*, Suffolk County Education Offices, Ipswich.

Gray, H.L. (ed.) (1982) *The Management of Educational Institutions: Theory Research and Consultancy*, Falmer Press, Lewes.

Gray, H.L. (1984) *Contributions*, no. 6, p. 1, Centre for the Study of Comprehensive Schools, Nene College, Northampton.

Gray, H.L. (ed.) (1988) *Management Consultancy in Schools*, Cassell, London.

Hamilton, N. (1981) *Monty*, Hamish Hamilton, London.

Handy, C.B. (1985) *Understanding Organizations* (3rd edn), Penguin, Harmondsworth.

Handy, C.B. (1984) *Taken for Granted: Looking at Schools as Organizations*, Longman, Harlow.

Handy, C.B. and Aitken, R. (1986) *Understanding Schools as Organizations*, Penguin, Harmondsworth.

Hargreaves, D. (1984) *Improving Secondary Schools*, ILEA, London.

Harris, T.A. (1973) *I'm OK You're OK*, Pan, London.

Harrison, R. (1972) How to describe your organization, *Harvard Business Review*, Sept.-Oct.

Harvey-Jones, J.H. (1988) *Making It Happen*, Collins, London.

Hastings, C., Bixby, P. and Chaudhry-Lawton, R. (1986) *Superteams*, Fontana, London.

Havelock, R.G. (1973) *The Change Agents' Guide to Innovation in Education*, Educational Technology Publications, Englewood Cliffs, N.J.

Heller, H. (1982) *Management Development for Headteachers*, in H.L. Gray (ed.) *op. cit.*

Her Majesty's Inspectorate (1977) *Ten Good Schools*, DES London: HMSO.

Hersey, P. and Blanchard, K.H. (1977) *Management of Organizational Resources Utilising Human Resources*, Prentice-Hall, Englewood Cliffs, NJ.

Herzberg, F. (1966) *Work and the Nature of Man*, World Publishing, Cleveland, Ohio.

Holmes, S. (1985) Using industrial managers as a resource for INSET, in I. Jamieson (ed.) *Industry in Education*, Longman, Harlow.

Honey, P. and Mumford, A. (1982) *Manual of Learning Styles*, Honey, Maidenhead.

Hughes, M.G., Carter, J. and Fidler, B. (1981) *Professional Development Provision for Senior Staff in Schools and Colleges*, University of Birmingham.

Huxley, J. (1984) How ICI pulled itself into shape, *The Sunday Times*, 29 July, p. 57.

Jones, A. (1987) *Leadership for Tomorrow's Schools*, Blackwell, Oxford.

Kolb, D.A. (1984) *Experiential Learning: Experience as the Source of Learning*

and Development, Prentice-Hall, Englewood Cliffs N.J.
Kyriacou, C. (1980) Coping actions and occupational stress among schoolteachers, *Research in Education*, vol. 24, pp. 57–61.

Lavelle, M. (1984) The role of consultancy and OD in innovation in education, *School Organization*, vol. 4, no. 2, p. 161.
Lawrence P.R. and Lorach, J.W. (1967) *Organization and Environment*, Harvard Business School Division of Research, Harvard.
Likert, R. (1967) *The Human Organization*, McGraw Hill, New York.

Mant, A. (1983) *The Leaders We Deserve*, Martin Robertson, Oxford.
Maslow, A.H. (1943) A theory of human motivation, *Psychological Review*, vol. 50, pp. 370–96.
Maw, J., Fielding, M., Mitchell, P., White, J., Young, P., Ouston, J. and White, P. (1984) *Education plc?*, London Institute of Education, Heinemann.
McClelland, D.C. (1961) *The Achieving Society*, Van Nostrand, Princeton.
McGregor, D. (1960) *The Human Side of Enterprise*, McGraw-Hill, New York.
Mortimore, P., Sammons, P., Stoll, L., Lewis, D. and Ecob, R. (1988) Key factors in effective junior schooling, in Glatter *et al.* (eds.) *op. cit.*
Myers, S.M. (1970) *Every Employee a Manager*, McGraw-Hill, New York.

Paisey, A. (1981) *Organization and Management in Schools*, Longman, Harlow.
Paisey, A. (1984) *School Management: A Case Approach*, Paul Chapman Publishing, London.
Perrow, C. (1970) *Organizational Analysis*, Tavistock Institute of Human Relations, London.
Peters, T.J. and Waterman, R.H. (1982) *In Search of Excellence*, Harper and Row, New York.
Pettigrew, A.M. (1985) *The Awakening Giant: Continuity and Change in Imperial Chemical Industries*, Blackwell, Oxford.
Plant, R. (1987) *Managing Change and Making it Stick*, Fontana, London.

Rackham, N., Honey, P, and Colbert, M. (1971) *Developing Interactive Skills*, Wellens Publishing, Northampton.
Reddin, W.J. (1971) *Managerial Effectiveness*, McGraw-Hill, New York.
Rice, A.K. (1963) *The Enterprise and the Environment*, Tavistock, London.
Rutter, M., Maugham, B., Mortimore, P. and Ouston, J. (1980) *Fifteen Thousand Hours*, in Bush *et al.* (eds.) *op. cit.*

Schmuck, R., Runkel, P., Arends, J. and Arends, R. (1977) *The Second Handbook of Organizational Development in Schools*, Mayfield, Palo Alto.
School Management Taskforce (1990) *Developing School Management – The Way Forward*, DES, HMSO, London.
Sloan, A. (1980) *My Years with General Motors*, Sidgwick and Jackson, London.

Stewart, V. (1983) *Change: The Challenge for Management*, McGraw-Hill, London.

Tannenbaum, R. and Schmidt, W.H. (1958) How to Choose a Leadership Pattern, *Harvard Business Review*, vol. 36, pp. 95-101.

Taylor, F.W. (1947) *Principles of Scientific Management*, Harper and Row, New York.

Taylor, J. (1984) Bridging the gap: A county council's approach to the management development of head teachers, *BACIE Journal*, March/April, p. 67.

Taylor, M. (1979) *Coverdale on Management*, Heinemann, Oxford.

Trist, E.L. (1960) *Socio-technical Systems*, Tavistock Institute of Human Relations, London.

Urwick, L. (1952) *Notes on the Theory of Organization*, American Management Association, New York.

Weindling, D. (1989) The process of school improvement, *School Organization*, vol. 9, no. 1, pp. 53-64.

Woodward, J. (1965) *Industrial Organization*, Oxford University Press, Oxford.

INDEX